ON THE CUTTING EDGE

On the Cutting Edge

THE STUDY OF WOMEN
IN BIBLICAL WORLDS

Essays in Honor of
Elisabeth Schüssler Fiorenza

Edited by
Jane Schaberg
Alice Bach
and
Esther Fuchs

continuum
NEW YORK • LONDON

2004

The Continuum International Publishing Group Inc
15 East 26th Street, New York NY 10010

The Continuum International Publishing Group Ltd
The Tower Building, 11 York Road, London SE1 7NX

Printed in the United States of America

Library of Congress Cataloging-in-Publication Data

On the cutting edge : the study of women in biblical worlds : essays in
   honor of Elisabeth Schüssler Fiorenza / edited by Jane Schaberg, Alice
   Bach, and Esther Fuchs.
      p. cm.
   ISBN 0-8264-1589-X (hardcover: alk. paper) – ISBN 0-8264-1582-2
   1. Bible—Feminist criticism. I. Schüssler Fiorenza, Elisabeth,
1938- II. Schaberg, Jane. III. Bach, Alice. IV. Fuchs, Esther, 1953- V.
Title.
BS521.4.O5 2003
220.6'982—dc21

                                                           2003010803

Contents

Preface

THESE ESSAYS IN HONOR OF ELISABETH SCHÜSSLER FIORENZA DRAW ON international feminist scholarship indebted to her ground-breaking achievements. The body of her work up to now ensures her a prominent place in the history and the future of biblical studies, feminist thought, ecumenical studies, and revitalization movements worldwide. That prominence can only grow: in biblical studies when gender and kyriarchal analysis is not as marginal as it is today in many quarters; in feminist studies in general, when the subject of religion is once more central and of interest to a wide audience, and when gender analysis is expanded to include the intertwined structures of domination; in ecumenical studies, when the focus and concerted effort to address issues of Christian anti-Judaism and to deal with gender issues in fundamentalism become a standard; in revitalization movements, when education in her seven steps of a critical theory of interpretation is even more widely extended.[1]

Her boldness, clarity, and persistence have helped many, inside and outside the academy, craft new understandings of the past and therefore of the present and future. For her, the "search for history and roots is neither antiquarian nor nostalgic: it is political."[2] The aim is not to promote religion but to produce emancipatory knowledge. A socially engaged biblical scholar, Schüssler Fiorenza teaches the constant, critical, invigorating interrogation of our reading practices and frameworks. The critical theory she has developed makes history and texts more readable and releases creativity. Hers is historical, sociological, rhetorical, theological study that tells us something about what compels people—ourselves always included—to take positions and to act in certain ways, then and now. It also directs and helps us to evaluate those positions in the light of our own experience and in the light of the egalitarian, democratizing impulses of the tradition. And it empowers us to act: by revolutionizing consciousness to participate in struggles to transform the world by meeting basic, concrete human needs.

"On the cutting edge" is a fitting description of Elisabeth's own work, which brings biblical studies into alliance and dialogue with feminist studies in general. Early on, the introduction of feminist concepts, theory, and terms into the field was her concern. She has constantly refined theories, expanding them to include newer and more complex, hybrid interpretive strategies. She has explored how religious, class, racial, national, ethnic, and local variations influence women's and men's interpretations of biblical worlds. Ever attuned to the politics of scholarship, she has pushed the envelope methodologically and politically, denying the usual separations between the worlds of academia, ethics, and political activism. So she has always been one step ahead.

One of the themes that emerges again and again in this collection of essays is that of the agency of wo/men in the past, the memory of which can sometimes be reconstructed in spite of distortion and loss and silence. This agency is valued as encouraging and energizing. The contributers to this volume come from a great variety of backgrounds, commitments, talents, and interests—a spectrum full of vitality. There are important convergences, intersections, and what Schüssler Fiorenza has called critical collaboration: more than conversation and not the same as consensus[3]—wo/men thinking together and creating together not in spite of but because of acknowledged and appreciated differences. Some of the contributions here deal directly with aspects of Schüssler Fiorenza's thought (Fuchs, Castelli, Joseph). Others deal with related hermeneutical theories (Pippin, Eisen); with issues of vital interest to Schüssler Fiorenza, such as violence against women (Brenner) or memory and popular culture (Bach, Reinhartz); or with historical reconstruction of women and women's self-understanding (Ilan, Taylor). Still others follow Schüssler Fiorenza's lead exploring dimensions of the resurrection faith and wo/men's leadership (Briggs, Wire, Schaberg).

This selection of essays offers only a suggestion of the breadth and depth of Schüssler Fiorenza's influence. With Catherine Clark Kroeger, she founded the section on Women in the Biblical World of the Society of Biblical Literature, which has given established and younger scholars a national forum for presenting their feminist research for over twenty-five years. The two-volume work she edited, *Searching the Scriptures: A Feminist Introduction* and *A Feminist Commentary* (New York: Crossroad, 1993, 1994) testifies to her desire to be inclusive of the growing diversity and plurality of approaches. We wish we had been able to include here all the scholars who have expressed a desire to honor Schüssler Fiorenza's work, and we invite them to celebrate with us. This volume is a Festschrift for *all* wo/men in the field, which has been radically and permanently (if slowly) changed by her work. Only a more inventive (and more expensive) means of communication, such as, perhaps, an ongoing website representing "the open cosmopolitan house" of Wisdom could properly host such a celebration in what she calls "the radical democratic learning space of Wisdom" and "the public radical democratic space of Wisdom's movements."[4] Royalties from this book will be contributed to the Center for Feminist Theology and Ministry in Japan[5] and to the *Journal of Feminist Studies in Religion.*[6]

To all of us, Elisabeth offers the compliment of taking our work seriously, of dialogue and disagreement and questioning and sharpening. Always honest, frank, and vulnerable, she has often been there before us on many paths that are becoming roads. She insists, all along, that we look at the larger picture, the currents of struggle and counterstruggle, the social and political implications of our work—as she herself strives to do in her own.

At the beginning of the third millennium C.E., the deadly potential of sacred texts in fundamentalist and hegemonic readings supports crusades and occupations and terrorist attacks of all kinds. In emancipatory readings, different possibilities emerge because wo/men find their voices, shifting values and ideals, and inspiring new commitments and creativity. Reading for these possibilities is the focus of Elisabeth Schüssler Fiorenza's career. The contributors to this volume are united by our appreciation for her as scholar, teacher, mentor, colleague, and friend.

JANE SCHABERG — ALICE BACH — ESTHER FUCHS
MARCH, 2003

Notes

1. Elisabeth Schüssler Fiorenza, *Wisdom Ways: Introducing Feminist Biblical Interpretation* (Maryknoll, N.Y.: Orbis, 2001), chapter 7.

2. Elisabeth Schüssler Fiorenza, *But She Said: Feminist Practices of Biblical Interpretation* (Boston: Beacon, 1992), 101.

3. Elisabeth Schüssler Fiorenza, "Commitment and Critical Inquiry:

Harvard Divnity School 1988 Convocation," in *The Discipleship of Equals: A Critical Feminist* Ekklēsia-*logy of Liberation* (New York: Crossroad, 1998), 275–89.

4. See Schüssler Fiorenza, *Wisdom Ways,* chapters 1 and 3.

5. C/o Oizumi Church, Oizumi Gakuen-cho 2-23-54, Nerima-ku, Tokyo 178-0061, Japan; contact persons Satoko Yamaguchi and Kisako Kinukawa.

6. This journal is currently edited by Elisabeth Schüssler Fiorenza and Kwok Pui-lan.

1

Points of Resonance

Esther Fuchs

W HAT DO I, AN ISRAELI-AMERICAN AGNOSTIC WITH SERIOUS leanings toward atheism, have to say about the work of Elisabeth Schüssler Fiorenza, a German-American Catholic theologian? Given our radically different points of provenance, is there something, anything I can offer? What can I, who for the better part of my career have focused on the Hebrew Bible as a literary/ideological meta-narrative, say about the work of this prominent historian of the New Testament? What possible intersection can there be between our respective preoccupations, positions, and locations? Because to a considerable extent the answer to these questions may be little, or not much, I will confine myself in what follows not to an evaluation of Elisabeth's work *in toto* or even of a part of her work. Rather, what I will do is focus on a few themes in her work as points of resonance for me.

I documented these points of resonance over the years with exclamation marks in the margins of her books, underlining certain paragraphs, highlighting others, and stuffing my own notes into them. When I was asked last year to contribute to a Festschrift on her biblical work, I began to unpack Elisabeth's shelf in my office. I must confess that I had a rather difficult time deciphering some of my scribbled notes as well as the exclamation points, the yeses and the nos in the margins. I therefore decided to limit myself in this brief overview to the responses that I did manage to understand after my first reading. The main points of resonance, for me, seem to revolve around the making of a biblical feminist historiography, the reconstruction of biblical women's history, the hermeneutics of suspicion, the problem of "malestream"

1

scholarship, the problem of anti-Judaism in feminist theological work, and the position of the "foreigner" as exegetical standpoint.

THE MAKING OF FEMINIST BIBLICAL HISTORIOGRAPHY

In the late 1980s I published what may perhaps be considered the first feminist critique of Israeli letters.[1] While I did not expect the male authorities in the field to celebrate my work as a "first" of sorts, I naively hoped that their graduate students would reassess their mentors' resistance and indifference to feminist theory. Within a decade, however, I realized that these mentors presented themselves as the benevolent feminist fathers who parented creative, original feminist daughters, thus obviating the need to acknowledge the first works published in the field. It should not have surprised me that the protégées of my male colleagues either ignored or made light of my work, which cost me dearly in professional terms. Within a decade I learned that androgynous and gender-bending approaches have become the forefront of feminist theory in Hebrew literature and have superseded my "outdated" focus on women as such. It was not, however, until I read Elisabeth Schüssler Fiorenza's critique of the politics of periodization in feminist biblical scholarship that the deep betrayal of intellectual motherhood and the importance of the concept of feminist genealogy became clear to me. Schüssler Fiorenza brilliantly analyzes the need of younger scholars to dismiss their mothers and anchor themselves in the authority of their academic fathers as the "Athena Complex."[2] She puts it as follows:

> Feminist scholars do not have the same power and standing in the academy as "doctor-fathers" do. Hence young women scholars must prove themselves to be the "daughters" of their intellectual academic father-mentors and must learn to understand themselves as the "motherless" offspring engendered from the brains of powerful "fathers." They have to prove their loyalty by denying or belittling their intellectual "mothers" in order to compete with them for respect and confirmation of their intellectual fathers.[3]

Schüssler Fiorenza highlights the dismissal of women's pioneering work as "naïve" simply for lacking the sophistication that would not have come about were it not for the earlier contributions of the allegedly less sophisticated mothers. Furthermore, the alleged sophistication of more recent generations is often anchored in categories of analysis produced by the male-dominated coterie of academic stars who promote the imitation of their own discourses as part of professional advancement. Schüssler Fiorenza advocates, instead of the recent repudiation of pioneering feminists, the collaboration of academic and activist feminists and a breakdown of the recent opposition between a certain brand of postmodern theory and politics.

It would be hypocritical of me to deny my disappointment at later appropriations of my political reading of the biblical narrative, readings that did not so much as mention my name in footnotes. With very few exceptions, biblical scholars whose reading was explicitly against the grain of the ideological text of the Hebrew Bible did not mention their indebtedness to my early articles. Yet in the early 1980s the dominant method of reading the biblical text was "depatriarchalizing" argument that the Hebrew text must be distinguished from later sexist readings. Only a few subsequent feminist critical readings of the Hebrew Bible mentioned my work as a methodological or theoretical precursor.[4] It is crucial, when reconstructing a biblical feminist historiography to remember our crucial methodological and theoretical divisions, as well as the common ground we share. In *Bread Not Stone* and in all her subsequent books about feminist approaches to the Bible, Schüssler Fiorenza offers categories and classifications that highlight the differences and theoretical distinctions between and among various approaches, without subsuming or derogating any one of them. This, along with her insistence on recognizing pioneering work in both the first and the second wave of feminist thought, is probably among her most important contributions to our field. To see all critical readers as the inheritors of Elizabeth Cady Stanton's *Woman's Bible* is to obliterate the important insights of the second wave, the innovations engendered by the concept of sexual politics and the paradigm of the resisting reader. No matter what we do, we must remember the pioneers, the mothers, the forerunners of each theory and method. Only this will allow us to reconstruct a truthful and responsible feminist biblical historiography and help us acknowledge the contribution of each phase in the development of what is now a thriving field of biblical criticism.

THE RECONSTRUCTION OF WOMEN'S HISTORY

In the 1980s and 1990s, increasing numbers of historical works appeared claiming that the social status of women in ancient Israel was different but equal to, or at least as valued as, men's. These works claimed for themselves the authority of the social "sciences," relying on an objective stance, typical of the discourse and style of German Enlightenment models of the late nineteenth century. Such works continue to be published by so-called male feminists who claim an interpretive authority based on their expertise in ancient Near Eastern languages, history, and archaeology. That much of their interpretation is subjective, tangential, and reconstructive rarely enters their descriptions of *actual* life and social structure in ancient Israel. What alarms me is the positivist stance of some of these works, reflecting little or no awareness of feminist critiques of objective neutrality and the scientist illusion.

It is instructive to juxtapose the positivist depictions of women's history in the Iron Age with Schüssler Fiorenza's approach to the history of women in the first century, a period that is equally (though certainly not more) shrouded in mystery and reliant on guesswork. Where the "objective" historians present the past as something one can see through a window, clouded as it may be, she goes out of her way to call attention to the process of reconstruction, the tentative interpretation, and the partial accessibility involved in any historical writing. Here is how she presents the problem: "Androcentric texts and documents do not mirror historical reality, report historical facts, or tell us how it actually was. As androcentric texts our early Christian sources are theological interpretations, argumentations, projections and selections rooted in patriarchal culture. Such texts must be evaluated *historically* in terms of their own time and culture and assessed *theologically* in terms of a feminist scale of values."[5]

Though Schüssler Fiorenza focuses on the New Testament, her cautious extrapolations as style and strategy ought to be heard by historians of the Hebrew Bible as well. Whereas they continue to use objective discourse referring to "data," "evidence," and "reality," Schüssler Fiorenza is acutely aware of history writing as a process of reconstruction and narration. She repeatedly refers to "models" and "paradigms" that by necessity mediate between the historian's perception and his or her object of interest. As she puts it: "A critical feminist theory and rhetorical paradigm of history recognizes that all representations of the world are informed by our own historical-cultural location as well as by the ways we are implicated in power-relations."[6] She carefully stresses in her historical writing the importance of inserting the location of the historian him/herself into his/her own reconstruction of biblical reality as part of the act of accurate historical reconstruction: "A critical feminist theory and rhetorical paradigm of history recognizes that all representations of the world are informed by our own historical-cultural location as well as by the ways we are implicated in power-relations."[7] She rejects the postmodern new historicism, insisting on the "provisionality and multiplicity of historical knowledge."[8] Though she stresses the discursiveness of historiography, she nevertheless affirms the freedom of the individual subject, or her agency. She reminds us constantly of the embodied and situated nature of knowledge and of the need for a free and open acknowledgment of the historian's position, but she refuses to bow to the relativism of postmodern concepts of ideological interpellation. She insists that women's agency be reconstructed, but questions certainty, positivism, and scientific authority. Her historical analysis is rarely removed from the position and location of her feminist interests or theological beliefs: "A feminist hermeneutics of remembrance desires to recover from historical silences the traces of the lives and faint echoes of their voices because of our need for a memory of women who have not only suffered and resisted patriarchal oppression but who have also spoken and acted in the power of the Spirit Sophia."[9] At the same time she assures us that the textual colonization of women's history ought not discourage us from exploring past models of struggles against oppression: "The experience and analysis of patriarchal colonization, however, tells us that women are and always have been historical subjects and agents. Women and other nonpersons have shaped culture and religion, even though androcentric records do not mention our existence and work."[10] As in her textual-hermeneutic work, the "both-and" attempt to include the best insights from disparate fields of scholarship, in this case history and philosophy, animates her historical-reconstructive work. She refuses to abdicate the possibility of historical reconstruction, yet she practices it with caution, always aware of the interpretive mediations and political interests entailed in her work.

A HERMENEUTICS OF SUSPICION

When I first began to distance myself from appropriative feminist-literary approaches to the Hebrew Bible, which dominated the critical scene in the early 1980s, I rejected the term "hermeneutics of suspicion" because of its identification with Paul Ricoeur, whom I saw as a theologian rather than a literary critic. I was suspicious of his own indebtedness to Freudian and Marxist ("malestream") suspicious readings of Western culture as a meta-narrative. Understanding the Bible as primarily a text, I rejected any and all approaches that pre-authorized it as a religious text requiring "exegesis" or "hermeneutics." It was not until I read Elisabeth Schüssler Fiorenza's feminist translation and evolving definition of the expression "hermeneutics of suspicion" that I realized to what extent this term could aptly identify some of the reading strategies I recommended as a resisting reader. Though over the years I learned to enjoy feminist uses of other hermeneutic strategies, I remained staunchly "Old Testament"—to use a classification playfully coined in the mid-1970s to designate the growing rift in feminist theory between feminist criticism and gynocentric appropriations of Western traditions.[11] For me, a feminist hermeneutics of suspicion liberates the reader even as it exposes textual oppression. In *But She Said* Schüssler Fiorenza articulates the dialectic tension in this strategy using New Testament examples:

> A *hermeneutics of suspicion* seeks to explore the liberating or oppressive values and visions inscribed in the text by identifying the androcentric patriarchal character and dynamics of the text. Since biblical texts are written in androcentric language within patriarchal cultures, a hermeneutics of suspicion does not start with the assumption that the Martha and Mary story is a feminist liberating text just because its central characters are women. Rather it seeks to investigate *how and why* the text constructs the story of these women as it does.[12]

Schüssler Fiorenza does not shrink from identifying androcentric discourse in the biblical text. She does not apologize for it by displacing the blame onto later generations of exegetes. By referring to the "character" and "dynamics" of the text, she highlights both a structural approach to the text and one indebted to the process of reading. She also highlights the fact that a hermeneutics of suspicion is not merely "negative," as many would have it. It is rather a method that explores "liberating *or* oppressive" [emphasis added] elements in the texts. Thus, I would argue, she captures here the paradox of resisting readings that "liberate" the reader—who is already constructed by patriarchal epistemologies—even as they expose the oppressive implications of biblical representations. In an earlier concise and articulate definition of a feminist hermeneutics of suspicion, Schüssler Fiorenza puts it as follows:

> A *hermeneutics of suspicion* does not presuppose the feminist authority and truth of the Bible, but takes as its starting point the assumption that biblical texts and their interpretations are androcentric and serve patriarchal functions. Since most of the biblical writings are ascribed to male authors and most of the biblical interpreters in church and academy are men, such an assumption is justified.[13]

A hermeneutics of suspicion for Schüssler Fiorenza is the opposite of the traditional hermeneutics of consent, the obedient reading of the Bible as religious scripture, a reading that presupposes the inerrancy and truth claims of the text.

In *But She Said* Schüssler Fiorenza further elaborates her understanding of the hermeneutics of suspicion by appropriately examining patriarchy as a term and an analytic category. Drawing on materialist, womanist, and third world analyses of patriarchy as an interlocking system of multiple oppressions, including class, race, and colonialism, Schüssler Fiorenza, instead of renouncing the concept of patriarchy as others have done, has sought to "reconceptualize patriarchy as a key heuristic category of feminist theology and biblical interpretation in such a way that it can make visible the complex interstructuring of the conflict-producing oppressions of different groups of women that are obscured by the ideology of patriarchy as binary sex-gender system." Rather than abandon "patriarchy" as a reified, essentialist term, she complicates, diversifies and multiplies its meaning as a "pyramid of multiplicative oppressions."[14]

In *Sharing Her Word*, Schüssler Fiorenza further extends the boundaries of a feminist hermeneutics of suspicion by focusing on language as a mode of communication and on what she calls "andro-kyriocentric," that is, male-master dominated, language: "In my view a hermeneutics of suspicion does not have the task of unearthing or uncovering historical or theological truth but of disentangling the ideological workings of andro-kyriocentric language. Grammatically androcentric language is not a closed system of signs but is historically and socially constructed."[15] By shifting our focus to language—to textual manipulations of grammar, syntax, and word formations—she emphasizes the importance of our literary competence, as critics who primarily deal with texts, be they "original" or interpretive. In this sense her later definition of a feminist hermeneutics of suspicion confirms my own understanding of "reading" as I presented it in my own work. Despite Schüssler Fiorenza's appreciation of language as the ultimate configuration of patriarchy, I would argue that she rejects postmodern representations of *Woman* or sexual difference as the "dark" continent, or ineffable underside of civilized discourse, or the law of the father. Instead, she refuses the essentialist, natural, and stabilizing contours of this term, which usually refers to elite, white, and privileged women, in favor of a fluid understanding of "woman" as a sociopolitical location.[16] This political understanding of "reading as a woman" is precisely what I gestured toward in my use of the expression "as a woman," with an emphasis on "as," which signifies the locus of, in place of, "as if" rather than actuality and presence.[17] From a unitary understanding of patriarchy as a sex-gender hierarchy, Schüssler Fiorenza moves us toward a multiple, heterogeneous, and complex definition of patriarchy as a system of interlocking oppressions, just as she moves us from an essentialist understanding of Woman or women, to a political definition of a radical democratic space she calls "women-church" or *ekklēsia gynaikōn* as a site of contradictory and heterogeneous feminist discourses.

In addition to the clarity and focus she brings to her taxonomy of feminist approaches, I believe that Schüssler Fiorenza's abiding contribution to biblical feminism is her ability to reduce the theoretical and political divisions between and among feminist interpreters to questions of method. By elaborating the differences between the approaches in a nonhierarchical manner, by defining ideological differences between readers as strategic variations, she succeeded in offering a bridge over the serious gap that Catharine Stimpson and Carolyn Heilbrun already saw emerging in feminist criticism in the mid-1970s.[18] Schüssler Fiorenza managed to create a context for a plural, democratic multilogue, one that ought to confront the individual interpreter as she comes to the biblical text, offering her various options, rather than a choice between rejecting the Bible and endorsing it. As one who opts for a careful reading of the Bible, I cannot possibly agree with those who reject it out of hand as inappropriate for any feminist reading whatsoever. The position of the reader who follows a hermeneutics of suspicion or of resistance will then always be paradoxical: one of deep intellectual engagement and of ideological difference.

At the end, what I find methodologically significant in Schüssler Fiorenza's hermeneutic classifications is her implicit advocacy to reject a theoretical "either-or" approach in favor of a "both-and" approach. In the early 1990s she elegantly summarized her own earlier project as based on a combination of deconstruction and reconstruction.[19] The importance of combining and including various feminist hermeneutic paradigms rather than rejecting and excluding some in favor of others cannot be overestimated. Though she has not avoided critiques of feminist scholars with whom she disagrees, she sought in her work to synthesize and to articulate a shared agenda and a unifying activist vision. As she moves from the identification of oppression in universal terms of gender hierarchy to an understanding of oppression as class- and race-specific manifestations of disempowerment, she takes the hermeneutics of suspicion into a new level of consciousness, developing her concept of a radical democratic *ekklēsia* of women as the social location of this kind of hermeneutics. Again, the Christian-theological term *ekklēsia* or "women-church" as a rhetorical figure may not resonate with Jewish feminists, as we shall see later; but as a site of political articulations of respective differences, it is a vital concept for any faith-based or even cultural community, because every community consists of differences. It is the location of the radical democratic community as the site for the articulation of a counter-hegemonic critique that holds promise, I would argue, for diverse, non-Catholic, non-Christian communities.[20] In the mid 1990s Schüssler Fiorenza elaborated her theory of a hermeneutics of suspicion in materialist, radical terms, focusing on the social location of the feminist critic, on the multivocal and contradictory discourses articulated by a democratic assembly of feminist critics, and on the agenda of social transformation and political action. The imagined space of the assembly of wo/men is to sustain "critical practices of struggle for transforming societal and religious kyriarchal institutional discourses. Such a theoretical space and frame of meaning seeks to displace the feminist anthropological construct 'woman' or the 'feminine' to replace it with a political construct that is at once a historical and an imagined political religious reality, already partially realized but still to be struggled for."[21] In her typical way of rearticulating, elaborating, theorizing, and reinterpreting her own previous work, she offers here a radicalizing, materialist revisioning of a feminist hermeneutics of suspicion, shifting its emphasis from the biblical text to the world, as it were, to social action and political commitment. Her search for theoretical and political inclusiveness leads in its most recent configurations to a recognition of the serious gaps, divisions, and contradictions within the assembly of feminist critics, yet by identifying this paradoxical community as "an oxymoron, a combination of contradictory terms for the purpose of articulating a feminist political site from where to speak" she sustains her original vision of plural inclusivity along ideological, racial, religious, national, and class lines.[22]

THE PROBLEM OF MALESTREAM SCHOLARSHIP

Recently, I began to witness a growing number of male scholars evaluating and categorizing feminist analyses of texts, correcting their women colleagues in public, as they adjudicate and evaluate, enumerate and praise, classify and criticize feminist scholars as they see fit. These discursive interventions in a field that emerged specifically as a challenge to male institutional and academic authority augur a reversal of earlier feminist gains. Some male scholars and journalists capitalize on feminist work by publishing feminist anthologies, still reasserting their final authority and control of women's means of intellectual production and distribution. This reemergence of male academic control and evaluative discourse in biblical feminist scholarship signals both the success and the demise of feminist biblical studies, as it becomes normalized as an academic field and appropriated, often by scholars who obstructed and ridiculed earlier pioneering feminist work. For male scholars—no matter how "feminist" they believe they are—to dictate to women scholars how to understand feminism properly is the final ironic twist in the long journey of feminist scholars toward recognition, a journey that began with a rebellious separation and distancing from both institutional structures and a style of knowledge that Schüssler Fiorenza calls "malestream" scholarship. It is ironic, because one of the questions feminist scholarship raised was the connection between the gender of the speaker or the scholar and the validity of her insights. For male scholars to appropriate feminism in an attempt to reassert their scholarly authority in biblical studies is a travesty of the very meaning of feminist knowledge.

Schüssler Fiorenza has reminded us time and again how resilient malestream academic authority is and warned us of the risks of patriarchal recuperation and appropriation of feminist knowledge. In the mid-1980s she pointed to the male domination of biblical studies as a field. The problem at that time was the posture of objective-scientific knowledge, oblivious to the gender of the object of knowledge as well as of the subject or producer of knowledge. The "feminist claim runs counter to the assertion of traditional historical-critical biblical scholarship that prides itself on being impartial, objective, and value-neutral."[23] In the 1990s, with the growing recognition by committed scholars of what came to be called ideological criticism, the problem was transformed from masculinist objectivity to co-optation and male appropriations of feminist theory as yet another academic discourse. Feminist scholarship in biblical studies and religious studies is in an especially risky situation because of the constant need to collaborate with academic and institutional structures that are fundamentally male dominated. Even as feminist scholars are engaged in a struggle to change these structures, they are implicated in them and often must comply with standards of excellence that are formulated by patriarchal authorities in the field. Here is how Schüssler Fiorenza articulates the problem: "Feminist biblical interpretation risks partial 'collaboration' with the patriarchal academy and biblical religions in order to change and transform them. . . . Women's studies in religion are often forced to engage in a calculated compromise in order to establish their discourses, since academic standards of excellence have been formulated by elite Euro-American men."[24] She points out that the survival of professional women in academic (and ecclesiastical) institutions requires a discursive and practical collusion. She accepts the price of calculated collusion, as long as it is used as a survival strategy or as a means of subverting patriarchal knowledge systems. It is not the sex of the thinker she rejects as dangerous, for she admittedly uses and elaborates male theories that lend themselves to feminist sensibilities. Instead, she refers to a "new" epistemology masquerading itself as having transcended all gender dualisms. She warns that the recent dependence of feminist scholars on the postmodern fathers will return us to a position of "kyriarchal" subservience to male scholarship: "Malestream scholarship rarely grants that feminists provide alternative knowledges that are equally valid although based on a different procedure of validation. Hence the malestream academy continues to insist that feminist work be measured by the prevailing intellectual standards of excellence."[25]

She points out that the increasing number of female students in seminaries and academic religious studies classes has not resulted in structural and institutional change. Malestream academic communities continue to police the discursive boundaries of their respective disciplines, thus perpetuating the automatic identification of male-produced knowledge as normative or universal. Instead, she proposes a shift from the pedagogical paradigm of domination to one of radical equality, empowering women students in their search for authority and voice. This will allow feminist academicians to create a counterdiscourse, no longer dependent on pedagogic domination and mastery as an instructional paradigm.[26]

In an article entitled "Feminist and Womanist Criticism" in a recent collection, an anonymous author takes Elisabeth Schüssler Fiorenza to task for questioning the relevance to feminism of malestream postmodern scholarship.[27] Though it may very well be the case that Jacques Derrida, Michel Foucault, Roland Barthes, and Jacques Lacan have been used by feminist critics, it is nevertheless appropriate to question their constructions of femininity as a discursive phenomenon, separating it from historical agency. It is indeed no accident that the rise of male continental theory, and the valorization of theory itself, has paralleled the rise of feminist criticism. It would seem that just when experience is named as a source of authority, and just as women enter history as producers of an alternative knowledge, sexual difference as such is being questioned. Again, it is not merely the biological or sexual provenance

of the theory that Schüssler Fiorenza questions, but rather the risk of returning women to the eternal mystique of universal femininity as inescapable trope
and metaphor. She puts it as follows: "Still, this essentialist Euro-American
discourse on Woman as Man's Other has not only been interrupted by feminist theory but has often also been incorporated by it."[28]

In *Sharing Her Word*, Schüssler Fiorenza rejects the tendency to evaluate
her own work in terms of its indebtedness to the male greats of hermeneutics,
which fails to appreciate her connection to female predecessors. Though she
herself acknowledged and credited male-authored sources when appropriate,
she is right to resist the exclusive emphasis on male provenance. With typical
clarity and forcefulness she argues for a maternal genealogy as a feminist strategy: "By constructing the genealogy of feminist hermeneutics primarily in
light of malestream biblical hermeneutics, or by spanning it into the pro-
crustean bed of the 'great fathers' of hermeneutics, feminist scholars are in
danger of collaborating in the continuing kyriarchal silencing and marginal-
izing of feminist theoretical work."[29]

Though feminist scholarship has decidedly made serious inroads into biblical studies, the academic process of evaluation that decides who receives a
grant and who gets published and where is still largely in male hands. Feminist
students must get the approval of malestream professors, and even feminist
professors continue to depend on malestream colleagues and administrators
for approval and advancement. That male scholars continue to control the
means of production of feminist knowledge means that this knowledge has
been interpreted largely as yet another ingredient to be added to and stirred
into the pot of biblical studies. The current co-optation of feminist studies
makes it impossible to use it as a means of transforming the entire field of biblical studies into an ethically committed and institutionally independent field
that values both social action and scholarship. The current state of affairs
makes it impossible for biblical feminism to change the field into one that
could "critically address public political discourses and individual questions
seeking for a world of justice and well being."[30]

In *Rhetoric and Ethic: The Politics of Biblical Studies*, Schüssler Fiorenza
argues that "scholarly discussions on rhetorical method and theory remain
firmly anchored in the malestream of academic discourses that marginalize
feminist work as ideological, if they mention it at all."[31] Only when rhetorical criticism accepts feminist criticism as an equal partner will the field be
able to transform itself from a scholarly discourse removed from the world

into a discourse that has the ability to change social relations of exploitation and dehumanization.

ANTI-JUDAISM IN CHRISTIAN FEMINISM AND BIBLICAL STUDIES

As a Jew, secular or not, I have never been able to remain indifferent to discussions of anti-Semitism or anti-Judaism in the profession. Judith Plaskow, Susannah Heschel, Amy-Jill Levine, and others have raised the important problem of anti-Judaism in biblical and religious studies in the American academy in general and in feminist theology in particular. Having recently reread *In Memory of Her*, I was struck by Schüssler Fiorenza's awareness of anti-Jewish sentiment in Christian popular culture and New Testament scholarship. When she wrote the book in 1983 there was a small number of articles on this subject. Some Jewish feminist scholars found her presentation of the Jesus movement as a reform, renewal, or protest movement within Judaism problematic because it implies that Second Temple Judaism—a highly diverse and complex civilization—as such was patriarchal.

I would suggest that Schüssler Fiorenza rejects a totalizing definition of Judaism as patriarchal. Her statements reveal a challenge to other Christian feminists who constructed a dichotomy between Judaism and Christianity. As she put it (and again the date is 1983): "The issue is not whether or not Jesus overturned patriarchy but whether Judaism had elements of a critical feminist impulse that came to the fore in the vision and ministry of Jesus. . . . The praxis and vision of Jesus and his movement is best understood as an inner-Jewish renewal movement that presented an alternative option to the dominant patriarchal structures rather than an oppositional formation rejecting the values and praxis of Judaism."[32] Schüssler Fiorenza makes it clear that in her understanding, the women who followed Jesus, like Jesus himself, were part of a Jewish movement. She also takes to task Christian feminist theologians who fail to reject anti-Jewish elements in the Gospels, in this case Luke: "Christian feminists who want to claim the revelatory authority of this text as liberating for women also highlight the tension between the action of Jesus and the argument of the synagogue leader. However, they too tend to neglect to question the anti-Jewish tendencies inscribed in the controversy dialogue."[33]

In *But She Said*, Schüssler Fiorenza calls for a hermeneutic sensitivity to implications of feminist readings of New Testament texts assigning Jewish women an inferior position, while highlighting the alleged liberation of women in early Christianity. Though she explains that feminist interpreters who follow this paradigm tend to repeat malestream anti-Judaic traditions, she warns against perpetuating such errors: "Nevertheless, a feminist critical hermeneutics of liberation must reject such an anti-Jewish interpretation, because it seeks to eliminate the oppression and marginality of Christian women by historically perpetuating that of Jewish women."[34]

In *Jesus: Miriam's Child, Sophia's Prophet,* Schüssler Fiorenza clarifies that the Jesus movement she described in her earlier work was not merely a renewal movement within Judaism (a claim some interpret as supersessionist) but mainly a political, anti-imperial, apocalyptic movement, one among several Jewish resistance groups. In addition to emphasizing the oppressive impact of the Roman Empire on Jewish men, and especially women of all classes, she emphasizes that "Jesus was not crucified because of his theological teachings but because of their potentially subversive character and the political threat to the imperial colonial system."[35] In this context she avoids idealizing the Jesus movement, noting the social divisions and hierarchical tensions within it, and the anti-Jewish and anti-woman rhetoric in the Gospels' articulation of an emerging Christian identity.[36]

In *Jesus and the Politics of Interpretation,* she argues that "anti-Judaism and antifeminism are two sides of one and the same kyriarchal coin."[37] By ignoring the presence of Jewish women in the Jesus movement, historians manifest an antifeminist stance, as they endorse an anti-Judaic position. Repudiating the idealization of the Jesus movement as an exclusive movement for reform, seeking to redress the inequality of women as women, Schüssler Fiorenza suggests that her own work was directed at exposing egalitarian elements in the earliest Jesus traditions.[38] She admits the deep roots and unconscious residues that continue to mar feminist analyses of New Testament texts and histories. She agrees with several Jewish feminist critiques regarding the need for a new scholarly method of investigating Christian traditions of origins. Finally, she goes on to offer a detailed list of practical steps that scholars of the New Testament can take to remedy what she sees as the "kyriarchal virus of anti-Judaism."[39]

While some may contest the use of such terms as *women-church, ekklēsia,* and *basileia* as both Christocentric and exclusive, we should remember that Elisabeth does not deny her own religious position and theological location. Her terminology is clearly indebted in some cases to this social context. There is, however, a difference between contextual provenance and intentional anti-Judaism. Elisabeth puts it in the following terms: "In the context of the Roman Catholic women's movement in the United States I coined the expression *ekklesia gynaikon* as 'women-church' as a counterterm to patriarchy in order to assert that, although silenced by the patriarchal church, women are church—*ekklesia*—and we have always been church."[40] By definition, a commitment to a particular community of faith would make it impossible for anyone to transcend fully that community's discursive practices. It is up to us to consider what terms apply to our specific faith community, if we "belong" to one. In my personal case, I would prefer a more neutral term for the radical, egalitarian democratic community of feminist interpreters, one that would be inclusive of both secular and religious feminists. But then this contested *ekklēsia* is meant to offer a site for interpretive struggle and, as such, to be the perfect occasion for clarifying our disagreements. The democratic and egalitarian community of women is not the occasion for denunciation and exclusion but is a space for "clarifying and adjudicating contested concepts and proposals. It seeks to engender biblical interpretation as a process of moral deliberation and practical solidarity in the midst of diverse and often competing struggles for liberation."[41] Deliberations about language and discourse should be part of this community, and therefore, what Elisabeth calls an "invitation to wisdom-sophia" should be accepted, rather than rejected. We may pick and choose our preferred terms, and let go of those that do not resonate with our cultural background and religious contexts.

In *Bread Not Stone,* Schüssler Fiorenza makes a comment that I would construe as a challenge to Jewish feminists to create a hermeneutics of their own, that is, to elaborate specifically Jewish questions and approaches to the biblical text. She puts it as follows: "Therefore we cannot speak about a feminist biblical interpretation as long as Jewish feminist hermeneutics has not developed in its own right and articulated its own specific questions and approaches."[42] Though we have witnessed a proliferation of Jewish feminist midrash in the last decade, and though numerous Jewish feminist critics have blazed new and innovative paths to the Hebrew Bible (and the New Testament), I would agree with Elisabeth here, that a coherent, or even incoherent Jewish feminist interpretive genealogy has not yet been reconstructed. Much as I regret to admit it, a recognizable Jewish feminist hermeneutics has not yet been produced, though we can point to numerous Jewish feminist interpretations (in the plural). No systematic taxonomy of the kind Schüssler

Fiorenza has produced for the Christian feminist community has yet been created, perhaps because systematic theological and interpretive taxonomies have never been a priority within Jewish tradition. This is also not to say that a Jewish reading of my reading of the Bible and the readings of other Jewish feminists are not amenable to a theoretical articulation of a specifically Jewish feminist hermeneutics. In *Sexual Politics in the Biblical Narrative,* I approached the Hebrew Bible as a literary-political text. Having been educated in a secular public school system, I never approached the Bible as anything but literature (though I spent the first years of my schooling in an Orthodox school for girls). Though in hindsight I may argue that the radical questioning and investigative hermeneutics I proposed in my early essays are Jewish as a matter of style and exegetical discourse, I was not aware of it at the time. When I suggested earlier that we ask ideological questions of the text, I could not know that this would become a major critical concern in the 1990s. I thought I was asking specifically feminist questions from the text, rather than Jewish questions. In the 1990s ideology came to encompass gender, as well as racial, class, and national differences. "Difference" has replaced, or has been added to "identity" as the primary heuristic category of feminist biblical analysis, and therefore it is time for those who identify as Jewish feminists to create a different hermeneutic genealogy and tradition, a different *kehila* or *havurah* that will be inclusive of all stripes and varieties of Jewish expression—radically democratic, egalitarian, and open to deliberation, struggle for change, and disagreement. In the spirit of Elisabeth's practical guidelines, I would add the need for establishing a Jewish women's section of the Society of Biblical Literature, an organization that has assigned special sections to all other "different" communities, but so far not to Jews.

THE POSITION OF THE RESIDENT ALIEN

Another suggestive category of difference that lends itself to a doubled interpretation as political location and hermeneutic position is described by Schüssler Fiorenza as the position of the woman immigrant, or foreigner. Before I begin, I should stress that as a white, heterosexual woman tenured in an academic institution and a naturalized citizen in the United States, I am unquestionably in a position of privilege, and I would venture to assume that Elisabeth would join me in sharing this description as fitting her social location as well. Nevertheless, having been born in Israel, I am reminded on a daily basis that no matter how well adapted, I am still a foreigner here, living in a national, ethnic, geographical, and cultural exile.[43] As an immigrant who abandoned the Zionist dream and the Holy Land, I was doubly suspect especially within the traditional Jewish American (even academic) community. I often found that I walked a tightrope between malestream academia and the local Jewish community in Tucson, an outsider in "my" professional and cultural contexts.

In *Sharing Her Word,* Schüssler Fiorenza proposes that we conceptualize the "foreigner" as a category of analysis in our reading of biblical texts.[44] Like the immigrant who is both American and non-American, the feminist reader is both an insider and an interloper in the academic fields of biblical studies and religious studies. In addition to religious identity, national difference can and should be theorized as part of a broader feminist hermeneutic project, and the repressed language of the feminist interpreter should be conceptualized as a resource of interpretive strength rather than as an inferior accent. This is how she puts it: "The notion of resident alien positions one as both insider and outsider: insider by virtue of residence or family affiliation to a citizen or institutions; outsider in terms of language, experience, culture and history."[45] What she seeks to prevent is the "naturalization" of feminists within the academic (or theological) institutions as yet another constituency, a normalization that will surely lead to the dissipation of the feminist quest for change. To maintain the political commitment to social transformation, one must experience institutionally and materially a sense of alienation. The dilemma that faces feminists as members of the academe (and of theological institutions) today differs remarkably from the dilemma we faced in the 1970s as we strove for recognition and authority. Now that male "feminists" seek to imitate and appropriate feminist discourse, the dilemma is different. It has metamorphosed within a period of barely two decades from alienation and isolation to co-optation and institutionalization. It is therefore apt that the original sense of alienation be maintained as a political and hermeneutic perspective, even as we share the academic, professional, or religious language of our respective communities of knowledge and faith.

In her typical way, Schüssler Fiorenza once again suggests a way of self-transformation from weakness and marginality to empowerment, not by abandoning the former but by owning and flaunting it. Her theoretical use of her personal social location is yet another manifestation of what I have repeatedly named here as her insistence on the "both-and" dialectics. Just as she keeps a hermeneutics of suspicion in vital tension with a hermeneutics of reconstruction and affirmation, so does she now advocate an insistence on a doubled status of insider and outsider, realizing full well that success—that is, institutional recognition—often leads to atrophy and loss of purpose. Even as privileged feminist scholars are to keep their focus on the pyramid of oppression, including class, race, and ethnicity, they are to always maintain a vivid memory of their/our history as outsiders. As Jews or blacks, we may wish to maintain our own special memory or continued sense of alienation. As feminists, Elisabeth tells us, the insider/outsider status is a condition that is at the same time an irritant, a necessary vigilance, and a useful hermeneutic strategy, as we produce interpretations in the language of the fathers about concepts and spaces that are our mothers'—however we wish to define them.

Notes

1. Esther Fuchs, *Israeli Mythogynies: Women in Contemporary Israeli Fiction* (Albany: State University of New York Press, 1987).

2. Elisabeth Schüssler Fiorenza, *Sharing Her Word: Feminist Biblical Interpretation in Context* (Boston: Beacon, 1998), 13. I refer to "Elisabeth" as well as to "Schüssler Fiorenza" in my piece not only to avoid monotony but also to highlight various aspects of the person discussed.

3. Schüssler Fiorenza, *Sharing Her Word*, 14.

4. Ilana Pardes situates my work in theoretical terms in *Countertraditions in the Bible: A Feminist Approach* (Cambridge, Mass./London: Harvard University Press, 1992); see also Pamela J. Milne, "Toward Feminist Companionship: The Future of Feminist Biblical Studies and Feminism," in *Reading the Bible: Approaches, Methods and Strategies,* ed. Athalya Brenner and Carole Fontaine (Sheffield: Sheffield Academic Press, 1997), 39–60.

5. Elisabeth Schüssler Fiorenza, *In Memory of Her: A Feminist Theological Reconstruction of Christian Origins* (New York: Crossroad, 1983), 60.

6. Elisabeth Schüssler Fiorenza, *But She Said: Feminist Practices of Biblical Interpretation* (Boston: Beacon, 1992), 91.

7. Ibid., 91.

8. Ibid., 87.

9. Ibid., 101

10. Ibid., 86.

11. Carolyn Heilbrun and Catharine Stimpson, "Theories of Feminist Criticism: A Dialogue," in *Feminist Literary Criticism: Explorations in Theory,* ed. Josephine Donovan (Lexington: University Press of Kentucky, 1975), 61–73.

12. Schüssler Fiorenza, *But She Said*, 57.

13. Elisabeth Schüssler Fiorenza, *Bread Not Stone: The Challenge of Feminist Biblical Interpretation* (Boston: Beacon, 1984), 15–16.

14. Schüssler Fiorenza, *But She Said*, 115, 114.

15. Schüssler Fiorenza, *Sharing Her Word*, 90.

16. See Schüssler Fiorenza, *But She Said*, 93.

17. See my *Sexual Politics in the Biblical Narrative: Reading the Hebrew Bible as a Woman* (Sheffield: Sheffield Academic Press, 2000).

18. See n. 11 above.

19. Schüssler Fiorenza, *But She Said*, 5.

20. Elisabeth Schüssler Fiorenza, *Jesus: Miriam's Child, Sophia's Prophet: Critical Issues in Feminist Christology* (New York: Continuum, 1994), 27.

21. Ibid., 28.

22. Ibid., 8.

23. Schüssler Fiorenza, *Bread Not Stone*, 107.

24. Schüssler Fiorenza, *But She Said*, 184.

25. Schüssler Fiorenza, *Sharing Her Word*, 45.

26. Ibid., 46.

27. The article is included in *The Postmodern Bible* authored and edited by the Bible and Culture Collective (New Haven/London: Yale University Press, 1995), 225–71.

28. Schüssler Fiorenza, *But She Said*, 136.

29. Schüssler Fiorenza, *Sharing Her Word*, 73.

30. Elisabeth Schüssler Fiorenza, *Rhetoric and Ethic: The Politics of Biblical Studies* (Minneapolis: Fortress, 1999), 193.

31. Ibid., 91.

32. Schüssler Fiorenza, *In Memory of Her*, 107.

33. Schüssler Fiorenza, *But She Said*, 209. See also her critique of the anti-Judaism of the *Woman's Bible* in *Sharing Her Word*, 68.

34. Schüssler Fiorenza, *But She Said*, 59.

35. Schüssler Fiorenza, *Jesus: Miriam's Child*, 93.

36. Ibid., 95.

37. Elisabeth Schüssler Fiorenza, *Jesus and the Politics of Interpretation* (New York/London: Continuum, 2000), 122.

38. Ibid., 133.

39. Ibid., 142–44.

40. Schüssler Fiorenza, *But She Said*, 131.

41. Ibid., 132.

42. Schüssler Fiorenza, *Bread Not Stone*.

43. See Esther Fuchs, "Exiles, Jews, Women, *Yordim*, I: An Interim Report," in *Women's Writing in Exile*, ed. Mary Lyn Broe and Angela Ingram (Chapel Hill/Lon-

don: University of North Carolina Press, 1989), 295–300; eadem, "Exile, Memory, Subjectivity: A *Yoredet* Reflects on National Identity and Gender," in *Women and the Politics of Military Confrontation: Palestinian and Israeli Gendered Narratives of Dislocation,* ed. Nahla Abdo and Ronit Lentin (New York/Oxford: Berghahn Books, 2002), 279–94.

44. Schüssler Fiorenza, *Sharing Her Word,* 8.

45. Ibid., 44–45.

2

Women's Altars

Lived Religion from Now to Then

Alice Bach

T O HONOR ELISABETH SCHÜSSLER FIORENZA'S CENTRAL CON-
tributions to and influence in the field of women and religion affords one
the opportunity of combining many subdisciplines in the examination of a
question involving women's lives in the ancient Mediterranean world. While
Elisabeth's work has focused primarily on the historical and theological roads
leading to and from the New Testament and on the effect of Christianity on
women since the earliest times of the religion, her insistence on gender as a
valid scholarly lens through which to analyze early Christianity opened up a
vast field of inquiry. Since we have so little literary evidence from the ancient
world reflecting women's voices, one needs to use a bit of auditory magic to
elicit these voices. The more time I have spent listening to women's voices
struggling with questions of identity in our contemporary world, the more
tempted I have been to link our voices back to the silent women of antiquity.
Although my own research is based more on literary texts than historical evidence, the lifelong attention to women's issues that Elisabeth's work has
reflected has convinced many feminist scholars of the possibility and accept-
ability of experimentation, of pushing out the boundaries of what has been
termed "correct" scholarship.

Through stories, women communicate the rhythms of dailiness. While
men surely have been storytellers, they have had law codes and political ora-
tions and philosophical treatises from the earliest written times to document

21

their thoughts and reflect their lives. Because the shape of women's lives tends not to be linear, not directed toward a goal, one often finds women's stories to be circular, complex, circumstantial, often cloudlike, plump with feeling and desire. Some records of dailiness are woven into quilts; some are planted into gardens; others are sculpted into clay, painted onto pottery, inscribed into journals and letters. Women's stories tend to be laden with details—what we ate, what we wore, what we said, each to the other. We have few literary records and few artifacts from the ancient Mediterranean world that reveal women's world through women's eyes. Thus, what is real in our records of women's lives must be imagined in the world of ancient Mediterranean women.

Feminist poet Judy Grahn has expressed the frustration we have with trying to focus on what is not there, words and pictures of the lives of women of antiquity. In her collection of poems, *The Queen of Wands,* Grahn expresses the frustration of a woman struggling against the silence of her foremothers.

> They say she is veiled
> And a mystery. That is
> One way of looking.
> Another
> is that she is where
> she always has been,
> exactly in place,
> and it is we,
> we who are mystified,
> we who are veiled
> and without faces.[1]

Even a queen and a legendary beauty like Helen had not the power to carve her way through the world in which she lived. While we have splinters of the literary lives of the privileged in this world through the male-authored epic texts, we lack the sense of dailiness or intimate contact with the women from that time. Thus we remain veiled, wishing for the power to see and hear across time. Grahn's realization that it is we who are veiled seems right to me. Poets are allowed to spend their days squinting across time. Scholars are meant to devise a method that will reveal that world without a trace of our handprints on the creation. Fortunately, some scholars have been as frustrated as poets, wanting to sense that ancient time, acknowledging that the reified tradition of impartiality and *truth* needs to crumble. The process of tumbling backwards through time is what I think many feminist scholars are trying to refine. I connect this process with Schüssler Fiorenza's term *slippage*, which I understand to be a gap or lacuna in thinking, a gap in which the feminine resides.[2]

Another approach to studying religion and culture embeds the religious person and community in history, that sees history and culture not as something that religious persons are "in" but as the media through which they fundamentally are. This method, the study of lived religion, is supported by what Pierre Bourdieu has named the *habitus*—the power of cultural structures and inherited idioms both to shape and to discipline thought as well as to give rise to religious creativity and interpretation.[3] According to Robert Orsi, a colleague of Elisabeth Schüssler Fiorenza at Harvard, "what is called for is the recognition that it is the historicized and enculturated religious imagination that is also the imagination by means of which in Marx's well-quoted expression, the frozen circumstances of our worlds are forced to dance by our singing to them their own melodies. Orsi is talking about "lived religion," a method for examining religious practice through the realia and religious imagery that reflect the way people live their religious beliefs as part of their daily lives. What excited me about this approach of lived religion is precisely what is anathema to many in the discipline of biblical studies, that is, establishing a link between the practices one studies and one's own everyday concerns. As Orsi has noted (and this study and its fruits are permeated with Orsi's method and sensibility), "the acknowledgment of a resonance between our experiences in the present and those of people in the past is so fearsome to historians that they have branded it a heresy and history departments strain to ensure that their neophytes are free of any taint of this notion."[4]

I have welcomed the taint in order to look at women's altars and shrines as images of visual piety that reflect women's culture, with its domestic locus and fragmented use of everyday objects. Schüssler Fiorenza would approve such a theoretical leap she would understand the desire for experimentation, which might further the understanding of women's history in any of its particularities. One such intellectual leap might look like this: I look at several sixth-century B.C.E. vases from Corinth showing scenes of women in a line holding hands. They are clearly involved in some sort of women's religious ritual . . . *dancing, walking in processions, and making offerings.* Southeast of Corinth, across the Mediterranean, to the Phoenician and Israelite cultures—were there women's festivals, similar to the rituals to Demeter and Kore? Were there flowers, aromatic as the marigolds in the Latina Day of the Dead festi-

vals? How did ancient women express the elements of interiority and dailiness that we have come to recognize as a defining element in contemporary
women artists' visions?

I have tried to focus on Orsi's lived religion scheme, what anthropologist
James Clifford has called "that moment in which the possibility of comparison exists in unmediated tension with the sheer incongruity . . . a permanent
ironic play of similarity and difference, the familiar and the strange, the here
and the elsewhere."[5] Leaning on these two scholars and woman wisdom, I
have tried not to explain away those missing elements in ancient Mediterranean cultures that render our own culture newly incomprehensible.

An altar of sacrifice, an altar of devotion, an altar tended by a priest to a
deity, these are the altars of ceremony, of public religious ritual. But there
have been personal or household altars tended by women in each of these
patriarchal religions. A domestic altar contains a woman's artistic as well as
her religious expression and therefore bears evaluation purely in terms of its
material arrangement and the motives this arrangement reveals. Women's
altars promote an aesthetic of relationship. It can be argued that a domestic
altar may be the prototype for many of women's domestic arts, such as quilting, needlepoint, and appliqué, which evolve from the art-making process
that artist Miriam Schapiro has named *femmage*. *Femmage* (a play on collage
and assemblage) is women's artistic process of collecting and joining seemingly disparate elements into a functional whole.[6]

In the domestic altars I have analyzed, elements of *femmage* project
women's chosen social and spiritual values. Notably heterogeneous, *femmage*
is still unintentional as it drives a cycle that constantly turns fragmentation to
wholeness and then back again. As a sacred, symbolic manifestation of this
cycle, the home altar demonstrates the value of fragments, which, when
linked together, provide a center of focus derived not by imposition but
organically through layering and accretion. Are there markers of women's
altars in the Hebrew Bible and other ancient literary texts?

When they fled with Jacob from their father's house, Leah and Rachel took
their household gods with them. The Greek hearth altar dedicated to Hestia
became the Roman one devoted to Vesta. The altar to the Virgin Mary occupying a niche in the home of a thirteenth-century woman of Lucca finds its
counterpart in an Italian Catholic home in Brooklyn. An American Buddhist
in California tends the Shinto altar of his deceased Japanese father-in-law,
while his wife constructs a domestic altar of bark and stone to the Great
Mother Goddess. My own home altars are varied: dried flowers, carved

figures of women amid the flames of purgatory, the Mexican *anima sola,* the traditional figures of the popular celebration of All Souls' Day next to a peace button on top of my grandfather's childhood Bible resting against a Santos figure of St. Francis. The connections that my eye makes to each of these objects narrate a personal story, intimate as prayer, but visible, tangible. For the creator of the altar or shrine, a seemingly random arrangement of objects is orderly and full of meaning; the altar can be read like a lyric poem, with verbal metaphors replaced by visual images—experimentation with the meaning and use of objects, images, and symbols. A landscape of memory, a personal altar gives old memories new contexts. Having an altar within the house allows one to integrate the daily world and the shrine world, crossing seamlessly the boundaries between the sacred and the profane. As one continually revises the altar, the reification of belief and the symbols that recall tradition change, keeping the spiritual life reflective of and concurrent with daily life.

A reflection of personal spirituality, the domestic altar is a site of subversion and insistence on the evolutionary nature of institutional religion. Women's domestic altars have in my opinion changed little across time. As women have reinvigorated old practices with new symbols, the consideration of women's altars as important elements of women's culture can be seen through an examination of hybridized Catholic ritual practices: within altars for Mexican Day of the Dead celebrations, and within Vodou altars from Haiti and the southern Mississippi Delta region. In a recent study of American folklore, the placement of memorial poetry and photography in local newspapers suggests that a woman's role is to mark family occasions during the calendar year and the life cycle, and that women regard it as their privilege, as representatives of the family, to report and publicize both joyous and mournful changes in life. Displaying their visual metaphors, altars provide women with a cherished mnemonic device for discerning a narrative order in their lives. Narrative memory works with popular religious imagery in creating and installing its shrines and also falls upon devotional images associated with rites of passage. Read through a spiritual lens, then, the primary function of the altar may be to disclose the benevolent and constant presence of God within the house. Read as a proponent of "lived religion" methodology, the altar reflects the elimination of boundaries between people doing religious things in the past and us today.

What arguments are there for envisioning invisible altars, not altars of death and sacrifice, but altars of spiritual connection between the sacred and the profane? Instead of scattered with blood and oil, were there altars redolent of spices and perfume, containing household gods, a scrap of silver, a shard of pottery that had personal meaning to the family who walked past it each day. Did women fashion special plates to hold the raisin cakes (*kawwānîm*[7]) for the Queen of Heaven? Did ritual objects associated with private devotions fill the spiritual space between what Pierre Bourdieu has called the "objective order and the subjective principle of organization?"

Were aromatic oils such as cinnamon, spice, incense, myrrh, and frankincense more widely used than the biblical texts have mentioned? Listen to the female voice in Jeremiah 44:19, "And the women said, 'Indeed we will go on making offerings to the queen of heaven and pouring out libations to her; do you think that we made cakes for her, marked with her image, and poured out libations to her without our husbands' being involved?'" Though the prophets cry out against making altars to other gods, though the Hebrew biblical texts continually remind the people of Israel of God's loyalty, we are reminded that both men and women turn to other gods, some of whom apparently delight in raisin cakes.

Susan Ackerman's descriptions of popular religion (another term for lived religion) during the time of the writing prophets in Israel provide arguments for the existence of rituals and traditions clearly despised by the prophets, priests, and Deuteronomists.[8] But there is very little actual data about the rituals, or the realia connected to women's religion or, more broadly, popular religion. One exception is a clay mold found at Mari that has been connected with cakes that are baked to honor the Queen of Heaven. This mold has the impression of a female figure with her hands cupping her breasts.[9] While many scholars line up to affirm that this figure is the deity referred to as the Queen of Heaven, Ackerman sensibly notes that there is no indication that the nude female figure is divine, since the Mari mold was found in a collection of animal and flower molds that are clearly decorative. I think it would be curious to offer cakes molded in the shape of a nude woman unless the figure was meant to represent a deity. Regardless of where one stands in the scholarly debate about the identity of the woman on the mold, my point is that there is a strong undercurrent of women's celebration, women's ritual, that has been a continuous element of lived religion throughout various cultures.

Further irritation at popular rituals appears in the collection of warnings and prophecies of Jeremiah, offering more proof that the subversive activities of the people of Israel continue to provoke God. "The children gather wood, the fathers kindle fire, and the women knead dough, to make cakes for the queen of heaven; and they pour out drink offerings to other gods" (Jer. 7:18). What better description can one offer for an entire family worshiping together, collaborating in their stiff-necked refusal to ignore all gods but YHWH. More than most biblical scholars, savant Robert Carroll has taken delight in this verse, referring to it as "a family that prays together stays together."[10] Central to this complaint of the prophet is the reflection that all these activities, gathering wood, kindling fire, and kneading dough, are the components of everyday life, common tasks that are being dedicated to the Queen of Heaven instead of YHWH. Evoking this connection between the spiritual and the mundane provides a clue to the subtle interweaving of the indigenous worship of the so-called pagan gods into the observable behavior of Israelite families.

Many scholars have noted the connection of the Great Mother to the Roman goddess Cybele and other female deities of the Mediterranean world, and to Isis and local female goddesses. Aspects of each of these deities participate in the evolution of the visual images of the Virgin Mary during the Middle Ages. Cybele, a mother goddess in the Roman pantheon, was contradictorily considered by some worshipers to be a virgin goddess, although this delineation seems dubious, given her mythic identification. Male scholars who have written about the cult of Mary have in general considered the cult masochistic, marginal, and somewhat bizarre. There is a particular interest in the *galli*, the priests who perform self-castration, cutting, and flagellation as part of their rituals in the cult of the mother goddess, and then of the Virgin Mary.

From the time of St. Augustine, the negative attitudes toward the "pagan" cults, particularly that of the Great Mother, proliferated, and the cults were considered to contain the vilest of religious practices. The righteous outrage of Augustine is an echo of the prophetic warnings of Jeremiah.

> The Great Mother has surpassed all her sons, not in greatness of deity, but of crime. To this monster not even the monstrosity of Janus is to be compared. His deformity was only in his image; hers was the deformity of cruelty in her sacred rites. . . . This abomination [the Great Mother] is not surpassed by the licentious deeds of Jupiter, so many and so great. He with all his seductions of women, only disgraced heaven, and with one Ganymede; she [the Great Mother] . . . has both defiled the earth and outraged heaven. (Augustine, *City of God* 7.26)

At the same time that visual messages of the Virgin as perfect mother came to dominate the production of images for the church, verbal messages pronouncing the innate inferiority of women were part of the traditional Catholic theology. This contrast has been examined by Margaret Miles, who has argued that women's personal interpretations of visual images have produced a strategy for self-empowerment over and against verbal misogyny. Miles looks at the Virgin Mary and sees not the testimony to her purity and passivity glorified by the church, but rather an understanding of her freedom from the entailment of marriage and sexuality, and hence her spiritual autonomy. I wonder what items from the practitioners of the old earth-based religions in the Middle Ages, the potions, amulets, incarnations, blessings at births and healings, what part of these elements of lived religion have disappeared, hidden under the weight of established religious propriety.

ALTARS OF THE DAY OF THE DEAD

There are vibrant examples of women's spirituality vividly interwoven within religious festivals and rituals. While we have no specific parallels from the ancient world, it seems clear from looking at differing cultural ritual shrines and altars—some intentionally temporary, such as cakes, flowers, or cut paper—that the creative impulses motivating women to make shrines or altars in our own times were probably operative in the Mediterranean cultures under consideration. One sense of "it might have been" comes through the voice of Epiphanius in the fourth century C.E. The concern was that Arabian women were baking cakes to the Virgin Mary.

> They prepare a kind of cake in the name of the ever-Virgin. They assemble together, and in the name of the holy Virgin they attempt to undertake a deed that is irreverent and blasphemous beyond measure—they function as priests for women. . . . For some women prepare a certain kind of little cake with four indentations, cover it with a fine linen veil on a solemn day of the year, and on certain (other) days, they set forth bread and offer it in the name of Mary. They all partake of the bread. (*Medicine Box* 78.23, 79)[11]

One of the most exuberant of the modern feasts with women creating and tending impromptu altars occurs on November 2, the feast of All Souls in the Catholic Church, celebrated in Mexico and Chicano-America as the Day of the Dead. A quick examination of this traditional holiday illustrates ways in which women have worked to share their resources of food and flowers and household care, which have resulted in a process of hybridization between older pagan or primal religious traditions with the dicta of the church. A study of the impudent imagery of the Day of the Dead underscores its subversive nature and destabilizes our reified expectations about the visual systems of religious value and representation to which we have become attached. I take personal delight in the shock of the uninitiated as they come upon these figures in my house and gaze transfixed at the skeletal heads—blinding them to the comedy of the figures engaged in daily activities, talking on the phone, enjoying a massage, performing surgery.

The Day of the Dead is a time when Mexican families spend hours at the cemetery, visiting the graves of their relatives. Women clean and decorate the headstones, arrange flowers, especially flowers of the dead (marigolds) and light candles. It is a time for eating and drinking, surrounded by reminders of the relative's favorite earthly objects, a subversion of the grim threat of death itself, and also the time to construct special domestic altars dedicated to the spirits of deceased loved ones. Such altars range from simple to very elaborate and are usually filled with objects that provided pleasure to the departed person in life, including favorite food and drink. Altars dedicated to the spirits of deceased children often include toys, candy, and other sweets. Because the altars are created by those who knew intimately the deceased, the private desires and tastes of the departed person can be heaped on the altars for the living to savor. Although the home altars change and add objects, a few items persist. A holy image, usually of the Virgen de Guadalupe, is situated in the center of the altar, and a photograph of the dead relative and his/her favorite foods are placed upon the altar—an echo of the raisin cakes made for the Queen of Heaven and an extension of the cult of the Virgin Mary.

The altars, or *ofrendas* as they are called, also usually contain objects made from sugar or sugar sculpture known as *alfenique*. These sculpted objects may be small animals, such as lambs, miniature plates of food (enchiladas with mole), small coffins, often with pop-up skeletons, and of course, the sugar skull, or *calavera*. The skulls are made by pouring a mixture of boiling water, confectioner's sugar and lime into clay molds that have been previously soaked in water. The *calaveras* are decorated with paper foil for eyes and a kind of colored icing for hair. Names can be added to the skull and Mexican children often exchange them. While to the uninitiated these wide-eyed skulls may seem grisly, to those familiar with the ritual, the Day of the Dead is a joyous time and the symbols a joking nod to death. If the tradition had not continued through time, the sugar *alfenique* and *calavera* would have dissolved into invisibility, and the aroma of marigolds would have left no trace of their peppery scent. And as in the instance of the raisin cakes baked for the Queen of Heaven and the cakes baked by the Christian Arabian women, we would have gleaned crumbs from some report by an unfriendly observer.

Vodou Altars

Vodou is a low-budget religion that thrives on the bits and pieces of daily life. It cycles all the world that comes its way; its altars move and vibrate like dances for the eyes. The plump head of a doll that arrives on an airplane from Miami as a Christmas present may be adorning an altar in Haiti three hours later. As with the Day of the Dead figures, some "high-art" critics have questioned whether these personal altars are art. Is it art *trouvé*, assemblage? Is it even sacred art at all? In Vodou ceremonies, objects are chosen, assembled, and dedicated to deities whose tastes are shaped as often by fashion as by tradition. Thus, any object may be sacred if it pleases the deities, since its reason for being positioned on an altar is to summon, appease, contain, or direct divine energies. Just as the skeletal figures that reflect the daily lives of dead ancestors on All Souls' Day, are considered sacred by the Latinos who create them and are sustained by them, a Voodoo practitioner from Brooklyn explained to me that "any object could do *mystique* if you believe in it. You do some kind of prayer and you touch the objects and the prayer becomes reality." To connect this *obeah* woman with the vital role that material goods play in the process of meaning-making is to wrap her in the theories of Pierre Bourdieu. In a prose that is at least as dense as a Vodou shrine, Bourdieu's *habitus* theory reflects a collective structure that is not rigidly predetermined. For those for whom theory is a shrine, Bourdieu's *habitus* is "a system of lasting transposable dispositions that integrate historical experience into a body of schemes that can be transferred analogously to new situations in order to solve new problems."[12]

Altars are the ideal form, and dolls, glittery objects, and handmade toys are the *habitus* for all Vodou's sacred arts.[13] They are palimpsests of Haiti's twisted history, made coherent through the eyes of synchronous gods. To look at an altar cluttered with whiskey bottles, satin pomanders, clay pots dressed in lace, sequins, feathers, plaster statues of Catholic saints, laughing Buddha figures, rosaries, crucifixes, bug-eyed kewpie dolls is to enter the ghost lives of slaves and free, indigenous and colonial, all the dances for the eyes, conflicting beliefs, traditions, from Dahomey and Kongo to the country houses of the south of France.

The scraps of dailiness used in Vodou also provide special ingredients and objects to create the *mojo,* or magic, that has been central for black women to achieve a kind of resurrection from lives of poverty and oppression to works of art. In the tradition of African women, excavating and connecting African-Caribbean, African, and southern black women's rituals and culture, recycling the artifacts of women's everyday lives, Betye Saar uses fabrics, photographs, laces, hats, boxes, bottles, and urban artifacts to assemble collages of protest art. Writing about one of her best-known works, "The Liberation of Aunt Jemima," Saar describes her *femmage,* "As a shaman gleans the environment for special ingredients and objects to fabricate the *mojo,* I glean the flea markets, estate sales, and thrift shops around my home in Los Angeles or places I visit such as Alaska, Maine and Texas. Marketplaces in Africa, Brazil, Crete, Mexico have also divulged special materials for my work."[14]

The impact of Vodou altars has been described as visual jazz, constantly reworked and revised, representing the music of time. The aesthetic of these altars is certainly improvisational; they can never be finished. Nobel-Prize–winning poet Derek Walcott has described the altars of his homeland, the Caribbean island of St. Lucia, in a collage of poetic words.

> Break a vase, and the love that reassembles the fragments is stronger than that love which took its symmetry for granted when it was whole. . . . This gathering of broken pieces is the care and pain of the Antilles, and if the pieces are disparate, ill-fitting, they contain more pain than their original sculpture, those icons and sacred vessels taken for granted in their ancestral places. Antillean art is this restoration of our shattered histories, our shards of vocabulary, our archipelago becoming a synonym for pieces broken off that the original continent.[15]

NEW YORK CITY

When I first became interested in the phenomenon of contemporary women's altars, and the possibility of ancient domestic altars maintained by women, I had no idea that my own hometown, the greatest city in the world, would itself become an altar. Its most public spaces would become private; its secular rushing rhythms would become a dirge. The clang of garbage trucks would be replaced with the keening of women and men searching for loved ones, and finding not twisted bodies, but rather twisted steel girders and pulverized concrete. Suddenly on a cloudless blue-skied morning at the beginning of a new academic year, my idea of altars and sacred spaces changed forever. The material has been transformed into the spiritual; the differences between the sacred and the mundane have been erased.

An altar makes visible what has been invisible. With flowers, snapshots, toys, and teddy bears, broken-hearted people wandering New York sought to connect the worlds of the human and the divine. Rather than a crucifix, a firefighter's hat was surrounded by votive candles. Rather than a Star of David a policeman's shield gleamed among hastily scrawled notes: Have you seen my husband, my sister, my neighbor, my friend? One of the extraordinary results of the tragedy of September 11 has been the creation of hundreds of altars, a spontaneous visual creation of religious art, a tangible testament to the terror of separation, the need for comfort and connection.

Often, the memorials draw clusters of people, commuters who have broken out of their rush to pause in silence and reflect on lives lost on September 11. These shrines create within small portions of ordinary public space private spaces, set apart, sanctified, silent amid the commotion, by what people have placed there. Such sacred spaces bring healing, allowing us to bridge our grief or find a form of solace, to be quiet at a time of turmoil.

The mass eruption of grief in New York City left behind its own kind of debris. The parks were lined with butcher paper; restaurants in lower Manhattan surrendered their walls and turned them into vast bulletin boards. Sidewalks called out in colored chalk, pleading for peace, insisting on war. These spontaneous altars have convinced me that altars and shrines that we know from antiquity, remains of stone, bone, shards of pottery, do not tell the entire story.

It is not surprising that we have nothing left of ancient personal shrines. The shrines in New York are already disappearing. The fact that most of the posters have been drenched with rain and sleet, torn by autumn winds, is part of the point. Decay seems to be part of the life of these spontaneous shrines. Symbols of grief are not designed as instruments of cheer. Candles, for instance, are not prized merely for the flickering vitality of their light. They must also melt and vanish—the flame must consume the flesh, the paper posters will blacken and curl, flowers are offered up because they bloom and rot. But the emotion has neither flickered nor decayed. As Marshall Sella wrote in the *New York Times Magazine*, a few weeks after the calamity:

> The second waves of fliers, which cropped up on the weekend after the attacks, were suddenly leaning heavily on detail, ostensibly for the sake of victims'

recovery and identification. Photos and text became brutally disconnected; with each lovingly chosen photograph came spikes of forensic data. A proud man in a tuxedo, we were told, had "very distinctive thick brown discolored toenails." The merry lady with the white dog had "a tribal tattoo along the lower back above the tailbone."[16]

In their desperation to find the living person, the secrets hidden in the visual images had to be revealed. The altar memories were being turned into a search for relics, an arthritic finger, a warted toe, any body part that would identify the loved one would be beautiful, sanctified.

CONCLUSION

The theory of popular religious visual culture advanced here posits that by becoming continual and transparent features of daily experience, embedded in the quotidian rituals, narratives, and collective memories that people take for granted, religious images help form half-forgotten textures of everyday life. As part of the very fabric of consciousness, religious images participate fundamentally in the social construction of reality. It is not the image itself, as an intrinsically meaningful entity, but the image as it is articulated within the context of the other visual metaphors present in the shrine that creates and stabilizes the sense of lived religion within the domicile. As one can see in both the traditional and spontaneous altars from Oaxaca to New York, religious imagery anchors everyday life to reliable religious routines in the home and provides historical traces of the worlds they helped to construct. Shrines and altars contain the visual images that help belief work.

NOTES

1. Judy Grahn, "They Say She is Veiled," in *The Queen of Wands* (Freedom, Calif.: Crossing Press, 1982).

2. Elisabeth Schüssler Fiorenza, *Jesus: Miriam's Child, Sophia's Prophet: Critical Issues in Feminist Christology* (New York: Continuum, 1994).

3. Pierre Bourdieu, *Outline of a Theory of Practice* (London: Cambridge University Press, 1977), 76–81, 86–89, et passim.

4. Robert Orsi, "Everyday Miracles: The Study of Lived Religion," in *Lived Religion,* ed. David Hal (Princeton: Princeton University Press), 7. Much of Orsi's work preceded the term "lived religion," and I would recommend his classic, *The Madonna*

on 115th Street: Faith and Community in Italian Harlem, 1880–1950 (New Haven: Yale University Press, 1985). On the danger of the polarity of "us/them," see Jonathan Z. Smith, *Imagining Religion: From Babylon to Jerusalem* (Chicago: University of Chicago Press, 1982), 6.

5. James Clifford, *The Predicament of Culture: Twentieth Century Ethnography, Literature and Art* (Cambridge, Mass.: Harvard University Press, 1998).

6. Schapiro is probably best known for an installation entitled *Womanhouse* (1971), which she created in collaboration with Judy Chicago and other pioneering feminist artists to emphasize the influence of dailiness of women's lives on their artistic output. For a discussion of Schapiro's development as an artist, see Eleanor Munro, *Originals: American Women Artists* (New York: Simon & Schuster, 1982), 272–81. See also Judy Chicago, *The Dinner Party: A Symbol of Our Heritage* (New York: Doubleday, 1979). For her review of how difficult it was to keep the 1979 *Dinner Party* installation "alive," and the failure to get a museum to house the project permanently, see Chicago's *Beyond the Flower: The Autobiography of a Feminist Artist* (rpt., New York: Penguin, 1997). Fortunately the art of *female* has been taken more seriously in the past few years, and Chicago and other *female* artists are no longer the butt of male art critics' jokes. See Edward Lucie-Smith, *Judy Chicago: An American Vision* (New York: Watson Guptill, 2000), an appreciative study of Chicago that focuses on her work rather than on her role as a feminist icon. Edward Lucie-Smith honors the *femmage* techniques such as quilting, tapestry design, and china painting.

7. *Kawwānîm* is a loanword from the Akkadian *kamanu*, meaning "cake." In various Akkadian texts these cakes are associated with the cult of Ishtar. See Moshe Held, "Studies in Biblical Lexicography in the Light of Akkadian," *Eretz Israel* 16 (1982): 76–77. See also W. E. Rast, "Cakes for the Queen of Heaven," in *Scripture in History and Theology: Studies in Honor of J. Coert Rylaarsdam*, ed. A. L. Merrill and T. W. Overholt, Pittsburgh Theological Monograph Series 17 (Pittsburgh, Pa.: Pickwick, 1977), 167–80.

8. Susan Ackerman, *Under Every Green Tree: Popular Religion in Sixth-Century Judah*, Harvard Semitic Monographs 46 (Atlanta: Scholars Press, 1992).

9. A picture of this mold can be found in Marvin Pope, *Song of Songs,* Anchor Bible 7C (New York: Doubleday, 1977), plate 1, opposite p. 360. See for a contrasting view, "And the Women Make Cakes for the Queen of Heaven," in Ackerman, *Under Every Green Tree,* 22–33. According to classical tradition, the goddess Cybele was sleeping on Mt. Ida, either as a rock or as the ground itself, when Jupiter, the ruler of the Pantheon, ejaculated on her. The child she bore was a monster, who ended up castrating himself. For the arguments about the connections between Cybele and Mary, see Michael P. Carroll, *The Cult of Mary: Psychological Origins* (Princeton: Princeton University Press, 1986), 90–124.

10. Personal communication.

11. I have used the translation from the collection edited by Ross Kraemer, *Maenads, Martyrs, Matrons, Monastics* (Minneapolis: Fortress, 1988), 51–58.

12. Bourdieu, *Outline of a Theory of Practice.*

13. For vivid descriptions of the music, dance, and artistic expressions that form the heart of Vodou, see Sallie Ann Glassman, *Vodou Visions: An Encounter with Divine Mystery* (New York: Villard Books, 2000); also for the *habitus* of art *trouvé,* see Stuart Plattner, *High Art Down Home: An Economic Ethnography of a Local Art Market* (Chicago: University of Chicago Press, 1997). For a classic ethnographic study of Vodou in New York, see Karen McCarthy Brown, *Mama Lola: A Vodou Priestess in Brooklyn,* Comparative Studies in Religion and Society (rev. ed.; Berkeley: University of California press, 2001).

14. "The Liberation of Aunt Jemima" depicts the mammy picture of Aunt Jemima found on the pancake boxes transformed into an icon, a woman warrior, holding a rifle in one hand, a white baby in the other; in the foreground a clenched black fist explodes. Saar's explanation of her process comes from the catalogue of her 1987 exhibit at Massachusetts Institute of Technology, called *Mojo Tech.*

15. Derek Walcott, *Omeros* (New York: Farrar, Straus, and Giroux, 1990), 2. A member of a small minority English-speaking Protestant mulatto elite in an overwhelmingly French-Creole Roman Catholic black society, Walcott reflects the fragmented nature of his life. *Omeros is* Walcott's prism for envisioning his own life of wandering and exile against that of Homer.

13. Marshall Sella, "Missing," *New York Times Magazine,* October 7, 2001.

3

The *Ekklēsia* of Women and/as Utopian Space

Locating the Work of Elisabeth Schüssler Fiorenza in Feminist Utopian Thought

Elizabeth A. Castelli

I N THE FIFTEENTH CENTURY, CHRISTINE DE PIZAN WROTE *THE BOOK of the City of Ladies,* a book that would become a classic of European proto-feminist writing, offering a portrait of an alternative polity in which women's intellectual, moral, and material labor were, counterculturally, given their due.[1] Writing both within and against received traditions, Christine de Pizan imagined society and its institutions radically otherwise. With Augustine's otherworldly *City of God* as an ironic intertext, *The Book of the City of Ladies* focused on the transformation of earthly, historical existence. However else this text might be understood to intervene in the cultural and political debates in Europe at the time, at least one feminist interpreter has argued persuasively that Christine's *Book* is a precursor text, pointing forward to the emergence of a critical literature in the European Renaissance—utopian writing.[2]

In the twentieth century, biblical scholar Elisabeth Schüssler Fiorenza produced a feminist theoretical vision that would become a classic within Christian feminist theological writing and in which "the *ekklēsia* of women" occupies a central and critical place.[3] This *ekklēsia* of women, like Christine's city of ladies, is the product of a process of critical reimagining and imaginative projection. In both Christine's city and Schüssler Fiorenza's *ekklēsia,* the past and the present are critically reconceived in the service of a transformative and hopeful vision for a possible future. In Schüssler Fiorenza's framing, the *ekklēsia* serves as a multivalent category for describing, simultaneously, a sociopolitical communal formation in the past and present *and* a critical idea whose full liberatory potential remains as yet unrealized. Because of the "already but not yet" quality of this category, it resonates with important aspects of utopian thinking. So, among the other kinds of important work that this concept might do, it invites us to situate Schüssler Fiorenza's work (among its other, equally important lineages) within the strong, historically varied, utopian strands of (especially nineteenth- and twentieth-century) European and North American feminist thought. This essay is devoted to a brief consideration of the complex history of feminist utopianism and to a reflection on the *ekklēsia* of women as utopian space.

FEMINIST UTOPIANISMS

Like many other aspects of feminist cultural and political work, feminist utopianism both participates in utopian discourse *tout court* and reads/writes/acts in critical relationship to—and often explicitly against—this discourse, seeking to transform it. In framing the relationship between feminist and other forms of utopianism in this way, I mean to highlight the fact that both the very existence and the critical character of feminist utopianism actually demand a recasting of the history of utopianism as a whole. That is, feminist utopianism—in all its variety—is sufficiently different from and critical of other forms of utopianism that it requires an alternative historical narrative to explain the collective significance and lineage of such modes of thought.[4] Moreover, like many other feminisms, feminist utopianism is multivocal and diversely positioned: there is not a single feminist utopia or utopianism; rather there are multiple transformative visions of feminist futures.[5] A dimension of feminist utopianism's particularity involves this multiplicity since feminist utopianism tends not to promote a monolithic vision or to insist on the reframing of social life around a precise blueprint for social change. Instead, the utopian strand within feminist thinking involves creating space—physical space, psychic space, imaginative space—for sustaining a hope that injustices can be overturned and more egalitarian arrangements can be conjured, built, and sustained.

Before proceeding, it is important to make some distinctions about the terms of the discussion. Although considerable theoretical debate circulates around terms like "utopia," "utopian," and "utopianism," for the purposes of this essay, these terms will function broadly in the following ways: "utopia" can mean the literary genre that imagines an alternative social/political reality. It can also refer to the alternative social formation generated out of such texts or individual/collective imaginings. The adjective "utopian" refers in this essay broadly to texts, institutions, and worldviews that critique the historical or contemporary situation and promote an alternative vision of social and individual existence—generally, a vision committed to more egalitarian and just structures and stances. "Utopianism," meanwhile, is an umbrella term for various related stances toward the world—equal parts critique, hope, and alternative vision. Common usage often emphasizes the inherent impossibilities and idealisms of the notion of utopia—so that a feminist critic like Sally Kitch can, for example, pejoratively situate "utopia" in binary opposition to a more positively charged "realism."[6] However, my discussion seeks to come at feminist utopianism from another angle, to consider it as a politically generative and productive refusal of the reductions and determinisms of the status quo. Although one can sensibly observe that utopianism alone is an insufficient form of critique, I will argue here that historically it nevertheless has created an important space for thinking otherwise.

While there are many differences between and among feminist utopias/utopianisms, there are a number of things they seem to share. They are, by definition, political—most often in the sense of turning a discerning and critical eye upon reigning systems of power and making visible their invisible scaffolding and rationales. Although they bring this critical energy to the project of social critique, feminist utopias/utopianisms generally reject one of the central tenets of utopian thinking as it has been practiced and articulated by many male writers: the aim or desire to produce a particular utopia as a perfect, closed, and static system characterized by the end of both politics and history.[7] Where traditionally construed classic models of the genre may have tinkered with the institutional structures whereby power is deployed in society, they left notoriously unexamined the question of power itself. Into the no-man's-land of radically rethinking the relations of power—at the level of the subject, her relationships with others, and the collective—feminist utopianism entered.[8] If, for example, one were to compare feminist and nonfeminist utopian fiction from the nineteenth century in Britain and the United States, one would encounter a range of differences. For example, utopias imagined by men give virtually no consideration to the power dynamics within the domestic sphere. Men's utopias keep the patriarchal household intact, though generally the utopian household manages (rather miraculously, to be sure) to be both cleaner and quieter than the nonutopian one. Technology is often evaluated differently in men's utopias than in feminist ones. The story of industrialization and the rise of capital meant different things to men and women in these societies; feminist utopias tend to be rather more suspicious of the impact of these broad changes in the economic and social systems around them. Meanwhile, feminist utopias tend to offer broader critiques of the androcentric or patriarchal status quo, and they have less unquestioning confidence in the very idea of political structures and concentrations of power.[9]

Different feminist theorists of utopianism have produced diverse mappings of the history of this mode of criticism and political thought and varying assessments of the multiplicity of feminist utopianism. German-American feminist literary critic Angelika Bammer argues that the feminist utopianism of the 1970s in the United States and Europe was in some critical respects the historical product of the collapse of the Left.[10] Looking at the heritage of Marxism in utopian thought from Karl Mannheim and Ernst Bloch, tracing a lineage through neo-Marxist theorizing about ideology and utopia through Louis Althusser and Fredric Jameson, Bammer positions twentieth-century feminist utopianism as the double heir of nineteenth- and early-twentieth-century feminists—such as Charlotte Perkins Gilman, Mary E. Bradley Lane, Elizabeth Burgoyne Corbett, and many others[11]—and twentieth-century leftist social theory written by men. In her characterization of the literary and intellectual history here, the feminist utopian project did not involve simply finding a way to include women in an existing utopian discourse. Instead, it sought to emerge with an altogether alternative *feminist* version of utopian discourse, liberating "utopia" from some of its history and reclaiming it as a necessary component of radical thinking and action. This project was organized around problematics and reconceptualizations of both historical time and political space. Just so, Bammer's discussion of fictional utopias produced by feminist writers during the 1970s in the United States, France, and Germany literally maps the possible options for utopia in different conceptual and lived spaces: "elsewhere," in the borderlands between the "real" and the "possible," and in the in-between space of the not-yet.[12]

Feminist critic and political theorist Lucy Sargisson offers a slightly different mapping of the feminist utopian terrain. Attempting to move beyond the conventional understandings of utopia which, she argues, are rooted in mod-

els that value stasis and closure, Sargisson privileges modes of utopian thinking that she categorizes as oppositional, critical, and transgressive.[13] Like
Bammer, she believes that feminist utopianism is not an add-women-and-stir
version of utopianism, but rather a critical practice of creatively imagining
the world otherwise. In Sargisson's reading, the challenges raised by contemporary feminist utopianism engage large, historical questions (thus interro-
gating reigning concepts of time) and reconceptualize notions of social space.

As Sargisson maps this terrain, she observes that the different modes of
utopianism she identifies place their emphases on different aspects of social
critique and social change. Under the banner of the *oppositional,* Sargisson
groups those forms of feminist utopianism that have acknowledged the limitations of traditional socialist utopianism (as found in the thought of writers
like Mannheim, E. P. Thompson, and others) and have sought to produce an
oppositionalism that is not grounded in an unnuanced and unreflective bina-
rism. Feminist oppositional utopianism here learns from the broader feminist
engagement with poststructuralism and psychoanalysis, which have produced
compelling critiques of essentialism and universalism; at the same time, it
also stays in and with the political struggles of the present. Sargisson sum-
marizes the impact of this mode of feminist utopian thought in these terms:

> The function of utopian thought, thus approached, is to anticipate the possi-
> bility of radically different "nows" (hence utopia as a paradigm shift in con-
> sciousness). This new utopian function operates in the political present, not in
> a desired future. This is an important shift that moves utopia from a specula-
> tive (or concrete) future to a no place/good place that is an alternative reading
> of the present. In this way the dominant understandings of what is possible are
> undermined, new conceptual spaces are opened and different perspectives of
> the possible are forged.[14]

In Sargisson's model, the *critical* offers another way of imagining how
utopian thinking works in relation to things as they are. In conversation with
an important study of utopianism and science fiction by Tom Moylan (who
himself builds on Jameson), Sargisson charts the importance of critique—not
as simple negation or opposition, but as a mode of discourse that interrupts
reigning systems.[15] "Critical opposition," in Sargisson's understanding of
Moylan's terms, troubles the underlying structures of social organization and
rhetorical terms of debate. It "opposes the existing space of opposition. . . .
Opposition thus understood is a bigger concept than the either/or structure
of exploitation, hierarchy and alienation."[16] Yet both the oppositional and
the critical dimensions of utopianism highlight the political effectiveness of

what Sargisson calls utopianism's tactic of estrangement. Hence, in this version of feminist utopianism, the project involves using critique as a fulcrum for opening up foreclosed systems (of social structure or, indeed, of meaning) by noticing and confronting the uncanny unfamiliarity that resides deep within the familiar. This tool is wielded in order to create a space for something else—even though the content of "something else" remains necessarily opaque or, indeed, as yet unimagined.

Sargisson's assessment of the utopian within feminism presses the case still further. The utopian is not only oppositional and critical, but potentially also *transgressive.* She uses the term to signal utopian troublings of both time and consciousness, and as an alternative to the more philosophically and theologically loaded term "transcendent."[17] The overall impact of her framing of feminist utopianism is to produce a field within which conceptual space is opened up for thinking about time (past, present, future) in new ways.

Meanwhile, in her book *Notes from Nowhere,* literary critic Jennifer Burwell addresses the tensions embedded in utopian imaginings in a related way but employs both a different language and a different conceptual framework. She situates her own theoretical contribution in conversation with Marxist, feminist, and postmodern anxieties about and critiques of the tendency of utopianism toward absolutes, ideals, and unities. But whereas some of these critiques have imagined utopianism in a simple, binary opposition to criticism, Burwell argues for the usefulness of theorizing the interrelationship of these two poles. As she puts it, "In fact, however, these two poles [the anticipatory/utopian pole and the critical/diagnostic pole[18]] already imply one another: utopia implicitly critiques existing conditions by explicitly thematizing a set of wishes and hopes for an alternative society; critique implicitly draws upon the utopian impulse to establish the 'outside' of existing conditions upon which our notion of critical distance rests."[19] Burwell's project involves attention to both the "figures of subjectivity" and "conceptions of social space," especially to the relationships between these two elements. Believing that "no theory of social transformation escapes some relation to the utopian impulse insofar as this impulse, most generally, funds our attempts to imagine the 'other' of what is," Burwell seeks to understand the logics of utopian thinking in feminist theory in order to uncover the stakes involved in any particular argument for change.[20]

These three feminist theorists—Bammer, Sargisson, and Burwell—focus on feminist fiction (utopias, science fiction, fantasy) and speculative writing (philosophy, theology, theory) and produce close readings of some of the most classic utopian texts of each feminist genre. All are aware of the cultural and political weight and complex historical legacy borne by the categories "utopia," "utopian," "utopianism." All seek in some way to recuperate the term from its dismissal as absolutist and totalizing. Each one believes that *feminist* utopianism functions repeatedly as an alternative to such absolutisms and totalizing ideological structures. Hence, for these theorists, *feminist* utopianism critiques and transforms the very terms of its own generic existence and emerges as a crucial tool in the feminist theoretical and imaginative toolbox.[21]

THE *EKKLĒSIA* OF WOMEN AS PAST AND AS PROCESS

Elisabeth Schüssler Fiorenza's interdisciplinary project—in which the *ekklēsia* of women functions as a central category for historical analysis, political and ethical evaluation, and creative imagining—resists easy reduction. The *ekklēsia* of women is at once political, sociological, theological, and indeed visionary. It is a critical building block of a much broader political and theological critique, offering itself as both alternative history and alternative future. The alternative future is, as we have seen, the stuff of feminist utopian thought. What this future might look like and how it is generated imaginatively in Schüssler Fiorenza's thought are the focus of this section.

Schüssler Fiorenza begins to outline the concept of the *ekklēsia* of women in her groundbreaking 1984 book *In Memory of Her*. In the chapter entitled "The Patriarchal Household and the *Ekklēsia* of Women," the first two centuries of Christian history emerge as a period of intense contestation over competing ideas about communal decision making, church leadership, and the proper institutional locations of power and authority. Some scholars have sought to explain the consolidation of ecclesiastical power in the episcopacy as a recognizable historical process of routinization and institutionalization. Although there are some points of overlap between this explanatory model and Schüssler Fiorenza's, she makes this distinction: "The shift which took place in the second century was not a shift from charismatic leadership to institutional consolidation, but from charismatic and communal authority to an authority vested in local officers, who . . . absorb . . . authority of the prophet and apostle but also the decision-making power of the community."[22] Since this authority is tied to church offices to which only men have access, women stand as a reminder of more democratic forms of church order—the discipleship of equals ("women as paradigms of true disciple-ship"[23]) and the *ekklēsia* of women.

The *ekklēsia* of women is thus understood, in part, as a historical reality. However, it is much more centrally an activist site within Christian communities in the present day and, perhaps even more importantly, an imagined future possibility. As Schüssler Fiorenza puts it in the epilogue to *In Memory of Her,* "*Ekklēsia* . . . is not so much a religious as a civil-political concept. It means the actual assembly of free citizens gathering for deciding their own spiritual-political affairs. *Since women in a patriarchal church cannot decide their own theological-religious affairs and that of their own people—women— the* ekklēsia *of women is as much a future hope as it is a reality today.*"[24] Elsewhere, Schüssler Fiorenza places more emphasis on the present activist impulse embedded in the concept. In these contexts, the *ekklēsia* of women emerges as a political site of debate, persuasion, and opposition within the framework of Christian community and intellectual work. Hence, in *Bread Not Stone,* her first systematic working-out of a theoretical and methodological model for feminist biblical interpretation, Schüssler Fiorenza puts the *ekklēsia* of women at the heart of the feminist interpretive project: "The hermeneutical center of such a feminist biblical interpretation . . . is the *ekklēsia gynaikōn* or women-church, the movement of self-identified women and women-identified men in biblical religion. When as a Christian I use the expression *women-church,* I do not use it as an exclusionary but as a political-oppositional term to patriarchy."[25] (Later on, Schüssler Fiorenza will refine the terms of this discussion further, replacing "patriarchy" with the more specifying term "kyriarchy."[26])

Also critical to Schüssler Fiorenza's articulation of the *ekklēsia* of women is the essentially dialectical character of the relationship between and among the past/present and future that it presupposes. The centrality of this dialectic appears repeatedly in Schüssler Fiorenza's theoretical formulations, and she identifies the failure of some readers to understand its centrality as a serious misreading of her arguments. For example, she opens her 1992 book *But She Said* with an answer to critics who have charged that her model problematically produces a continuous and unbroken lineage between contemporary feminist struggles and the earliest church's discipleship of equals. "Such readings of my text," she responds, "misapprehend, however *the tension between the 'already' and 'not yet' of the* ekklēsia *of women.*"[27] This dialectical tension between "the already" and "the not-yet" attempts to keep the category poised primarily in a posture of critique.

Historical memory, activist space in the present, hoped-for future—all of these are dimensions of the *ekklēsia* of women in Schüssler Fiorenza's thought. The notion is multifaceted and highly mobile. It appears in a wide range of positions in the broader rhetoric of Schüssler Fiorenza's interpretive model and reconstructive history. Women-church uses the Bible as "a formative root-model" that produces "models and traditions of emancipatory praxis" as supplements to (and implicitly as destabilizers of) the traditional patriarchal understandings.[28] Women-church operates in counterpoint, as I have already shown, to patriarchy/kyriarchy (both in/as the church and in/as society as a whole), but also to a range of other institutional settings and practices. The academy, both in general and as the space in which mainstream biblical interpretation takes place,[29] is posited as women-church's opposite as are feminist poststructuralist and psychoanalytic theories that focus on understanding the dynamics of subject formation and sexual difference.[30] It is simultaneously a place for critical interpretation, a discursive site, "the practical center and normative space for the hermeneutical circle-dance of a critical feminist rereading of the Bible for liberation,"[31] a democratic political assembly set in explicit opposition to other (hierarchical) political structures, and a symbolic space for the staging of a future vision.

THE HERITAGE OF SCHÜSSLER FIORENZA'S WORK AND THE *EKKLĒSIA* OF WOMEN AS UTOPIAN SPACE

Many different writers have suggested various intellectual lineages into which the work of Elisabeth Schüssler Fiorenza might fruitfully be placed.[32] Schüssler Fiorenza has critiqued this gesture at various moments in her writing, recognizing the implicit bestowal of authority-by-association that is often involved—and the potential concomitant suppression of other lineages and authorities in the process. Nowhere does her critique appear more pointedly than in the recent *Sharing Her Word,* where she observes;

> [M]y theoretical-theological framework and proposal is usually assessed as to whether and how much it is stamped by or in line with the intellectual tradition of the "great men" or "fathers" of hermeneutics, rhetorics, or dogmatics. Whereas reviewers have suggested that the intellectual framework of my work is articulated in dialogue with or dependence on one or another of the "masters" of hermeneutics, such as Gadamer, Bultmann, Ricoeur, the Frankfurt School, Dworkin, or the American pragmatist philosophical tradition, they have not inquired as to its intellectual "foresisters."[33]

In this same context, she claims for herself a lineage that includes Anna Julia Cooper, the African American writer and orator, and other nineteenth-century women intellectuals. In suggesting that feminist utopian thinkers and writers may also be an important part of the visionary inheritance of Schüssler Fiorenza, I hope to introduce another strand of the intellectual inheritance that is reflected in her thought. Suggesting that Schüssler Fiorenza stands in a lineage with other important utopian thinkers, both feminist and nonfeminist, does not of course diminish the importance of the other intellectual genealogies she and others may trace.

This said, it seems to me that the utopian is a particularly illuminating category through which to approach Schüssler Fiorenza's feminist project and, in particular, her understanding of the *ekklēsia* of women. When women-church is invoked in her writings, it clearly aligns with the characteristics other feminist critics have identified as crucial to *feminist* utopianism.

First, the *ekklēsia* of women is firmly positioned within a broad political critique, that is, within a critique of existing relationships of public power. Offered as an alternative political space, it exists both apart from and in direct critique of dominant spaces—institutions such as the androcentric church and the "malestream" academy and, indeed, the broader *kyriarchy* that these institutions serve and sustain.

Second, the *ekklēsia* of women is not a blueprint for a concrete future but an alternative space within which the future might be reimagined and renegotiated in light of a critical vision of the past and present. The *ekklēsia* of women is described by a variety of terms—as a discursive space and critical site, as a "discursive feminist public and democratic polity," as "feminist counterpublic open space," as "the congress or synod of women . . . not to be envisioned as a coherent, consistent web but rather as a heterogeneous, polyglot arena of competing discourses," as "a political 'open space' in which Divine Presence as mutual recognition and respect of self and others, of identity and difference, of oneness and separation can be experienced."[34] All of these forms of description resist any simple mapping onto or containment within a concrete political plan or blueprint for particular forms of activism in and against particular institutions and settings. They operate in a different register from that of the political blueprint, and in doing so find alliance with feminist utopianism expressed most often in other literary genres.

Third, the *ekklēsia* of women aims at a radical reconceptualization of both time and space. Situated in a historical past to which access is most easily achieved through processes of critical memory, the *ekklēsia* of women reperiodizes the history of the church and offers a broad counternarrative to challenge the traditional and dominant meta-narratives. In place of the meta-narratives of progress or decline, the story of the *ekklēsia* of women requires a narrative of ongoing struggle.[35] Moreover, this transformed historical narrative establishes diachronic connections across time. When these connections are read in tandem with the "already, not yet" character of the *ekklēsia* of women, time is reconceptualized and the past operates as both object of critique in the present and resource for rethinking the future.

At the same time, in another echoing of feminist utopianism, Schüssler Fiorenza emphasizes the ways in which the *ekklēsia* of women has the potential for reconceptualizing and reorganizing notions of space. In her essay "The Ethics and Politics of Liberation: Theorizing the *Ekklēsia* of Women,"[36] she engages in a brief dialogue with the work of feminist psychoanalyst Jessica Benjamin on domination and submission, extracting from Benjamin's discussion the notion of "open space."[37] Benjamin's own use of this concept focuses on the subject formation of infants, drawing upon the work of infant psychologist Louis Sander, which describes a stage of "optimal disengagement" of the infant from the mother during which time the child can begin to experience itself in the world as a separate being.[38] Schüssler Fiorenza takes the notion of "open space" from this location within theories of infant development and subject formation and replants it in a quite different setting.

> The notion of "open space" applies not just to the individual but also suggests a place from which to envision the *ekklēsia* of women as an open rhetorical space bounded by its struggles against multiform oppression. The *ekklēsia* of women metaphorized as "bounded open space," rather than as sisterhood or daughterhood, can engender historical community and continuity without denying existence of differences of experience and power between women and between women and men."[39]

There are a number of interesting dimensions to the use of this term in relation to its precursor text. Whereas Benjamin's discussion is concerned with the emergence of a differentiated subject who is produced through experiences of "open space" within a familial framework, Schüssler Fiorenza makes use of the category in an attempt to interrupt the familial metaphors that have had a particularly fraught history within feminism.[40] How this translation from the psychoanalytic to the political works could be the interesting subject of another discussion. What is particularly striking about the appropriation of this language in Schüssler Fiorenza's essay is that the notion of "open space" has another lineage, tracing back to the utopian theorizing of

Bloch and Mannheim. As critic Tom Moylan, whose work is significantly influenced by both of these earlier thinkers, characterizes the political character of utopia, the notion of "open space" emerges front and center. "Utopia," Moylan writes, "negates the contradictions of a social system by forging visions of what is not yet realized either in theory or practice. In generating such figures of hope, *utopia contributes to the open space of opposition.*"[41] The *ekklēsia* of women, "metaphorized as 'bounded open space,'" can then quite easily be read as an oppositional, *utopian* space and also situated within this utopian intellectual trajectory.

Whether taking up Lucy Sargisson's interpretive model of oppositional, critical, and transgressive utopianisms within feminism or Jennifer Burwell's critique of the traditional opposition between the utopian and the critical, one cannot help but register the deep utopian resonances that echo through the *ekklēsia* of women and, indeed, the broader feminist theoretical/theological framework within which it is situated. It bears the same characteristics as Moylan's "plebeian public sphere"—"a liberated cultural and ideological zone seized from the totalized society from which the anti-hegemonic forces can attack the present and move openly towards an emancipated and radically open future."[42]

What is the significance of such a reading of the *ekklēsia* of women? I think there are several important implications that might be drawn from this reading. First, it responds to Schüssler Fiorenza's own call for her readership to place her thought within a feminist history of ideas rather than to focus solely on an intellectual genealogy comprised only of fathers and sons. If Anna Julia Cooper is a foresister, and surely she is, then so too are the many women engaged in imaginative critique of things as they are, from Christine de Pizan forward into our own time. Second, recognizing the utopian within this body of work invites a broader comparison of the categories and directions of Schüssler Fiorenza's thought with those of other feminist writers and theorists working in other disciplines and cultural spaces. Those of us who work in the field of feminist studies in religion know all too well how frequently work in our field escapes the notice of our colleagues in both religious studies and women's studies. Given the ongoing interest among feminist critics in the history (both literary and theoretical) and analytic power of the utopian for feminist struggles, making visible the utopian impulses in Schüssler Fiorenza's work can make a useful intervention into these conversations.

Such a reading may have a range of other meanings attached to it. But it is my sincere hope that, among the other work this reading might do, it will also be received as the gift it is intended to be. I count myself among the many feminist scholars in the field of religion whose ability to imagine a place for her work in the field was greatly enabled by the fact that Elisabeth Schüssler Fiorenza has devoted her career to creating an opening for thinking and writing otherwise—in all sorts of institutional contexts, including the academy (the main site of my work for feminist change). We all continue to labor within the tension of the "already and not yet" potential of which Schüssler Fiorenza so passionately writes, operating under a principle of hope that allows us to imagine transformed institutions for learning and living. Elisabeth Schüssler Fiorenza's utopian vision has been consistently oppositional, critical, *and* transgressive in the reconceptualization of the field and the institutions in which the field's work continues to be carried out. With this essay, I am happy to honor the work *already* done by Elisabeth Schüssler Fiorenza and to join with her and the other authors whose work is gathered here in a renewed commitment to the ongoing pursuit of the *not yet*.

NOTES

1. Christine de Pizan, *The Book of the City of Ladies,* trans. E. J. Richards (New York: Persea Books, 1982); originally published in 1405.

2. Angelika Bammer, *Partial Visions: Feminism and Utopianism in the 1970s* (New York: Routledge, 1991), 10.

3. The systematic discussion of this category can be found in two works by Schüssler Fiorenza, both of which appeared in 1984: *In Memory of Her: A Feminist Theological Reconstruction of Christian Origins* (New York: Crossroad, 1984) and *Bread Not Stone: The Challenge of Feminist Biblical Interpretation* (Boston: Beacon, 1984). It subsequently played a crucial role in later works, including a collection of essays that had originally been published in various contexts between 1984 and 1992 but were brought together in *Discipleship of Equals: A Critical Feminist Ekklēsia-logy of Liberation* (New York: Crossroad, 1993). The *ekklēsia* of women appears in more explicitly theoretical works like *But She Said: Feminist Practices of Biblical Interpretation* (Boston: Beacon, 1992) and *Sharing Her Word: Feminist Biblical Interpretation in Context* (Boston: Beacon, 1998) as well as in more explicitly pragmatic writings such as "The *Ekklēsia* of Women: Re-Visioning the Past in Creating a Democratic Future," in *The Call to Serve: Biblical and Theological Perspectives on Ministry in Honour of Bishop Penny Jamieson,* ed. Douglas A. Campbell (Sheffield: Sheffield Academic, 1996), 239–55.

4. This observation, of course, can be extended to other forms of feminist writing and critique—including the writing of early Christian history, as Schüssler Fiorenza

and other feminist scholars of the Bible and early Christianity have argued persuasively and repeatedly. The incorporation of feminist history into the dominant narrative of early Christian history, despite the massive body of work that has *already* been produced, appears to languish in the realm of the *but not yet.*

5. The literature here is wide-ranging and copious. For a bibliography of utopias written by women in English from the mid-nineteenth century through the latter part of the twentieth century, see Daphne Patai, "British and American Utopias by Women (1836–1979): An Annotated Bibliography, Part I," *Alternative Futures* 4, nos. 2–3 (1981): 184–207. The theoretical framing provided by Bammer, *Partial Visions* (see n. 2 above), is extremely helpful, as is her bibliography (pp. 181–92). Other recent studies of the specificity of feminist utopianism that I have found particularly helpful include Frances Bartkowski, *Feminist Utopias* (Lincoln: University of Nebraska Press, 1989); Lucy Sargisson, *Contemporary Feminist Utopianism* (New York: Routledge, 1996); and Jennifer Burwell, *Notes on Nowhere: Feminism, Utopian Logic, and Social Transformation* (Minneapolis: University of Minnesota Press, 1997).

6. Sally L. Kitch, *Higher Ground: From Utopianism to Realism in American Feminist Thought and Theory* (Chicago: University of Chicago Press, 2000).

7. J. C. Davis argues that this sort of closure and finitude are a baseline characteristic of utopias ("The History of Utopia: The Chronology of Nowhere," in *Utopias,* ed. Peter Alexander and Roger Gill [London: Duckworth, 1984], 10). As a consequence, he understands utopia as the end of politics—not its goal or *telos,* but its foreclosure and conclusion.

8. Bammer blames this failure to rethink power in classic utopian thought on the genre itself and on its concomitant separation from other forms of writing—fantasy, romance, and the psychological novel (all genres traditionally associated with women) (*Partial Visions,* 13). As she puts it, "To the extent that the polity model defined the parameters, utopias addressed themselves to the changes that could be made within institutional structures. To rethink power altogether, to think not only of changing institutions and systems of state, but the structures of consciousness and human relationships, went beyond the boundaries of the genre."

9. This summary is necessarily broad and general. For a more nuanced discussion, see Bammer, *Partial Visions,* 28–47.

10. Ibid., 6.

11. Karl Mannheim, *Ideology and Utopia* (New York: Harcourt Brace & Co., 1936); Ernst Bloch, *The Principle of Hope,* trans. Neville Plaice, Stephen Plaice, and Paul Knight (1959; Cambridge, Mass.: MIT Press, 1986); idem, *Geist der Utopie* (1919/1923; Frankfurt am Main: Suhrkamp, 1964); Louis Althusser, "Ideology and Ideological State Apparatuses," in *Lenin and Philosophy and Other Essays,* trans. B. Brewster (New York: Monthly Review Press, 1971), 127–87; Fredric Jameson, *The Political Unconscious: Narrative as a Socially Symbolic Act* (Ithaca: Cornell University Press, 1981); idem, "Progress versus Utopia: Or, Can We Imagine the Future?" *Science Fiction Studies* 27 (1982): 147–59; Charlotte Perkins Gilman, *Herland* (1915;

rpt., New York: Pantheon, 1979); Mary E. Bradley Lane, *Mizora: A Prophecy. A Manuscript Found Among the Private Papers of the Princess Vera* (1889; rpt., Boston: Gregg, 1975); Elizabeth Burgoyne Corbett, *New Amazonia: A Foretaste of the Future* (1880). See the bibliography cited in n. 5 above for many other examples.

12. See her chapter titles: "Worlds Apart: Utopian Visions and Separate Spheres' Feminism"; "The End(s) of Struggle: The Dream of Utopia and the Call to Action"; and "Writing toward the Not-Yet: Utopia as Process."

13. Sargisson, *Contemporary Feminist Utopianism*, 39–60.

14. Ibid., 52.

15. Tom Moylan, *Demand the Impossible: Science Fiction and the Utopian Imagination* (London: Methuen, 1986).

16. Sargisson, *Contemporary Feminist Utopianism*, 55.

17. Ibid., 57–58.

18. These terms come from Seyla Benhabib, *Critique, Norm, and Utopia: A Study of the Foundations of Critical Theory* (New York: Columbia University Press, 1986).

19. Burwell, *Notes from Nowhere*, 3.

20. Ibid., 3–4.

21. An important dissenting voice in this chorus of feminist theorists of utopianism is Sally Kitch (*Higher Ground: From Utopianism to Realism in American Feminist Thought and Theory*), who does not accept the complicating countertheories offered by these other feminist thinkers. For Kitch, utopianism can only possibly be read as idealizing and essentializing; as a consequence, for Kitch, utopianism is completely irredeemable for feminist theorizing or action. In Kitch's analytic narrative, utopianism is diagnosed as infantile wish fulfillment (p. 40), the collective form of which is religious and mythic constructions of imagined perfection (p. 41). Within a couple of pages, the religious utopian impulse reaches its unsettlingly apocalyptic limits in the highly charged examples of the Jonestown suicides, the conflagration at the Branch Davidian compound outside Waco, and the willing deaths of the members of Heaven's Gate in San Diego (p. 43). "Utopianism must be held accountable if it does not provide restraining mechanisms to prevent its tenets from becoming poison punch or fire bombs," Kitch ominously intones (p. 45). In opposition to the perils of utopianism, defined crudely only in terms of absolutism, Kitch offers the category, "realism" which operates as utopianism's redemptive conceptual "other."

22. Schüssler Fiorenza, *In Memory of Her*, 286.

23. Ibid., 315–33.

24. Ibid., 344 (emphasis added).

25. Schüssler Fiorenza, *Bread Not Stone*, xiv.

26. The terms "kyriarchy" and "kyriarchal" first appear in Schüssler Fiorenza's work in the early 1990s. See her discussion of these categories in *But She Said*, 8. She later elaborates the role of the *ekklēsia* (now of wo/men rather than women) in the opposition to kyriarchy in *Sharing Her Word*, 131–36.

27. Schüssler Fiorenza, *But She Said*, 5–6 (emphasis added).

28. Ibid., xvii.

29. Ibid., xxiv, 103.

30. Schüssler Fiorenza, *Discipleship of Equals*, 344. In Schüssler Fiorenza's reading of these theories, both here and elsewhere in her writings in *But She Said* and *Sharing Her Word* (see, e.g., p. 104) especially, it seems that her critique takes two different but related forms. Her interests lie in institutional transformation and, as a consequence, her analysis emphasizes structural and external forms of oppression. Hence, she is less interested in theorizing about the complex dynamics of subject formation to which poststructuralist and psychoanalytic feminists devote their energies and attentions. In Schüssler Fiorenza's formulation of the relationship between these different forms of feminism, poststructuralist and psychoanalytic feminists are concerned with questions of identity—which Schüssler Fiorenza argues necessarily morph into a version of essentialism. Schüssler Fiorenza situates her own concerns around the category of democracy, which she sets in opposition to notions of identity. See, e.g., *But She Said*, 11. It strikes me that these different feminist modes of analysis and discourse are actually operating at quite different levels of thinking. Whereas Schüssler Fiorenza's theory is grounded in an on-the-ground form of political and pragmatic activism whose goal is the transformation of social institutions and structures, poststructuralist and psychoanalytic feminists are focused in a different arena—that of the unconscious, fantasy (in the psychoanalytic sense), and subject formation. Where Schüssler Fiorenza sees discussions of identity formation as necessarily essentializing or reifying, other feminists would argue that attention to these same matters are crucial to understanding how the subject comes to be constituted in and through power.

31. Schüssler Fiorenza, *But She Said*, 75.

32. One of the most interesting readings of Schüssler Fiorenza, from my perspective, is Marsha Aileen Hewitt's "Memory, Revolution, and Redemption: Walter Benjamin and Elisabeth Schüssler Fiorenza," in *Critical Theory of Religion: A Feminist Analysis* (Minneapolis: Augsburg Fortress, 1995), 147–70.

33. Schüssler Fiorenza, *Sharing Her Word*, 72.

34. All of these quotations come from Schüssler Fiorenza, *Discipleship of Equals*, 344–49.

35. Schüssler Fiorenza, *Bread Not Stone*, 153 n. 21.

36. In Schüssler Fiorenza, *Discipleship of Equals*, 332–52.

37. Jessica Benjamin, *The Bonds of Love: Psychoanalysis, Feminism, and the Problem of Domination* (New York: Pantheon, 1988).

38. Ibid., 41–42.

39. Schüssler Fiorenza, *Discipleship of Equals*, 348.

40. The familial metaphor of "sisterhood" has been resoundingly critiqued from many vantage points. These critiques emphasize the fact that the metaphor requires the submersion of critical elements of difference between and among women individually and collectively in the service of harmony within the family. It should be

noted that there is also a growing literature concerning the generational tensions within feminism within both activist and academic settings. See, e.g., Elspeth Probyn, "Re: Generation: Women's Studies and the Disciplining of *Ressentiment*," *Australian Feminist Studies* 13 (1998): 129–36; and Elizabeth Freeman, "Packing History, Count(er)ing Generations," *New Literary History* 31 (2000): 727–44.

41. Moylan, *Demand the Impossible*, 1–2 (emphasis added).

42. Ibid., 28.

4

Trailblazers

Elisabeth Schüssler Fiorenza
and
George M. Soares-Prabhu

Pushpa Joseph

THIS ESSAY IS A COMPARATIVE STUDY OF TWO BIBLICAL SCHOLARS: George M. Soares-Prabhu, an Indian exegete of the Christian Scriptures,[1] and Elisabeth Schüssler Fiorenza, a German scholar of the Christian Scriptures and a feminist theologian. I will present three important ideas of the two scholars and then specify the areas of convergence and also the divergent aspects of the methodologies of these two scholars. This comparison will lead to a reflection on how the different aspects of Schüssler Fiorenza's hermeneutics can prove feasible and significant for women in the Indian context.

The task of bringing together two towering personalities in critical collaboration is not only adventurous and fruitful but also replete with subtle ramifications and intricacies. The complexity increases when the dialogue envisioned involves an intermingling of traditions as diverse as the East and the West. Much ink has been spilled on detailed investigations of the irreconcilable differences between these two poles. Certain positions emphasize that these elements can never coalesce: "East is east and West is west," said Rudyard Kipling, and "never the twain shall meet."

Disciplines and perspectives as controversial and suspect as feminism and feminist theology add to the complexity. Too often the argument that feminism and feminist theology are the obsession of certain white women forestalls a profound engagement with the critical and insightful discipline. A feminist theologian, a leading writer and prophetic voice in the Indian church, reminisces, "When I did my Masters in Theology, ten years back, in one of the prominent seminaries in India I was counseled against reading Schüssler Fiorenza's classic in feminist theology, *In Memory of Her.*" That, one might maintain, is a decade ago. I agree that the nineties have seen an immense reception of critical theories and marginal theologies in Indian theologizing. However another student from the same institution who completed her theological training just last year testifies, "My professor and moderator instructed me to engage with some women's issues for my thesis, nonetheless without subscribing to the word feminism or feminist theology." On my inquiring about the logic behind such an instruction, I was told that the professor emphasized, "We [men] like to see you with your feminine qualities intact. On account of feminism we wouldn't want you to lose your gentleness and feminine grace. Feminist theology is fine in the Western/American context."[2]

Still another argument is that a tendency to subsume differences comes often from the dominant position, here the West. In my opinion, however, in analyzing such arguments we should be guided by two considerations: first, the question of commitment, and, second, the factor of involvement. In my estimation, both of these factors are evident in the life of Elisabeth Schüssler Fiorenza and have permeated her writings. In an interview with Julia Flatters, Schüssler Fiorenza explicates: "Participation is important because the great danger for feminist theology is that it will conform to that academic model which is cut off from the base and can therefore all too easily become coopted."[3] Her commitment to women's issues and empowerment, both ideological and structural, is acutely evident in the wide gamut of her *oeuvre.* Her involvement in women's movements, both within the church and in the secular and social realm, coupled with her intense association and affinity with third world feminist campaigns and the manner in which she brings these concerns to her exegesis and writings are credentials enough.

Substantiating the germaneness of George M. Soares-Prahbu's writings for the Indian context does not seem necessary, though as Soares-Prabhu himself notes, the Indian theologian and exegete is beset by a triple alienation:[4] cultural alienation (estrangement from the Indian people), academic alienation (estrangement from Indian intellectual life),[5] and alienation from popular religiosity (estrangement from the prevalent ceremonial and sacred practices of people). Although seminarians today hail from vernacular-speaking rural areas, Soares-Prabhu observes that they are drilled in the "knife-and-fork culture" that has become an essential part of priestly formation. The Roman Catholic priest is not only the pastor of a local Christian community but also belongs to a "transnational bureaucracy which has a Western bourgeoisie clerical culture of its own."[6] As a result, "[t[he theologian like the church itself is in India but not of it."[7]

While Soares-Prabhu's being an Indian and having theologized from the context of the concerns of marginal groups (such as tribals and *dalits*) in India can be *ipso facto* considered proof of his relevance, I submit that even his hermeneutic approach should be subjected to critical scrutiny by Indian feminists. To speak for the marginalized does not make one pro-women; nor does being a woman necessarily mean that one is a feminist. There is a danger here, as Schüssler Fiorenza herself would warn us: "One cannot assume that the reading of the Bible from a woman's point of view will necessarily amount to a feminist reading; it does not suffice to ask what it means to read the Bible as a woman. Rather, one must ask: What does it mean to interpret Scripture as a feminist, and what constitutes a feminist reading?" A feminist reading, in my opinion, is one that employs a systematic and critical analysis and avoids interpretations that reinscribe cultural and religious stereotypes, which are not favorable for the free growth and flowering of women. In addition, a feminist theoretical framework seeks to "enable readers to become subjects of interpretation and to give them the tools for engaging in a feminist approach when reading and interpreting texts."[8] Schüssler Fiorenza claims: "A history of women's biblical interpretation must not be taken as identical with the history of feminist biblical interpretation. Rather, it must be subjected to a critical analysis of its implicit and explicit feminist achievements and possibilities."[9]

Soares-Prabhu's contribution to Indian theologizing is profound. As an avant-garde and prophetic liberation theologian who has pioneered a method in theology well suited to the Indian context, he is our guide and beacon. "History," as Francis D'Sa rightly suggests, "will number Soares-Prabhu among such theologians."[10] It is definitely significant that Soares-Prabhu has pioneered the enterprise of contextual theologizing as a very relevant Indian liberation theologian. Nevertheless, a critical collaboration between feminist theologian Schüssler Fiorenza and Soares-Prabhu has much to offer the Indian church.

This article is part of my greater project of creating an ongoing conversation and collaboration between feminist theology and liberation theology in the Indian context. Some questions that guide my search are the following: Can we work toward a methodology for feminist theologizing that will be true to the specificity of the Indian context and yet open to catholic global sisterhood? What would be the contours of such an approach? What challenges does Schüssler Fiorenza's critical feminist methodology pose to feminist theologizing in the Indian context?

This said, I will explore the commonalities and differences between these two authors from the viewpoint of a few of their common themes: (1) their notions of the biblical poor; (2) their specific methodologies; and (3) their understanding of liberation.

THE POOR AND BIBLICAL POVERTY

The overwhelming mass of the poor makes it impossible for any scholar of the Bible to conduct a serious reflection on the scriptures without considering attentively the Bible's understanding of poverty and the poor. Solidarity with the ʿănāwîm is a heartfelt concern and a constant passionate commitment for both Soares-Prabhu and Schüssler Fiorenza. Their provocative and evocative readings of various passages from the Christian Scriptures take as "theologicus locus" the struggles in which we are involved. Both scholars critique the tendency to spiritualize the powerful message of the Bible about poverty and the poor, for they believe that spiritualizing blunts the prophetic thrust of the Gospels.

For example, Soares-Prabhu explains that the most frequently used word in the Hebrew Scriptures to designate the poor is ʿăniyyîm, which is derived from the root ʿnh, which means to be bent, bowed down, afflicted. The Hebrew ʿăniyyîm are the characteristic biblical figures of exploited powerlessness: the widow, the orphan, and the refugee. In the Christian Scriptures, the standard, indeed almost exclusive designation for the poor is ptōchos, from the root ptōssō, which means "to crouch or to cringe." In postexilic times the term ʿănāwîm (a late and secondary form of ʿăniyyîm) began to acquire religious connotations and was used to describe the pious and faithful Israelites (the poor of Yahweh), whose poverty and helplessness had taught them to rely absolutely and exclusively on God. Echoes of this development resonate in Matthew's "poor in spirit." But the religious connotation of one who puts trust in God alone is a secondary and derived meaning, built upon the primary sociological meaning of the word. The primary import of the word "poor" is social, not spiritual. It is the socially ostracized, the economically poor, and the culturally infringed who learn from their powerlessness to place their whole trust in God.

Set against the grim social reality of India, with its grisly and terrifying poverty, spiritualization offers little to the masses of the Indian poor. Confronted with the haggard and battered plight of the teeming poverty-stricken millions of India—a ghastly 290 million—Soares-Prabhu scrutinizes the Bible from the standpoint of the poor, the victims, the socially oppressed. The result is a very touching and dynamic picture of the poor and their role in God's dealings with humanity.

The Biblical Poor—A New Identity

The poor, Soares-Prabhu explains, are those who are utterly needy, desperately in want, so that one would be tempted to formulate the Jesus beatitude as: "Blessed are the destitute, for theirs is the kingdom of God." The poor Jesus addresses include not only the economically destitute but also the socially outcast, the simple and unlettered, the mentally ill, and the physically handicapped. In short, the poor comprise the "people of the land," a contemptuous designation employed by the religious leaders and the social elite of the time.

Indian society, constructed like a pyramid on the basis of a hierarchy of gender and classes, has also developed negative terms to refer to the lowest groups. In every culture, dominant groups make themselves the point of reference. To these upper sections of society the outcastes are nameless nonpersons. They are labeled the "rabble ignorant of the law." Soares-Prabhu's radical and materialistic description of the poor gives a new identity to these groups, who lack an identity of their own.

Soares-Prabhu places in the center of theological reflection the poor, the "others," the nonpersons who are absent from history. He has insisted over and against Western theology that the point of departure for Indian liberation theology is the struggle in general of the nonperson and particularly of the tribal, the *dalit* and so on. Going a step further, Schüssler Fiorenza emphasizes that the majority of the poor in the world are women and children dependent on women. This awareness leads her not only to "an incorporation of 'women questions' into the framework of liberation theology" but more prophetically to the delineation of a different analysis and theoretical framework. The insight that women are not just the "others" of white Euro-

American men but are the "others of the others"—in Indian terms the "*dalit of the dalit*"—has led Schüssler Fiorenza to an analysis of oppression in its multiplicative and multistructured incarnations. Thus she has offered us, through her neologisms, complex analytical categories that transcend a dualistic approach, and she has proposed a complex theory of interlocking kyriarchal structures.

The Schüsslerian inquiry includes the analysis of multiple structures of oppression such as sexism, racism, classism, casteism, and imperialism— hence the neologism *kyriarchy*. Derived from two Greek words—*kyrios*, meaning "lord" or "master," and *archein*, meaning "to rule"—this term seeks to redefine the analytic category of patriarchy in terms of multiplicative and intersecting structures of domination. Alternate metaphors and other neologisms coined by Schüssler Fiorenza help challenge the constructed nature of holy injunctions and exhortations that are propagated as "divine" and/or natural. Her analysis of the scriptures as a historical prototype and not a mythical archetype is significant, considering the fact that a mythical approach based on determinism has been used to propagate cultural and economic poverty. Schüssler Fiorenza, however, rightly identifies biblical poverty as an outcome of injustice.

Biblical Poverty as Injustice

Soares-Prabhu emphasizes that the poor in the Bible are always thought of as victims of injustice. Poverty in the Bible is not a natural condition but is always brought about by oppression, either human, as a result of economic destitution or social ostracism, or demonic, as a result of illness or possession.

> For according to the Bible, every Israelite (ultimately every human being) has a right to the "land"—a symbol which stands not just for territory, but for freedom, peace, community, independence, prosperity—in a word for all that is needed to achieve the fullness of a truly human existence. If anyone lacks these (if he [*sic*] is poor) he is being unjustly deprived of his due: he is being oppressed.[11]

In India, where the rich elite, comprising just 12 percent of India's population, own about 60 percent of the country's urban and rural property and consume nearly one-third of its total annual consumption, it is glaringly evident that injustice is the root cause of poverty. The implications of Soares-Prabhu's warning are drastically demanding. A good deal of rethinking is needed on the part of the Indian church. In a country like India, where the poor are deprived of land and where the basic problem is struggle for food, a rich church with enormous property, extensive landholdings, affluent religious houses, and elite institutions presents a sharp contrast. We must constantly reflect on the extent to which such possessions help the church to be the voice of the poor. A complacent attitude is a scandal to the conscience of the church.

Schüssler Fiorenza also criticizes the spiritualization and romanticization of poverty and the poor. Far from giving in to determinism, she notes that patriarchal structures in church and society are based on hierarchical notions that in turn foster unequal ideologies and institutions.

The Poor in the Bible as a Sociological Group

Soares-Prabhu strongly opposes the tendency to view poverty and the poor from an individualistic perspective. For him, "all through the Bible, then, the poor are a sociological rather than a religious group. Their identity is defined not by any spiritual attitude of openness or dependence on God, but simply by their sociological situation of powerlessness and need."[12] Thus, in the Bible the poor are not merely individuals, but a social unit marked by deprivation and marginalization, which includes but does not exhaust their plight of economic deprivation. In his own words, "The poor of the Bible are thus the 'wretched of the earth,' the marginalized, the exploited, all those who are actually or potentially oppressed."[13]

The Poor in the Bible as a Dialectical Group

The Bible consistently locates the basic cause of poverty in external factors. These include the exploitation of the poor by elite groups who dominate and oppress. The poor, according to Soares-Prabhu's analysis of the Bible, are thus a dialectical group. Their status is determined by and depends dialectically on that of other groups, which the Bible refers to as the powerful, the mighty, the haughty, and the rich—groups who stand in opposition to the poor. Soares-Prabhu's emphasis, which reveals the dialectical nature of poverty, is prophetic.

The Poor in the Bible as a Dynamic Group

Soares-Prabhu emphasizes that the Bible does not depict the poor as a passive group or as a pitiable group of unfortunates, objects of compassion with historical significance, waiting passively for the deliverance promised them.

Rather they are given a significant role in biblical history; they are active agents through whom God brings about radical changes in the world and society. Since they are the victims of oppression, they will be the beneficiaries of salvation and will mediate this salvation to others. The salvation they mediate is a salvation that is eschatological but not otherworldly. This salvation is communitarian, not an individual enterprise. Its image is the New Jerusalem.

Soares-Prabhu discovers great similarity between the Marxist understanding of the proletariat and the conception of the poor in the Bible as a group of people struggling to create a new order of society. But he argues that the biblical category of ʿănāwîm goes beyond the Marxist conception of the proletariat. Though biblical poverty is a sociological category, it should not be reduced to purely economic and Marxist terms. It has a wider sociological and religious meaning. "The poor in the Bible are an oppressed group in conflict, but it is doubtful whether their conflict can be usefully described as a class struggle. The bible goes beyond Marx's classless society in its affirmation of a religious basis for social justice."[14]

Schüssler Fiorenza also notes that the poor are not mere recipients of God's mercy and goodness. Through their total involvement and historical agency, they become active agents of their own empowerment. This is made possible through their own cooperation with God's goodness. She illustrates this point through her analysis of the Jesus movement and its origins.[15] The discipleship of equals, she argues, formed an important component of the vision of the basileia formulated by Jesus.

The Poor and the Basileia Vision

Schüssler Fiorenza rightly claims that the majority of the poor are women and children. This fact has not been sufficiently considered by liberation theologians. It calls for a different analysis and theoretical framework. Schüssler Fiorenza has qualified the understanding of the poor from two aspects. The poor are mostly women, and women are not only the "other" but also the "other of the others." The poor are viewed from the perspective of the basileia and the ekklēsia. The basileia is best understood as "God in the midst of us." Restoring humanity to the poor, as a collective group, is the central significance of the basileia. The experiential aspect of the basileia is emphasized by evoking a whole range of Isaianic images. Luke 7:22 best demonstrates this. "Go and tell John what you have seen and heard; the blind receive their sight, the lame walk, lepers are cleansed, and the deaf hear, the dead are raised up, the poor have good news preached to them."

The central image of the *basileia* is that of a festive meal and table sharing. Such an understanding is based on the logic of democracy, that is, "the notion of equal power among members of a community." For Schüssler Fiorenza, the poor herald God's reign. As a precursor of "God's gracious goodness," the Jesus movement articulates an understanding of God that calls Israel's underdogs. The God of gracious goodness was perceived in a woman's gestalt as divine Sophia. The Sophia-God is a God "of all inclusive love, letting the sun shine and the rain fall equally on the righteous and sinners."[16] This inclusive graciousness of God is seen in parables such as the man searching for his lost sheep, or the woman tirelessly sweeping for her lost coin. Jesus in the latter depicts God as a woman searching for one of her ten coins, as a woman looking for money that is terribly important to her. Jesus articulates God's own concern—a concern that determines Jesus' own praxis for table community with sinners and outcasts. The *basiliea* parable of laborers in the vineyard also shows God's gracious goodness. Those who are last receive a whole day's payment. God's gracious goodness thus establishes equality among all of us, righteous and sinner, rich and poor, men and women, Pharisees and Jesus' disciples.

The *ekklēsia,* moreover, is etymologically related to the church understood as a political group of equal citizens. Justice requires that it promise freedom and equality to all its citizens.

Schüssler Fiorenza thus adds to the analysis of the poor a holistic understanding and also talks about the multiplicative structures of oppression. Based on such an analysis, she highlights the need for a complex hermeneutic methodology. Her hermeneutical strategy is not closed-ended but moves in circling spirals and spiraling circles. It is a seven-step method, which gives importance to the moments of deconstruction and reconstruction. It emphasizes to both change of structures and change of hearts as defined by Soares-Prabhu.

HERMENEUTIC METHODOLOGY

The seven steps that make up the hermeneutical model proposed by Schüssler Fiorenza are the hermeneutics of experience, of social location, of suspicion, of critical evaluation, of imagination, of re-membering and reconstruction, and of transformation.

The main features of the feminist critical method will be spelled out as five elements.

First, the aim of the feminist rhetorical model is not merely to understand texts and traditions but also to transform them. In order to transform the kyriarchal structuring of biblical texts and interpretations, interpretation should be displaced from a privatized and individualized domain and be made a political and public discourse. Consciousness raising by engendering a systemic ethical, political, religious, and cultural analysis is the goal. This demands a movement from the kyriarchal lie of neutrality and objectivity to conscious commitment to the community of wo/men. Such an involvement calls for continued struggle in the interest of emancipation. Denoting dynamic process and rhythmic motion, it is best explained through metaphors that depict fluidity and change.

Second, symbols of struggle and process are employed in order to delineate the contours of the hermeneutical movement. Schüssler Fiorenza's favored metaphor is the symbol of dance, with which she designs the artistic and aesthetic layout of her critical approach. Dancing confounds hierarchical ordering, for "the circle of the dance is an enacted symbol."[17] Influenced by Plato's attack of rhetoric as "mere cookery," she likens biblical interpretation to the process of cooking a stew, "utilizing different herbs and spices to season the potatoes, meat and carrots, which, stirred together, produce a new and different flavor."[18] Such figurative usage points to the domain of quotidian existence. By attributing a specific emancipatory intent to these metaphors, Schüssler Fiorenza decentralizes the highly dogmatic discipline of biblical hermeneutics and makes it accessible to women as subjects of interpretation. Decentralization paves the way for accessibility, especially in a context such as India, where more than half the women are isolated from the highly technical province of biblical hermeneutics. It renders the dance of interpretation open-ended. It welcomes all into its ambience because it makes the gift of fullness a promise meant for all.

Third, the dance of interpretation takes us to the open house of wisdom, where boundaries or walls are absent. Whereas the classical hermeneutical circle is closed and static, the feminist critical model keeps the interpreter ever on the move. Its movement does not follow a linear progression. Propelling ahead in "circling spirals and spiraling circles," its renditions are ever new. In metaphors that denote struggle, its emphasis is on evolving and not arriving, for to arrive very often is to be static and all-knowing.

Fourth, the emancipatory hermeneutical dance recasts interpretation in rhetorical terms. Schüssler Fiorenza's ingenuity lies in having underscored the rhetorical nature of biblical texts and biblical interpretation. In highlighting the fact that religious texts were produced in and by particular historical debates and struggles, Schüssler Fiorenza was influenced by three factors: the notion of the four different senses of scripture in Christian medieval interpretation: literal, allegorical, moral, and anagogical;[19] the Jewish comparison of the Bible to a "palette of colours that an artist uses to create a painting, but it is not the painting itself";[20] the Jewish understanding that the Torah was written in black fire on white fire and that the white spaces around the black letters held meaning yet to be discovered. These "yet-to-be-discovered" gaps provide the space for a feminist interpretation.

Fifth, the goal of a feminist rhetorical model is consciousness raising. This includes a critical analysis of experience. Feminist liberation interpreters change the starting point of traditional biblical interpretation by beginning with the sociocultural and religious experiences of the marginalized and of those women traditionally excluded from interpreting the Bible. Experience thus becomes the takeoff point for the hermeneutical waltz.

Starting from the encounter of the unfathomable mystery within one's inner self, Soares-Prabhu points out that the Indian hermeneutic launch pad also is experience. Interpretation of sacred books is considered a *brahmajijnasa* (knowledge of Brahman), a quest toward a deeper *anubhava* (experience) and a progressive awakening to the divine truth. Progression is not perceived in a linear fashion. Intrinsically and intimately connected with the mystery of the subject (the seeker), the divine is not the object of one's search. Perceived as a complex phenomenon, the journey/dance to the divine is best illustrated in terms of an awakening to the highest state of realization called the *turiya* (perfect and total silence) in the Indian fourfold understanding of consciousness.

A DIALOGICAL HERMENEUTICS

Soares-Prabhu describes the hermeneutical process as a dialogue or conversation between the "I" of the interpreter and the "Thou" of the text. In such a hermeneutical conversation, as in any genuine dialogue, each is open to the other. The text will respond to the questions the interpreter brings, and the interpreter in turn will react to the claims of truth made on him (or her) by the text. Meaning thus emerges from a creative and dialogical encounter between the interpreter and the text.

In likening hermeneutics to a genuine conversation where the interlocutor will be open to his (or her) partner in dialogue, Soares-Prabhu has not considered sexist internalizations, in my opinion.

There are four chief elements in his methodology that, while together they form one indivisible process, must clearly be distinguished from one another. First comes a prophetic critique of oppressive elements in current exegesis; the second distinctive element is a conversion from alienation to inculturation; the third element is commitment to the poor; and finally revisiting the Bible from the perspective of the oppressed class within the sensibilities of the Indian *Weltanschauung*. Such a reading must take place in pluri-religious communities of men and women who are actively committed to the task of building up God's kingdom. The kingdom is realized only through an intense love and commitment to God and neighbor, especially the poor and oppressed. The experience of God's love urges us to an effective concern for our neighbor. Thus, the *Dharma* of Jesus encompasses personal, religious, and social dimensions. Such a reading will avoid the theological aridity of historical criticism and the irresponsible ahistoricism of naïve, precritical interpretations. This is a reading that is contextual and suited to real-life situations.

The category of experience (*anubhava*) thus is viewed from social, political, cultural, aesthetic, spiritual, and religious perspectives explained in terms of an integrated outlook. This does not point toward a negation of the varied possibilites of experience but toward an analysis. Professionalism is placed at the service of prophetism and authenticity of life. It is in this sphere of critical analysis and committed prophetism that Schüssler Fiorenza's method offers categories of analysis to the Indian hermeneutic approach thus enhancing its liberating thrust.

Schüssler Fiorenza's method demonstrates that any theorizing that centers on theological or cultural legitimacy or normative external authority does not concern itself with a feminist historical reconstruction. A feminist historical reconstruction commences with the presupposition that wo/men have been historical and cultural agents. The burden of proof is with those who think that they have not. From this standpoint, a feminist historical reconstruction through the sevenfold strategic method that Schüssler Fiorenza proposes critically analyzes scriptural passages, texts, and traditions, in order to retrieve hidden traces of the vision, sufferings, and struggles against kyriarchal oppression of our biblical foresisters. Such a search for lost traditions is done from the context of present-day movements for emancipation.

Bodies of wo/men are sites of violence, exclusion, and abuse. At the same time, experience tells us that they are also sources of agency and power that allow for the possibilities of negotiation, intervention, and transformation. Through Schüssler Fiorenza's hermeneutical dance, Indian Catholic wo/men can unlearn all the kyriarchal lies that have so far constricted them and can move from alienation to affirmation of their inner powers. This will help them realize that their bodies are not their destinies and will help them enjoy the gift of womanhood.

Schüssler Fiorenza presents a new metaphor for the understanding of scriptures in her book *Bread Not Stone.* She calls for an approach that understands scriptures as "bread for sustenance on the way" and not "tablets of stone" that prescribe a litany of rules and regulations. As *Bread Not Stone,* the Word of God cannot prescribe anything that oppresses. Therefore anything that is life-negating is not the Word of God but the word of Paul or Matthew or Luke. By employing such a critical and creative approach, which begins with the challenge to divine authorization and an understanding of the rhetorical nature of the Word, Indian Catholic wo/men also affirm their agencies.

In adopting a critical attitude to tradition and scripture, Indian Catholic wo/men can become free from their alienation. Schüssler Fiorenza also emphasizes that such a search for emancipation is a collaborative endeavor. This points to the importance of joining movements for liberation. Feminism is seen both as critique of ideology and critique of societal structures.

LIBERATION

For both Soares-Prabhu and Schüssler Fiorenza, all method is a path toward a goal. The goal both of them have in mind is liberation. What Francis D'Sa says of Soares-Prabhu can be adapted to apply to both.

> What he [Soares-Prabhu] meant by liberation was more comprehensive than even that of liberation theologians: liberation of our understanding of Jesus (and Mary) from dogmatic and a-historical approaches, liberation of the Bible, more especially of the Gospels from purely academic, emotional, pietistic, patriarchal and "spiritual" readings, liberation from one-sided methods of interpreting the Scriptures, liberation of the Church from authoritarianism and its mission from the "triumphalistic mission commands," liberation of the priesthood from ritualistic tendencies, liberation of theology and its method and goal from other-wordly or ideologically loaded starting-points, liberation of the poor from a pie-in-the-sky kind of hope, liberation of women, libera-

tion from consumerism, liberation from communalism, liberation for the tribals, liberation from a colonized mentality, liberation from oppressive practices of religious and social traditions, liberation of Christians from attitudes of superiority towards other faith-traditions, and towards the end of his life, liberation of the earth from the rapacity of humans.[21]

For Soares-Prabhu, theology does not end in words but in effective transformation of peoples and society. Genuine liberation is possible, he emphasizes, only if personal conversion complements social change and if a cultural revolution leavens a sociopolitical one. A merely individual concern will not usher in God's reign and the new society.[22]

Schüssler Fiorenza also argues that transformation and consciousness raising should be the main objectives of theologizing. Critiquing the tendency in Christian theology to understand redemption as merely spiritual, her understanding of liberation encompasses the various strands delineated by Soares-Prabhu. In addition, she goes a step further because her understanding also includes the need for a deconstruction and reconstruction of mythical archetypes. Offering us a complex methodology for the process, she offers Indian women a hermeneutic and analytical tool that will help them challenge inscribed identities and myths that often work toward their disempowerment. In doing so, she underscores the agency of women.

CONCLUSION

The main aim of this project has been to explore the manner in which Schüssler Fiorenza's method extends Soares-Prabhu's concerns and is therefore crucial for a reinvention of the Indian woman's identity. Soares-Prabhu maintained that it was a luxury to be involved with the issues of truth and method in a country like India, where the theologian ought to be absorbed in blood and sweat issues. Such a perspective nonetheless could consign women, "the other of the others," to theological amnesia because it fails to recognize methodologies that implicitly and explicitly perpetuate patriarchal and kyriarchal values. By consciously working toward the delineation of a new method Schüssler Fiorenza paves the path for a reconstruction of women's active and creative participation in the construction of a religious and social history and offers us tools for the transformation of the scriptures as bread for sustenance on the way. A conscientious involvement in method has also led to an empowering vocabulary and language that challenge patriarchal linguistic determinism and offers all "Others" life-generating possibilities. If Soares-Prabhu has given us a radical and wholesome definition of transformation as change of hearts and change of structures, Schüssler Fiorenza has generated the method to achieve this.

NOTES

1. George M. Soares-Prabhu was professor of scripture in the faculty of Jnana-Deepa-Vidyapeeth, Pune, India, for almost twenty-five years. He died in a road accident in July 1995.

2. In this context it is important to point out that very often the words feminism (a political construct) and feminine (cultural construct) are used as synonyms. This is another manner in which patriarchal forces try to blunt the prophetic and political thrust of feminism. Too often I have heard even women in the movement saying with concern that if the words feminist and feminism are used, many women will be reluctant to join us though they agree with the goals and objectives of the feminist movement.

3. Quoted in Hedwig Meyer Wilmes, *Rebellion on the Borders*, trans. Irene Smith-Bowman (Kampen: Kok Pharos, 1995), 190.

4. George M. Soares-Prabhu, "From Alienation to Inculturation: Some Reflections on Doing Theology in India Today," in *Bread and Breath: Essays in Honour of Samuel Rayan*, ed. T. K. John (Anand, Gujarat: Sathiya Prakash, 1991), 72–73.

5. In its effort to be strictly neutral toward competing religious groups, the Indian State refuses official recognition to any institute of religious training. Of the approximately 150 universities in India, only one university has a department for postgraduate and doctoral studies in Christian theology, and three other universities have chairs. In addition, the academic disciplines of the university rarely challenge the theologians in the seminary. Hence Soares-Prabhu rightly notes that the Indian theologians often remain alienated even from the world of Indian intellectual life.

6. Soares-Prabhu, "From Alienation to Inculturation," 73.

7. Aloysius Pieris, "Asia's Non-Semitic Religions and the Mission of the Local Churches," *Month* 15 (1982): 81–90.

8. Elisabeth Schüssler Fiorenza, *Wisdom Ways: Introducing Feminist Biblical Interpretation* (Maryknoll, N.Y.: Orbis Books, 2001), 3.

9. Schüssler Fiorenza, *Searching the Scriptures,* volume 1, *A Feminist Introduction* (New York: Crossroad, 1993), 3.

10. Francis D'Sa, "The Contribution of George M. Soares-Prabhu to Method in Theology," *Third Millennium II* (1999): 4, 103.

11. George M. Soares-Prabhu, "Jesus and Social Justice," in *Jesus for Our Times: Towards a Spirituality of Social Action* (Manila: FABC, 1986), 37.

12. George M. Soares-Prabhu, "Class in the Bible: The Biblical 'Poor' a Social Class?" *Vidyajyoti* 49 (1985): 332.

13. Ibid.

14. Ibid., 345.

15. For Schüssler Fiorenza's analysis of the origins of the Jesus movement, see *In Memory of Her: A Feminist Theological Reconstruction of Christian Origins* (New York: Crossroad, 1983).

16. Ibid., 131.

17. Schüssler Fiorenza, *Wisdom Ways*, 166–67.

18. Ibid., 166.

19. John H. Hayes and Carl R. Holladay, *Biblical Exegesis* (London: SCM Press, 1983), 21.

20. Schüssler Fiorenza, *Wisdom Ways*, 168.

21. Francis D'Sa, "The Contribution of George M. Soares-Prabhu," 4, 103.

22. George M. Soares-Prabhu, "The Kingdom of God: Jesus' Vision of a New Society," in *The Indian Church in the Struggle for a New Society*, ed. D. S. Amalor-paadass (Bangalore: NBCLC, 1981), 607.

5

Some Reflections
on Violence against Women
and the Image of the Hebrew God

The Prophetic Books Revisited

Athalya Brenner

ELISABETH SCHÜSSLER FIORENZA TAUGHT US ALL, AGAIN AND AGAIN, that we should use a judicious hermeneutics of suspicion as feminist women approaching biblical texts and that our reflective and reflexive suspicions, while profoundly informing our readings, should nevertheless be accompanied by a sense of [serious] fun and wonderment. This article is dedicated to you, Elisabeth, in the hope that you'll approve of how this very important lesson has been internalized.

In the following remarks on well-trodden, critical, feminist, and other ground regarding the Hebrew prophets, my intention is to problematize rather than to give answers.[1] Some tentative answers there will be—Who can withstand the temptation to prophesy, even a little?—but not too many, in this exercise of reading from today, while "remembering the past in order to create the future."[2]

Let us give another thought to the name conferred upon the texts to be discussed here, such as Jeremiah 2–5, Ezekiel 16 and 23, Isaiah 47, Nahum 3, Malachi 2, and other passages as well that conform to these typologies. Let me add Isaiah 3, although it does not deal with exactly the same topic, as a mirror image in the sense that husband–wife relations in times of collective trouble are imaged there too.

The name given to such texts in biblical criticism, feminist and otherwise, is the *marriage metaphor*. Renita Weems writes, as a matter of course: "[I]n recent years there have been a number of interesting studies on the *marriage metaphor*."

A longer title for such passages will read something like this: *The prophetic metaphor about the relationship between YHWH—metaphorized into a loving, wronged and enraged husband—and his people, metaphorized into a loved but unfaithful wife.* The first questions we have to consider, then, refer to the shorthand title, that is, the "marriage metaphor."

1. What, precisely or approximately, is the meaning of "marriage" here? Marriage is a social contract, time- and place-bound, to be sure. What kind of social contract is constructed/reflected in such passages, and how is it gendered?

2. How do we understand "metaphor" for the purpose of reading these passages?

3. It is widely acknowledged that the biblical descriptions contain violent, even pornographic images and assumptions about the nature of female sexuality and violent male responses to it. Why is this component absent from the name/title attached to the descriptions by readers and commentators?

It would seem, so far, that the first two points are methodological, while the third is more of an epistemological-philosophical as well as social-anthropological nature. However, if we consider the longer title, more questions emerge.

4. What is the nature of the partners, as disclosed through the focalizing description? The focalizer, clearly, is a divine first-person male (speaking directly or indirectly through the mouthpiece of the prophet, another religious male focalizer). Especially pertinent, then, is the nature of the divine [male] partner in this metaphor. This, of course, is a theological and moral issue.

5. What are the implications of the metaphor for the Hebrew Bible in general, for the contextualization of so-called prophetic literature within what came to be known as the Jewish canon, the post-Qumran library

of sacred writings? This would be a literary-historical issue with, once again, theological and ethical connotations.

6. What memories, what cultural constellation, could have created or advanced such descriptions? This would be a historical-cultural issue.

Let me go briefly through these points, introducing problems and difficulties of interpretation as I proceed. I do have some criticisms to make about the way the discussion is proceeding—from Drorah Setel's ground-breaking study of nearly twenty years ago to more recent studies such as those by Renita Weems, Yvonne Sherwood, Mary Shields, and Gerlinde Baumann.[4] These are valuable contributions to an ongoing debate. My purpose is not to undervalue these and other contributions. What I would like to add, after two decades of almost obsessive Jacob-like wrestling with such passages, is what is still missing from the debate—at least to my own taste. And criticism, by its very nature, points to absences as well as considering presences.

MARRIAGE

Do we know enough about marriage in "biblical" times to justify speaking about marriage in the passages listed above? The texts allude to taking a "wife," "divorcing" her, or taking her back. We try to step back and look at the texts from afar, as if we could suspend subjectivity for a while in favor of temporary objectivity,[5] to read the metaphor against its implied original setting[s]. But in spite of our honorable intentions, and because we know so very little about social practices in the biblical worlds—what we have are prescriptive and fictive texts, whose mirroring quality can be pondered again and again—we falter, we have no choice, and ultimately we return to rely, perhaps unconsciously, on our own marriage praxis. The result is an inevitable seesaw movement between vehicle and tenor (in the metaphor), past and present, in which some items are privileged and others are lost from view. For instance, we tend, alas, to read such texts using our own notions of Western, officially monogamous marriage practices, while forgetting something. But what we call a "wife" can also be, in the Hebrew Bible, a "concubine"—certainly one of several "wives" of varying social status. In biblical terms, I suppose, this would constitute a possible norm (for some classes at least). But I have not read many feminist critiques of the metaphor that problematize the attribution to the husband/YHWH of more than one "wife" (as in Ezekiel) and what this may mean for the metaphor as a whole, for depictions of YHWH's "nature," and for understanding better both the gender relations and the violence inherent in such passages—to our greater horror, perhaps. What do we do then? Do we derive the power language and structures (Weems) inherent in these passages also from the "one husband/several wives" situation, or do we let this aspect drop for (a) historical considerations and/or (b) assuming that this is in order, since the "wife" in the metaphor symbolizes a collective, meaning that "wives" are suitable partners as well? In short, we have not problematized the "family" background satisfactorily by assuming a single wife for a single husband, although the facts—in the form of Ohala and Ohalibah in Ezekiel—stare us in the face. Furthermore, and once again reading for today (and tomorrow), do we condone bigamy or pardon it because of ancient customs? How might a potential bigamous relationship impact the notion of husbandly love or the demand of exclusivity, once we see that it is not binding upon the "male" partner? He himself, as is clear, can have more than one partner. Have we stopped to think about that, not only in the Jacob stories but also in this one, of the "marriage metaphor"?

METAPHOR

The term "metaphor" indicates double trouble.[6] First, are we sure of the use we make of "metaphor"? This term is so overused as to become a cliché? What definition shall we adopt, and what are the implications for our analysis? To begin with, metaphor is not just a matter of speech or discourse, a tool to elucidate a point to be made; it goes so much deeper into the fabric of our thought structures and conceptualization of the inner and outer world. Furthermore, are we sure a metaphor is employed here, not a comparison? And if this is a metaphor we are dealing with, if the image of divine husband/ human wife is a metaphor and not a comparison or an allegory or another rhetorical device, are we sufficiently aware that in metaphor the vehicle and tenor, or signifier and signified, tend to blur or collapse into each other? In metaphor, the entity "metaphorized" *is*—at least after a fashion—the referent, not simply or complexly something similar to but other than it. To say otherwise is to use the term "metaphor" in an excusing and disarming manner. The prophets wanted to shock their audience into attention, but this is not the whole story. In this connection, we would do well to reread the contributions of Claudia Camp and Mieke Bal in the *Semeia* volume entitled

Women, War, and Metaphor.[7] Not only is this particular example, as Mieke Bal points out, one of the "Metaphors He Lives By"—that is, a male metaphor that should be defined as such in the "title" we attribute to the relevant texts—but also perhaps it is time to question our adoption of the term "metaphor" to describe such passages. It is no more metaphor than our ordinary speech and life conveyed by literary register. The term "metaphor" ultimately obscures more than it reveals. It softens the blow, so to speak: it allows us to think, in most cases, that when all is said and done, it is *only* a metaphor, not a "reality"—bad enough, surely, but open to change and surprise (Weems again). Of course, this is not so. Metaphors are life's texture, not just a rhetorical-literary phenomenon. Allowing the passages in question to become metaphors obscures the pain—and the relevance—by making them into literary phenomena more than life phenomena. Furthermore, can violence of any kind ever be considered only metaphorical? Predominantly metaphorical?

VIOLENCE

The component of violence is very much in evidence in the texts under discussion. The *verbal* abuse directed at the "wife" contains depictions of *physical* abuse. In my conceptual and "real" world, the coupling of sexual desire with violence, more often initiated by the male partner, for whatever reason, implies hardcore pornography as a fantasy framework and justification for battering. Why is this fact omitted from the name given to the metaphor? The answer may be that pornography may seem too outlandish a term for divine behavior, or religious propaganda—or simply because it is uncomfortable to consider. This is hardly the place to indulge in a discussion of the fondness some readers may have for sado-masochistic relationships. The s/m relationship in the text is not by mutual consent, let us remind ourselves once more, but is initiated by the male "partner." Is such violence a typical or an actual property of marriage? Should it be, then and now? Can this violent marriage be justified because women cheat on their spouses, as do men? These and other epistemological questions are not ignored in scholarly treatments of the relevant passages, especially feminist ones. However, they are softened by the mere consent to use the accepted coin.

So far I have tried to point out that even feminist critics—including me—have practiced complicity with accepted norms by not escaping the s/m vision drawn in the marriage passages simply because, even while discussing its contents with horror and distaste, we have retained the convenient short-hand title. To backtrack a little, did we, some of us at least, do it in order to salvage the Bible from itself, at least a little bit, to salvage the Hebrew god from himself (yes, himself), to lessen the blow to our own sensibilities? But as Mary Shields says about Jeremiah 3, "this text constructs gender in that it reveals a disguised pressure for female readers to conform to the patriarchal symbolic order. This imagery, however, works only as long as men hold the exclusive power to shape and define subjectivity. When women become resisting readers, the crisis in the patriarchal symbolic order is revealed."[8] Let us therefore move on to the issues contained in the longer description or title given to the metaphor. Our general aim will be to begin a contextualization of the gender relations and gender boundaries that inform the relevant biblical passages within the theological, cultural, and perhaps even historical worlds of the Hebrew Bible inasmuch as we can understand them from "this place," our place.

THE PARTNERS

What is the nature of the partners? Let us begin with the dominant, male, divine partner. We know from other biblical texts that he is violent by defin-ition: he is "the lord of hosts," the god of war. He takes revenge upon his ene-mies. He leads his people into battle. Of course, he has another side, a mercy side, for those who love him (see Exodus 20 and 34; Deuteronomy 5). But, in principle and to begin with, he is the god of battle and destruction. This is confirmed by the mythical remnants of the creation epic, such as Isaiah 27 (I do not refer here to the Priestly schema of the creation in Genesis 1:1–2:4a), to use Umberto Cassuto's language in his many discussions of the mythic/mythological traces in the Hebrew Bible. Destruction antedates construc-tion, for the Hebrew god as well as for others, such as the god Marduk. There is no doubt that YHWH, as a national god, fights—a property not unlike that of other dominant gods, such as Baʿal and ʿAnat of Ugarit (to whom we shall return later). Moreover, the legacy of violence, the "curse of Cain," to use Regina Schwartz's idiom,[9] permeates the whole of the Hebrew Bible. Have a look at the books of Joshua and Judges. No wonder, then, that YHWH's gen-der relations correspond to this dominant trait of his character. Unlike Bau-mann,[10] then, I would like to emphasize that god's behavior as a soldier/rapist, as in Isaiah 47 and elsewhere, is not different from his treatment of his "wife" or "wives" or other nations/"women" he encounters. As Mieke Bal poignantly observes, sex and control merge in both sex and war: Sex is war and war is sex.[11] But this is not all. Yнwн demands exclusivity from his "lovers." This appears already in the Decalogue (Exodus 20; Deuteronomy 5); however, with his tendency to universalize himself, does he also grant exclusivity to his "lovers" as well as demanding it? How many "wives" does he have? To begin with, "his" own people, no doubt, but then extending as universal god to other "wives"/nations? In "real" life, a violent man will be considered just that, a violent man, and he will be feared for that. Violence toward those he supposedly loves will be taken more seriously and justified less easily. Finally and by the way, Yнwн provides his "wife/wives" with everything apart from sexual gratification—food, shelter, clothing—and then blames her/them for searching for that elsewhere. He leaves "her," like Hosea's woman in chapter 3, sitting as no-man's property, and then blames her. What have we to say to that? In "life," this would be considered the product of passive-aggressive jealousy. In short, can virtues cancel out shortcomings?

I can almost hear the protest, but "he"—Yнwн—has other sides and other properties as well, apart from being a violent soldier and violent "husband." "He" may behave like a mother, as in several passages in, for example, Isaiah 40–66.[12] Now, how serious is this claim? In "life," once again, mothers are less idealized than they are in some passages of the Bible. There are good mothers and bad mothers; mothers can be conceptualized as good by their children at times and as bad at other times. Ambivalence toward offspring, offering a good breast and a bad breast to the baby at the same time—to use the language of psychoanalysts Melanie Klein, Donald Woods Winnicott, and others—is human and commonplace. This "god of the breasts" (ʾel šadday) is also similar to ʿAnat, the Ugaritic goddess who is ymmt lʿimm ("mother of nations") on the one hand, and a bloodthirsty warrior on the other hand (as in the Baʿal epic). My point is that the duality in the divine nature, in both instances, is *concurrent* rather than consecutive. Why is it, then, that when Yнwн behaves like a mother, which he doesn't do too often, we tend to see this as an antidote to his more pronounced violent behavior as soldier/man?

What about the female "partner/s"? As is now being increasingly recognized, the texts address communities of males and call upon them to recognize that if they behave "like females"; they are females,[13] with all the gender prejudices this implies (and let us also give some thought to the very interesting if rarely talked about gender-bending possibilities). Thus, in fact, both genders are abused in the relevant prophetic texts. Both genders are given very little opportunity to justify themselves in this imagined relationship. All too often, we as interpreters tend to accept the basic premises of the focalizer, the speaker-in-the-text, call him god or god's messenger or the prophet or what you will. Even if we object to the "vehicle," we accept the actual claim made and explain it away as historically correct, theologically understandable, a matter of opinion, or the like. We tend to *comprehend* and even *appreciate* the speaker's motivation—or frustration because of his (yes, his) audience's implied behavior. Once again, such a practice is far from satisfactory.

Love?

It is commonplace to argue that a love relationship and marital contract are highly appropriate for depicting the covenant between YHWH and his people. As an aside, let us remember once again that the covenant, in all its accounts and occurrences, is initiated by YHWH rather than by his people; and, other ancient Near Eastern parallels notwithstanding, this again is meaningful. Now, perhaps love is the appropriate image. The question is, What love— between a dominant partner and a subordinate one, a violent partner and a subdued one, a conqueror such as YHWH and a conquered one such as the wailing woman of Lamentations, a miserable mother as in Hosea, Malachi, and Trito-Isaiah and the divine husband who took her back? I have my doubts about the declared love component. No equal footing, no mutuality is afforded in biblical literature: the call, nay, the demand to "love YHWH your god with all your heart and all your mind and all your being" (Deut. 6:2) is a valiant attempt at equating religious belief and desire, an attempt that paradoxically evidences the difficulty of such love while anticipating the more graphic, violent, disappointed hankering for human love in the "marriage metaphor." (As is well known, threats of disenfranchisement, of the "if . . . then" format, are very much in evidence in Deuteronomy too.) In that sense, the view of the creation account as therapeutic (as seen by Phyllis Trible and Bal[14]) is, in my opinion, unfounded: no real theological or social gain can be found there.

Neither can we find a remedy for divine violence and battering love in the Song of Songs. Correction: as readers, we may find consolation both in the creation and garden stories in Genesis and in the garden in the Song of Songs.

But if we stop for a minute to consider the author's intent, although this has become unfashionable in the postmodern age, then an answer to the violence of love is to be found in postbiblical Jewish interpretation of the Song of Songs only. Like many other readers, I do not think that an allegorical understanding of the Song of Songs, as if it depicted an allegorical, gendered love story between the divine and his community, refers to the primary level of the Song of Songs. Basically, I read the Song of Songs as a collection of secular love poetry and consider Jewish allegorical interpretations of it secondary. However, and this should be borne in mind, it is quite conceivable that postbiblical Jewish interpreters found the so-called marriage metaphor much too harsh for their liking. Therefore, and since the Song of Songs was available to them as well as the prophetic writings, they interpreted it by way of *derash* as a happier love story between YHWH and his people. No "Batter my heart, three-person'd God" (John Donne) for them, in this connection. Once again, therefore, we have the anomaly of a metaphor/allegory using love to depict a same-sex relationship between a male god and his typically—nay, almost exclusively—male community. Without too much proof beyond the continuance of the same-gender participants, I wish to advance the hypothesis that the Jewish allegory for the Song of Songs was produced specifically to counter the marriage metaphor. Perhaps, too, we can see the liturgical coupling of passages such as Ezekiel 16 together with the Song of Songs in the Passover Haggadah as another signal in that direction. At any rate, such a remedy seems to me much more convincing than hailing YHWH's maternal or husband-on-the-rebound, inner-biblical qualities as the counterpart of the imge of the violent man/husband. Ultimately, and since a positive image of YHWH's love story with his people is already known from 4 Ezra (second century C.E.), we may surmise that the picture of YHWH's violent love, together with the prophetic books that contain it, was known and recognized as theologically and culturally troublesome at least as early as the time of 4 Ezra. Perhaps one may venture a guess as to the gender awareness of the "alternative" Song of Songs love story, as in the Jewish allegory. While at this time I have become less enthusiastic about the gender superiority of female figures in the Song of Songs—the general patriarchal framework is still there, and very much so; and the pendulum of scholarly readership is beginning to problematize this recent haven of feminist biblical content—at least, together with the relative disappearance of violence from the world of committed love, there appears an improvement in female status vis-à-vis her "lover" or even "lovers" in it. And she has a voice.

But this corrective measure is, in the main, a postbiblical development. I no longer argue—although I have done so in the past—that the Song of Songs itself can serve as an effective inner-biblical answer to the marriage metaphor, unless this is done purely as a conscious exercise of readerly response. All I am saying is that, in time and perhaps in the spirit of the time, the spirit eventually produced a Christian god much more loving, much more egalitarian (but, well, let us not forget the "batter my heart" syndrome, so beloved by Christian [male] mystics in their responses to the Song of Songs;[15] much less of a warrior, a bridegroom *not* of blood and uncircumsised. Slowly, and in Judaism too, the image of the divine warrior/lover was largely rejected for the present—be that "present" what it may in different periods, although retained for the past. But this did not happen in the Hebrew Bible itself: images of god as mother and ex-husband-turned-new-husband are too few to convince of a complete character transformation—within the metaphor of course, as it continues to evolve as a *topos*.

MEMORY, REMEMBRANCE

The issues of memory and remembrance come to mind here. Memories are an ever-shifting construct, much like the identities that are formed by them and shape them in return. One must therefore ask how and why the "memory" of a warrior/rapist/jealous husband/avenging god metamorphosed into another memory, that of a caring god of mercy. Both images have existed side by side; the question is how, why, and when the balance between the images shifted. It is tempting to view the metamorphosis as a response to political and military loss. This, however, does not always happen. Postexilic biblical literature prefers, by and large, to preserve the image of the divine warrior (see Isaiah 63 for instance) who can and does turn—at least in religious discourse—against his own people as well as against their enemies. So-called prophecies of salvation are still far outnumbered by so-called prophecies of doom. In prophetic literature as in other parts of the Hebrew Bible, it seems preferable for humans to carry the burden of guilt for their own sorry fate, while the violent god is being exonerated and justified. This is how the memory of god is sanitized and kept intact, how his image is preserved from imploding and exploding upon itself. But the mere memory of god's merciful side and the questioning of his motives as in the book of Job (or Jonah) witness the difficulties of creating a memory of a life-sustaining divine image in times of personal or collective trouble. Weems's consolation, in that the divine "husband" may surprise us all by yet taking his "wife" back,[16] is perhaps not sufficient grace for me because of this action's arbitrariness: discourse of grace may supplant, not only supplement, discourse of violence, but both spring from the same source of divine power politics (as Weems freely states).

To Conclude

Let me emphasize the obvious once more. I regard the violent description of YHWH as a professional soldier and dissatisfied husband who tortures his "wife" as unacceptable, on general humanistic-ethical as well as theological and social-gendered grounds. I regard the relevant passages as pornographic and beyond salvation not only for feminists but also for any objector to violence, be that violence divine or religious or otherwise. The Hebrew god is violent. We have to recognize that in the same way that we have to recognize how many crimes have been committed in the name of the peaceful religion that claimed it was an antidote to this violent streak. Ultimately, no reconsideration of the "original circumstances," whether grounded in reconstructed history or anthropology or religious studies or psychology or developmental theory or positivism, can change that or serve as an excuse for "understanding." No learned recognition of the violent prophetic coinage of the divine husband/human wife as metaphor of marriage or love can or should change that. Think for the present and future. Focus on the consequences rather than on excuses for the biblical prophets. Look, for instance, at women's fate in war—as in Isaiah 3 or 47, and Lamentations, and beyond.

Monotheistic gods must indeed be good and evil. Such gods are, by definition, powerful and absolute. Need I go on to state that absolute power corrupts absolutely? "Batter my heart, three-person'd God" (John Donne), is so often, and as I have already said twice above, the (mostly male) human response to the gods that humans create for themselves. And the gods comply: they indeed seem to batter. But is it love, this "battered" thing, or need we understand it some more? Apart from acknowledging that this model of faith exists, can we not regard it as an s/m model that is unacceptable to feminist readers? We can, and should, elect to use other models or to [re]create them.

The Bible, contrary to popular and even scholarly beliefs, does *not* speak or *say*. Its readers do. Because this is our heritage, because this is what we read and have been contemplating for millennia, it is up to us to choose to disown this description. We can also choose to use it as the mirror it is, a negative teacher so to speak, and draw our conclusions about our own nature. If, by doing that, we step back from fourth-wave feminist thinking to second-wave anger, so be it.

But, whatever our choice, merely condemning past practices is clearly not enough. Speaking in metaphors should be understood for what it represents, for readers perhaps more than for the authors of the "original" biblical texts— whoever they were, whenever and wherever they lived, if they did, and whatever they intended.

NOTES

1. The first version of this paper was read in Würzburg, Germany, on December 13, 2000. It focuses on the following texts (while mentioning others as well): Isaiah 3:14–4:1 (read also Isaiah 1 for the image of the Hebrew god); Jeremiah 2–5; Ezekiel 16 and 23. It covers ground similar to that covered by Renita Weems in her *Battered Love: Marriage, Sex, and Violence in the Hebrew Prophets* (Minneapolis: Fortress, 1995). For references to and critiques of Weems's and other scholars' analyses, see below. I wish, however, to state that I am indebted to Weems's many insights in this paper, although I take issue with some of her stated positions.

2. Elisabeth Schüssler Fiorenza, "Remembering the Past in Creating the Future: Historical-Critical Scholarship and Feminist Biblical Interpretation," in *Feminist Perspectives on Biblical Scholarship*, ed. Adela Yarbro Collins (Chico, Calif.: Scholars Press, 1985), 43–64.

3. Renita Weems, *Battered Love*, 4 (italics added), and many times throughout her book. Or see Gerlinde Baumann's automatic use of what I call the short title ("Connected by Marriage, Adultery and Violence: The Prophetic Marriage Metaphor in the Book of the Twelve and in the Major Prophets," in *Society of Biblical Literature 1999 Seminar Papers* [Atlanta: Scholars Press, 1999], 552–69; eadem, *Liebe und Gewalt: Die Ehe als Metapher für das Verhältnis JHWH-Israel in den Prophetenbüchern*, Stuttgarter Bibelstudien 185 [Stuttgart: Katholisches Bibelwerk, 2000]).

4. Drorah T. Setel, "Prophets and Pornography: Female Sexual Imagery in Hosea," in *Feminist Interpretations of the Bible*, ed. Letty M. Russell (Oxford: Basil Blackwell, 1985), 93–106; repr. in *A Feminist Companion to the Latter Prophets*, ed. A. Brenner (Sheffield: Sheffield Academic Press, 1995); Weems, *Battered Love;* Yvonne Sherwood, "Boxing Gomer: Controlling the Deviant Woman in Hosea 1–3," in *A Feminist Companion to the Latter Prophets*, ed. Brenner, 101–25; eadem,

The Prostitute and the Prophet: Hosea's Marriage in Literary-Historical Perspective (Journal for the Study of the Old Testament Supplement 212; Sheffield: Sheffield Academic Press, 1996); Mary E. Shields, "Circumcision of the Prostitute: Gender, Sexuality and the Call to Repentance in Jeremiah 2:1–4:1," in *A Feminist Companion to the Prophets and Daniel,* 2nd series, ed. A. Brenner (Sheffield: Sheffield Academic Press, 2001), 121–33; eadem, "Multiple Exposures: Body Rhetoric and Gender in Ezekiel 16," in *A Feminist Companion to Prophets and Daniel,* ed. Brenner, 137–53; Baumann, "Connected by Marriage"; eadem, "Prophetic Objections to YHWH as the Violent Husband of Israel: Reinterpretations of the Prophetic Marriage Metaphor in Second Isaiah (Isaiah 40–55)," in *A Feminist Companion to Prophets and Daniel,* ed. Brenner, 88–120.

5. See, e.g., Weems's attempt in *Battered Love,* 2–3, 78–80, and elsewhere.

6. See Weems, *Battered Love,* 12–30, for a convenient discussion.

7. Claudia Camp, "Introduction: Metaphor in Feminist biblical Interpretation: Theological Perspectives," and Mieke Bal, "Metaphors He Lives By," in *Women, War, and Metaphor,* ed. Claudia Camp and Carole R. Fontaine, *Semeia* 61 (Atlanta: Scholars Press, 1993), 3–36 and 185–207, respectively.

8. Shields, "Circumcision of the Prostitute," 133.

9. Regina Schwartz, *The Curse of Cain: The Violent Legacy of Monotheism* (Chicago/London: University of Chicago Press, 1997).

10. Baumann, "Prophetic Objections to YHWH as the Violent Husband."

11. Bal, "Metaphors He Lives By."

12. Mayer Gruber, "The Motherhood of God," in *The Motherhood of God and Other Studies* (Atlanta: Scholars Press, 1992), 3–15; see also Baumann, "Prophetic Objections to YHWH as the Violent Husband."

13. Fokkelien van Dijk Hemmes, "The Imagination of Power and the Power of Imagination: An Intertextual Analysis of Two Biblical Love Songs, The Song of Songs and Hosea 2," *Journal for the Study of the Old Testament* 44 (1989): 75–88; repr. in *A Feminist Companion to the Song of Songs,* ed. A. Brenner (Sheffield: Sheffield Academic Press, 1993), 156–79; Shields, "Circumcision of the Prostitute" and "Multiple Exposures."

14. Phyllis Trible, *God and the Rhetoric of Sexuality* (Philadelphia: Fortress, 1978); Mieke Bal, *Lethal Love: Feminist Literary Readings of Biblical Love Stories* (Bloomington: Indiana University Press, 1987), 104–30.

15. Stephen D. Moore, "The Song of Songs in the History of Sexuality," *Church History* 69 (2000): 328–49.

16. Weems, *Battered Love,* 80–81, for instance.

6

Paul and Pharisee Women

Tal Ilan

N *IN MEMORY OF HER,* IN THE CHAPTER DEVOTED TO THE JESUS
movement dubbed "A Renewal Movement within Judaism," Elisabeth
Schüssler Fiorenza wrote: "We do not know for sure whether the Pharisees
admitted women to their ranks, and especially to their table communities of
the *havuroth.*"[1] In this statement she voiced disappointment at the limited
availability of sources and, therefore, at the hopelessness of reclaiming a feminist past for the Pharisee movement. Such a history would, of course, have
been most convenient for the reconstruction of the past, as Schüssler Fiorenza
imagined it, provided that the most prominent Jewish group at the time—
the Pharisees—had been, like the Jesus movement, amicable to women. This
would imply that the Jesus movement was indeed an inner-Jewish movement
and not a revolutionary "feminist" one. The idea that the Jesus movement
should be viewed as a feminist revolution within Judaism was (and still is)
being promoted in Christian circles. Schüssler Fiorenza rightly viewed this
approach as promoting "anti-Judaism," and she sought to eradicate it.[2] In the
absence of further evidence from Jewish sources, however, Schüssler Fiorenza
could not make a further leap of faith and claim with authority that Jewish
women were members of Jewish sects, and primarily the Pharisee sect.
Although she had never been a staunch supporter of what she called "posi-
tivistic . . . historical-textual" writing and has often promoted what she called
"a hermeneutics of reconstruction," and recently even a "hermeneutics of
desire,"[3] Schüssler Fiorenza seems to have been reluctant to pursue such an
approach with regard to Jewish history. She felt that she was not trained to

cast doubt on or interfere with the scholarly consensus within Jewish academic circles. This was not, in her terms, her "site of struggle."[4] Thus, she ventured no further than to raise the remote possibility that the Pharisees had female supporters, or even members, but she qualified this statement with the appropriate amount of doubt for a sound scholarly essay.

I, on the other hand, have always been a "positivist historian."[5] In other words, even while I know we can know very little about the past, I still endow the sources with a certain amount of credibility (which, whenever possible, should be tested and retested), and I believe my reconstructions are based on the slight, reliable information gleaned from the sources. I have no doubt that the sources are ideologically bent, and I have always attempted to tease out of them their specific leanings. Furthermore, I am also well aware that ideological considerations ultimately direct me in the questions I ask of the sources, in the issues I pursue, and in the emphasis I place on one set of evidence over and against another. Unlike Schüssler Fiorenza, I do not describe my tendentious approach as a theology. I have no specific religious leanings and no belief that God (in any form) or scriptures (read in any fashion) can help save the world. Instead I describe it as an "ideology," a word that, during the twentieth century, has been used and abused by great social and other specifically nonreligious movements. Even as I see the collapse of great ideologies and understand the universal damage for which they are responsible, a return to religion as an alternative worldview is for me impossible. Thus I stick with ideology. I believe my ideology partly consists of reconstructing the past as an end in itself. This, however, does not imply that my historical research conforms to rigid, outdated research tools that were employed by historians of the nineteenth and early twentieth century. I use feminist theoretical observations and methodologies in my research, based on the premise that women were always present in history but only became invisible in the historiography. I employ Schüssler Fiorenza's "hermeneutics of suspicion"[6] as a major tool in my historical research, and I am a firm believer in the technique of placing women at the center so as to unbalance the old androcentric theoretical-historical paradigms.

I hope here to make a minor contribution to Elisabeth Schüssler Fiorenza's enormous project of feminist renewal by demonstrating how a rather conventional reading of Jewish sources indeed confirms her suspicion that women were members of the Pharisee movement. Even more so, it will demonstrate that they participated in the activities of the Pharisaic table fellowships, the *havurot* mentioned above in Schüssler Fiorenza's quotation. I shall do this by examining a corpus of data from rabbinic literature hitherto not discussed by feminist scholars. I shall then compare this data with material found in chapter 7 of Paul's First Letter to the Corinthians in the hope of showing the influence of one corpus on the other.

In another chapter in *In Memory of Her*, entitled "Neither Male nor Female," Schüssler Fiorenza discussed Paul's sexual politics. She examined his advice to Christians married to nonbelievers not to attempt actively to dissolve such marriage unions. She wrote: "Paul insists that because of the missionary situation (God has called us to peace!), the decision to continue or not to continue the marriage relationship is up to the unbelieving partner. . . ."[7] This advice, which she identifies as resulting from Paul's peace policy, is formulated in two parallel sentences, one directed to a Christian man and one directed to a Christian woman (1 Cor. 7:12–14). Because of this parallel formulation, Schüssler Fiorenza concluded that "Paul's interests . . . are missionary and not directed against the spiritual freedom and charismatic involvement of women in the community."[8] Thus, she recognizes as important the theoretical equality attempted by the linguistic formulation of the law. Antoinette Clark Wire went one step further and defined Paul's formulation as a "rhetoric of equality."[9] In what follows I shall attempt to demonstrate that the formulation suggested by Paul in this case could be the result of his Pharisee upbringing and of his thinking in terms of sectarian Pharisaism. I will do this by first defining the Pharisees and then examining their legislation on women as well as their rhetorical leanings

RESEARCH ON THE PHARISEES

The most pressing question associated with the study of the Pharisees today, as formulated recently by Daniel Schwartz, is whether the Pharisees were a sect or the "dominant variety of Judaism during the Second Temple Period."[10] Traditional scholarship, since the foundation of the *Wissenschaft des Judentums* in the middle of the nineteenth century, so he claimed, held the latter opinion, namely, that a minority of Jews belonged to sects and the rest, with no sectarian affiliation, were Pharisees. Over the last several decades, however, scholars have read the evidence about the Pharisees differently. For example, Joseph Sievers notes that Josephus claims that there were only six thousand Pharisees who refused to swear allegiance to Herod (*Antiquities* 17.42). This number certainly better describes a sect than the majority of the people.[11] In the late 1960s Morton Smith developed a thesis according to which our perspective of the Pharisees is distorted by the fact that both rabbinic literature and Josephus were writing about them in the post-70 C.E. era. By this time the Pharisees had indeed become the dominant variety of Judaism.[12] Thus the view we have of the early Pharisees is a projection of their later situation onto a completely different group. However, not all scholars concur with this view, and the pendulum has recently swung back to the old position, as Schwartz's above-mentioned article indicates.[13]

All these scholarly assertions have significant implications for a feminist critical reading of the Pharisees. What does a feminist reading of the Pharisees as a sect gain and what does it lose? In 1995 I claimed that, according to Josephus and rabbinic literature, we could deduce that Pharisaism held an attraction for Jewish women, particularly for aristocratic women.[14] A survey of the evidence makes it hard to deny such a claim: a queen shared her power with the Pharisees (Josephus, *Jewish War* 1.110–11; *Antiquities* 13.409); a king's sister-in-law paid a political fine imposed on the Pharisees (*Antiquities* 17.41–43). One derisive source claims that the Pharisees had a large female following (ibid.). I was very careful in my formulation, claiming that "there is some evidence for a relationship between aristocratic women and the Pharisees. . . . The Pharisees did not attract women's support by proposing egalitarian halakhah for women, but rather because they accepted their support and refrained from enacting detrimental rules against women."[15] Thus I did not claim that the women involved were Pharisees themselves but rather that

> the ruling parties were dominated by a male aristocracy, which by virtue of its political power found no need to seek support from larger segments of the population. Opposition movements, on the other hand, rallied support where they could, and thus had to adopt a more democratic attitude. Wealthy women could support opposition movements over and against their husbands' political leanings, demonstrating their financial independence by supporting charities of their choice. Through their financial contributions, such women may have influenced decision and policy making in the opposition parties they chose to support. Such a reconstruction is highly probable for early Christianity, and is just as plausible for the Pharisee movement.[16]

By making such a claim I placed myself squarely among scholars who uphold the view that the Pharisees were a sect. I refrained, however, from addressing the question of what membership in the Pharisee movement meant, and whether the women who supported the Pharisees were indeed Pharisees themselves. If the Pharisees were simply the majority of Palestinian

Jews, there need be no distinction between support and membership. If, however, they were merely one sect among many, they must have had strict membership requirements and period of probation. Scholars who first upheld the sectarian theory, beginning with Morton Smith, have indeed identified a sectarian document within rabbinic literature that outlines the initiation process by which a new member was enrolled in the sect.[17] The text is found in the Tosefta—a legal compilation akin to the Mishnah—*t. Demai* chapter 2. This text defines two sorts of members of the Jewish society: *am-haaretz* (sg.) (עמ־הארץ), literally translated "the people of the land" (pl. *amei-aratzot*) and *haverim* (pl.) (חברים), literally translated "companions" or alternatively "members" (sg. *haver*). These *haverim* belonged to a *havura* (sg.; pl. *havurot*), a group name derived from *haver*, meaning "companionship" or "fellowship." The term *am-haaretz*, on the other hand, applied to everyone else in society who were not members of the *havura*. The *havura* placed special emphasis on purity and applied stricter rules than the rest of the Jews to the kinds of food they ate.[18] The terms *haver* and *am-haaretz* are found often in rabbinic literature, and, by collecting and studying the occurrences of the terms, scholars such as A. Oppenheimer, and J. Neusner have attempted to draw a picture of the social and historical environment of this group. Both Oppenheimer and Neusner understood that the group was sectarian in character, namely, that it separated itself from the general society; and both assumed that, since the literature about it is located in rabbinic sources, they must be associated with the Pharisees. Yet both refrained from identifying the two as one and the same. Neusner wrote in 1969: "one must retain a distinction between the חבורה and the whole Pharisee sect since there is no evidence that all Pharisees were members of the fellowship."[19] I note here, however, that one may equally claim that there is no evidence that they were not, since no known Pharisee ever denied that he was a member of the *havura*. Similarly, Oppenheimer some years later claimed: "By the nature of things the *haverim* were very close to the Pharisees, in that the latter were scrupulous about the same areas in which the *haverim* adopted restrictive practices. But whereas the Pharisees constituted a spiritual social movement, the *haverim* belonged to closed associations."[20] One would expect such a statement to be backed up with supporting evidence, but it is not.

I would like to devote some space to the argument that the *havura* was the name the Pharisees chose for themselves, and to a careful text criticism and source analysis of the relevant documents, with the help of which I will show its sectarian character. I will then devote the remaining space to a gender analysis of the *havura* texts, revealing that they indeed counted women among their members.

THE HAVERIM ARE THE PHARISEES

When rabbinic literature refers to the Pharisees, it calls them by name—*perushim* (פרושים).[21] Thus, it is assumed by many scholars that when and if the rabbis wished to discuss the Pharisees, they would have had no difficulty naming them. Since they call the *haverim* by a different name, they obviously refer to another group. However, the term *perushim* (Pharisees) is derogatory in essence, since it derides its bearers as "separatists." Furthermore, as has already been shown, the term "Pharisees" in rabbinic literature is usually put in the mouth of this group's opponents.[22] At one point, where a dispute between two groups is staged, the Sadducees designate their opponents as "Pharisees (פרושים)," while the talmudic editor names the same group "the sages of Israel (חכמי ישראל)" (*b. Qidd.* 66a).

Thus, in texts that are not primarily polemical, we are hardly likely to find rabbinic literature employing the term *perushim*. What name would the group have chosen for itself? There is some textual evidence that they chose to call themselves *haverim*. *T. Shabbat* 1:15 records one of the disputes between Beit Shammai and Beit Hillel on a question associated with purity and separation from *am-haaretz*. The discussions between the Hillelites and the Shammaites are usually deemed very old, dating from Second Temple times.[23] In this discussion, where the status of a *zav* (a man with a gonorrheal discharge and therefore ritually impure) is decided, the Shammaites wish to distinguish between a *zav* who is reliable and another who belongs to the *am-haaretz* (therefore unreliable). Interestingly, the reliable *zav* is not described, as would be expected, as a *zav haver*, but rather as a *zav parush* (i.e., a Pharisee *zav*).

A second, more interesting proof text is found in *t. Hagigah* 3. This chapter discusses many issues pertaining to the differences between *haverim* and *am-haaretz*. There is some disagreement about the correct order of the verses in this chapter between the two prominent textual witnesses of the Tosefta—the Leiden and the Ehrfurt manuscripts[24]—but the last verse obviously refers to the *am-haaretz* imparting impurity to the temple vessels. The text then goes on to say, "Once they [i.e., the above-mentioned *haverim*] immersed the *menorah* (to remove impurity) and the Sadducees (צדוקים) exclaimed: Come see the Pharisees (פרושים) immersing the moon" (*t. Hag.* 3:35). In this case too the Pharisees are contrasted with the *am-haaretz*. One should note, however, that throughout chapter 3 the *am-haaretz* are contrasted with *haverim*, but here, since it is their political opponents (the Sadducees) who are speaking, they designate this group "Pharisees." I take these two texts to mean that the Pharisees should indeed be identified with the *haverim*.

Scholars initially viewed rabbinic literature as the internal documents of the (nonsectarian) Pharisees.[25] This view, however, has recently come under sharp criticism. Scholars have claimed that, rather than identify with the Pharisees, the rabbis, as we have seen, are occasionally critical of them, and in any case do not directly speak for them.[26] This means, of course, that we can no longer naively assume that everything voiced by the rabbis between 70 and 500 C.E. is, in fact, a Pharisee statement. Rather, we cannot assume out of hand that anything at all in our entire rabbinic corpus is in any way associated with the Pharisees.

The problem is a real one when we attempt to identify the *haverim* with the Pharisees, because, in contrast to the case of the Pharisees, rabbinic literature does indeed speak in the name of the *haverim*. The rabbis do indeed see themselves as the *haverim*. How should one approach this issue? Let us look at the problem from another angle. Women, I claimed, supported the Pharisees. How do women fare in rabbinic literature? Obviously, not very well. This discrepancy could be viewed as supporting the view that the rabbis were in no way associated with the Pharisees. The Pharisees welcomed women; the rabbis kept them at a distance. Yet recent scholarship has warned us time and again against reading rabbinic literature, early as well as late, legal as well as midrashic, as a seamless whole. Judith Hauptman, in studies directed to a completely different end, has shown that the two early tannaitic compilations —the Mishnah and the Tosefta—have a very different agenda when it comes to women.[27] The Mishnah is the official Jewish second canon. It was edited at the end of the second century, envisioned as the authoritative document of rabbinic Judaism. This vision indeed materialized, and the Mishnah achieved a sanctified status within Judaism. Those who rejected it were (and are) considered heretics.

The Tosefta, compiled (rather than edited) some time later along the same editorial lines as the Mishnah, was a collection of many traditions and rulings that the official Mishnah had discarded, and often specifically rejected. It never achieved any position of importance in Judaism, although it was never officially banned. Rather, only scholars who showed interest in the unconventional studied it. The survival of only two Tosefta manuscripts from antiquity indicates how little it interested ancient scholars. Judith Hauptman has shown that, in general, the Tosefta displays a more lenient, less domineering approach to the status of women. She explained this phenomenon as the result of a deliberate editorial move on the part of the Mishnaic redactor to narrow and contain women's freedom by excluding materials that manifested a less patriarchal approach to women. This type of material can be found in the Tosefta.

Hauptman's discovery, however, is only part of the picture. Elsewhere I have shown that a comparison of the two schools of thought prevalent in rabbinic circles around the time of the destruction of the temple—the schools of Hillel and Shammai—reveals a similar pattern. The school of Shammai, in general, put greater emphasis on the personhood, dignity, and economic independence of women than the school of Hillel.[28] Jewish tradition, however, while quoting the school of Shammai as often as the school of Hillel, discarded all the Shammaite rulings as nonbinding and chose to ally itself with the House of Hillel. Notwithstanding any benefit this decision may have had for Judaism, it certainly did not mean good news for women. It could also be viewed as a step in the process of containing women's freedom.

Further, I have recently compared the exegetical principles applied to the inclusion of women in or their exclusion from the term *ish* (איש, "man/person") by two competing midrashic schools of early rabbinic legal Bible exegesis (= tannaitic midrashim). The documents, one an exegesis of Numbers and the other of Deuteronomy, are traditionally assigned to the schools of the sages Rabbi Ishmael and Rabbi Aqiva in this order. I have discovered that, in the midrash assigned to the school of Rabbi Ishmael (*Sifre* on Numbers), the term איש is almost universally interpreted as inclusive of women. Conversely, in the midrash assigned to the school of Rabbi Aqiva (*Sifre* on Deuteronomy), the opposite is the case, and the term is universally interpreted as exclusive of women.[29] Although neither midrash became normative, it is probably no coincidence that the Mishnah, the document that did achieve normative status, was also the work of the school of Rabbi Aqiva. The attitude displayed in the midrash of Rabbi Ishmael was rejected, together with the other less-restrictive traditions present in the Tosefta, and with the whole corpus of Shammaite halakah, in favor of a stricter patriarchy, obviously promoted by the school of Rabbi Aqiva.

If all this is taken together, we can see in the editing of the Mishnah and its school a movement away from a less restrictive patriarchy. Can this less restrictive view be assigned to the Pharisees? When I attempted to explain to myself why the rabbis deemed these restrictive measures necessary, I suggested that "after 70 CE a slow process of evolution began within the Pharisee movement, transforming it from a sect to a religion, and from an opposition force to a position of leadership."[30] This process obviously meant that the rabbis did not want to be perceived as upholding sectarian notions or being endowed with sectarian characteristics. Curtailing women's freedom was a move in this direction. Since women are traditionally associated with marginal religious and sectarian associations, the rabbis, the heirs of the Pharisees, wanted nothing to do with them.

If we could detect a similar trend within early rabbinic compilations attempting to limit the importance of the *haverim* and *havurot*, this would be a further indication that the rabbis wished to distance themselves from their sectarian Pharisee forebears. Scholars in the past have used the material about the *haverim* in the Mishnah and the Tosefta to complement each other. However, a critical reading of the texts should reveal tensions rather than agreements, and thus perhaps disclose dialectics of struggle within the texts.

How, then, do the *haverim* fare in the Mishnah and the Tosefta? Is there a difference? My research definitely answers this question in the affirmative. The first difference is in the amount of material. In the Tosefta no fewer than eighty-four verses mention issues associated with either *haverim* or *amei-aratzot* or both. In the Mishnah there are only thirty-three such verses. While it is true that the Mishnah is considerably more concise than the Tosefta, it is certainly not shorter by two-thirds. Thus, the earlier interest in the rulings on the *havura* was greatly diminished by the time the Mishnah was edited. However, not just quantity but also quality is at stake here. The term *am-haaretz* seems to have acquired a new meaning in the tannaitic period, so that it now denoted an ignoramus, one who, out of negligence or ignorance, does not fulfill the commandments. In the Tosefta, *am-haaretz* is defined, according to sectarian categories, as one who eats consecrated food in a state of impurity and who does not tithe his food (*t. Avodah Zarah* 3:10). Both these negative definitions define him as "other" to the *haver*. In an early tradition in the Babylonian Talmud (a considerably later rabbinic compilation) the definition of the *am-haaretz* is broadened to include those who do not recite the *Shema*, those who forgo the commandment of the phylacteries, those who wear no fringes or have no *mezuzah* on their doors, those who do not raise their children as sages, and even those who do not minister to the sages (*b. Berakhot* 47b). In other words, the Tosefta definition is sectarian. Later rabbinic literature makes the *am-haaretz* into a bad Jew. The Mishnah in this respect is subtler. It attempts to retain the universalized *am-haaretz*, while greatly limiting the sectarian *haver*. In the Tosefta, *haver* is mentioned (with or without *am-haaretz*) sixty-two times (out of a total of eighty-four verses), that is, in more than three-quarters of the traditions. In the Mishnah *haver* is mentioned only ten times (out of thirty-three verses), that is, in fewer than one-third of the traditions. This means that in the Mishnah, the *am-haaretz* is not intrinsically associated with the *haver*, but has an independent status, while in the Tosefta such conclusions are unwarranted. Furthermore, in some of the verses in which a *haver* is mentioned in the Tosefta this term is edited out of the mishnaic parallel. For example, in the Tosefta (*t. Toharot* 8:3) we are informed of a *haver* who left an *am-haaretz* in his house, while in the Mishnah (*m. Toharot* 7:2) the wording of a similar halakah is simply "he who leaves an *am-haaretz* in his house." This sort of formulation removes the sectarian character of the ruling.

Chapter 2 of *Tosefta Demai* is the largest repository of sectarian rulings associated with the *havura*. It contains no fewer than sixteen verses dealing with the process of admission into the *havura*. In the Mishnah this entire text is reduced to two verses (*m. Demai* 2:2–3). Here too the difference is not just quantitative but qualitative. The Tosefta opens the entire discussion with the words "Whoever takes upon himself four things is accepted as a *haver*." Then it goes on to discuss "whoever takes it upon himself to be reliable" (i.e., becomes a member, but this is a formulation not using sectarian terminology). In the Mishnah the order of these verses is reversed. First the non-sectarian verse on reliability is quoted precisely, and only then is the sectarian verse on the *haver* cited. This second verse, however, has undergone severe editing. In the Tosefta the *haver* is required to give tithes only to priests who are members of the *havura* and to eat his unconsecrated food in a state of purity. Both these aspects have been removed from the text of the Mishnah. In other words, the sectarian character of the ruling is deleted. Instead Rabbi Judah of Usha (mid-second century) states that a *haver* may not raise small cattle in Palestine, that he should not make unnecessary vows or laugh too much and that he should not contract corpse impurity and then minister in the House of Study. In other words, he endows the *haver* with the characteristics of the rabbi in his day, ignoring those of the Second Temple sectarian Pharisees. All this evidence points to the fact that the editing of the Mishnah goes clearly in one direction. Anything that gave the impression that the rabbis' interests were sectarian was modified. Since this process has met with some success, it is hardly surprising that modern scholars find it hard to identify the Pharisees with the *havura*.

I am aware that I have engaged in a lengthy discussion of technical details relevant to rabbinics more than to feminist theory and practice. Yet this discussion was necessary because it is determined by feminist observations on the tensions between rabbinic compilations, and, in turn, determines a complex feminist analysis of the gender issues of the corpus we have just identified as Pharisee. To this analysis I now turn.

WOMEN IN THE PHARISAIC *HAVURA*

Were women included in the *havura*? The answer to this question should be an unequivocal yes, despite first impressions. Chapter 2 of *Tosefta Demai* opens with a general formulation:

> Whoever takes upon himself four things is accepted as a *haver:* not to give *terumah* or tithes to an *am-haaretz,* not to purify anything at an *am-haaretz*['s house], and that he eat his unconsecrated food in a state of purity. Whoever takes it upon himself to be reliable tithes what he eats and what he sells and what he buys. (*t. Demai* 2:2)

This text is formulated in male-generic language. The words "whoever takes upon himself" translate the Hebrew construct המקבל עליו, and though in English this formulation is only half gendered, in Hebrew both parts of the construct are male. In order to determine a similar formulation for women the forms המקבלת עליה would have had to be used. Hebrew, in general, is a much more gendered language than English because verbs and nouns as well as pronouns are gendered. It is for this reason that gender exclusion based on language is more easily "justified" in Hebrew texts. Furthermore, nowhere in the tannaitic or amoraic texts is the female equivalent of *haver* (*havera,* חברה) used. Thus one may conjecture that the text specifically singles out males as the recipients and practitioners of this halakah.

At first sight, vv. 16 and 17 make no difference to this general claim, because they do not refer to a female member—a *havera*—but rather to the wife of a *haver* (אשת חבר). Yet it is now very important to leave aside the question of terminology and gendered language and turn to contents, since, obviously, the language used here is rhetorical and androcentric rather than descriptive. Verse 16 reads as follows: "A daughter of an *am-haaretz* married to a *haver,* the wife of an *am-haaretz* married to a *haver* . . . should undergo initiation (in order to become trustworthy)." One could conclude from this verse that, when a *haver* marries a woman who had not been raised in a sectarian home, he should induct her into his sectarian lifestyle, so that she will not be an impediment to his righteous living. The assumption of such an interpretation here is that the *havura* was a group of male Israelites who took wives from all walks of life, since women, by definition, were not subject to sectarian loyalties and, as wives, were only instrumental in the man's correct observance of his sectarian obligations. One may further assume that their instrumental role required a limited amount of technical training, which the husband could impart to his wife briefly and rapidly. The only question that arises from this reconstruction is, Why, then, should such a woman undergo what I termed in my translation "initiation"? In the text the term is לקבל עליהן, which literally means, "to take upon themselves" and which is also the technical term used for the general initiation we encountered in v. 2. If women were required to actually undergo some form of formal induction into the group, does this mean that all wives automatically, after a short education period, underwent this rite, or was there a test required? Did some members of the sect remain married to women who failed the test and were thus never fully accepted into the sect? These questions cannot be answered by consulting v. 16 alone; v. 17, however, which is formulated in parallel terms, gives reasonable answers.

In v. 17 we read: "A daughter of a *haver* married to an *am-haaretz*, the wife of a *haver* married to an *am-haaretz* . . . they remain trustworthy, unless they become suspect." This verse imagines the opposite situation: a woman who grew up in a sectarian household, or was married to a sectarian and was then widowed or divorced and married someone from outside the sect. What is her position regarding the sect? Interestingly, the sect does not disown her. In the sect's mind, she continues to be trustworthy (נאמנת) until proved otherwise. What is she trustworthy for? She is no longer a necessary facilitator for her husband. Thus, she need no longer observe sectarian requirements. What does being trustworthy mean anyway? It seems that "trustworthy" (נאמן) is the technical term used by the sect to describe its members. A trustworthy person is someone a sect member can interact with: eat with or take food from, touch without fear of becoming unclean, and trust to warn the sectarian about uncleanness, if the person is in such a state. This, in fact, means that women who had once lived within the confines of the sect and then left to join a nonsectarian household are expected to continue observing sectarian practices. Such women must therefore have been members of the sect in their own right and not just as reliable appendages to their husband's sectarian household. Understanding the text in this way now helps us view in another light the formulation in v. 16. Rather than speak of all wives of sectarians as being facilitators in their husbands' sectarian service, this verse in fact states that marriage to a sect member does not automatically guarantee a sectarian status for the wife. Despite her marriage, she must undergo sectarian initiation and become a sectarian in her own right as any male novice. It suggests that a sectarian male could be married all his life to a nonsectarian woman and that she would become a member only if she accepted the practical (and probably also ideological) requirements that went with the membership. All this together, in my opinion, indicates that, despite the androcentric language and mind-set used in the formulation of these rulings, women must have been full and independent members of the *havura*. If the *havura* is synonymous with the Pharisees, as I have claimed above, women were full members of the Pharisee sect. When Rabbi Joshua mentions (very negatively) a Pharisee woman (אשה פרושה) in the Mishnah (*m. Sotah* 3:4), he knows what he is talking about.

SLAVES IN THE PHARISAIC HAVURA

The verses quoted above (16 and 17) refer not just to women but also to slaves. Verse 16 states: "a slave of an *am-haaretz* sold to a *haver* should undergo initiation (in order to become trustworthy)." Similarly, v. 17 states: "a slave of a *haver* sold to an *am-haaretz* remains trustworthy, unless he becomes suspect." Since my analysis of these verses with regard to women holds true also with regard to slaves, this is an indication that slaves too could become independent members of the Pharisee *havura*. Gender and class seem not to have been obstacles to membership in the Pharisees. In Christian language, we could state with the Pharisees that "there is neither male nor female, neither slave nor free" at this table.

PAUL AND THE DISCIPLESHIP OF EQUALS

When advising the Christians of Corinth, Paul suggests that, when married to non-Christians, they should attempt to preserve the marriage (1 Cor. 7:12–14). This he recommends in support of Jesus' logion against divorce.

Yet one would have thought, and some of the Corinthians obviously did think, that Jesus' words referred to Christians and were not relevant when non-Christians were involved. Paul's advice, over and against this assumption, imagines a situation very similar to that of Pharisee men and woman married to members of the *am-haaretz*.

When advising slaves about staying in non-Christian households, Paul suggests that they seek freedom, but he warns against any direct or violent action to that end (1 Cor. 7:21). Again he envisions the situation, parallel to the Pharisee slave whose owner is an *am-haaretz*, of a Christian slave whose master is a nonbeliever. Paul's letter to the Corinthians lacks the parallel situation of a Christian slave-owner and his non-Christian slave. We may fill in this lacuna with reference to Paul's letter to Philemon. In this letter Paul is sending Onesimus, a Christian slave, back to his master, Philemon, also a Christian. The problem that arises here is of Christians owning Christian slaves. Onesimus had obviously run away on the assumption that Christianity would protect him from slavery. Yet he was owned by Philemon before he converted to Christianity, as Paul's words in v. 11 indicate, for here he writes: "Onesimus, once so little use to you [because he was not a Christian and yet you kept him] but now useful indeed." Thus, Christians can obviously own slaves, non-Christian as well as Christian. Here again we see the influence of the sectarian *havura* legislation on Paul's outlook.

1 Corinthians 7	t. Demai 2
vv. 12, 14: If a Christian has a heathen wife and she is willing to live with him, he must not divorce her . . . for the heathen (husband) now belongs to God through his Christian (wife).	v. 16: A daughter of an *am-haaretz* married to a *haver*, the wife of an *am-haaretz* married to a *haver* . . . should undergo initiation (in order to become trustworthy)
vv. 13–14: and a woman who has a heathen husband willing to live with her must not divorce her husband . . . for the heathen (wife) now belongs to God through [her] Christian (husband).	v. 17: A daughter of a *haver* married to an *am-haaretz*, the wife of a *haver* married to an *am-haaretz* . . . they remain trustworthy, unless they become suspect.
v. 21: Were you a slave when you were called? Do not let that trouble you, but if a chance of liberty comes— take it.	v. 17: The slave of a *haver* sold to an *am-haaretz* remains trustworthy unless he becomes suspect.
	v. 16: The slave of an *am-haaretz* sold to a *haver* should undergo initiation (in order to become trustworthy).

In a recent demonstration of what she defines as a feminist hermeneutics of reconstruction, Schüssler Fiorenza shows how one may use the Christian Scriptures in order to draw a picture of an early Christian "discipleship of equals." She begins with the Jesus movement, but then goes on to state:

> Traces of the discipleship of equals that surface as "dangerous memory" in a critical radical reading of the Jesus traditions are also inscribed in the Pauline correspondence. Although they are articulated here differently, they still indicate that the ethos of the discipleship of equals was also at work in the *ekklesia* —the public assembly or congress of the Christian movements in the Greco-Roman urban centers. The key symbols of their self understanding were *soma* or body/corporation of Christ/Messiah and *ekklesia* or democratic assembly. . . . "In Christ"—that is, in the body politic, the messianic sphere of power— socioreligious status inequalities no longer pertain. Equally, social status inequalities and privileges between Jews and Gentiles, Greeks and barbarians, slave and free—both women and men—are no longer defining those who are "in Christ." . . . House-churches were crucial factors . . . insofar as they provided space and actual leadership in the Spirit. Women played a decisive role in the founding, sustaining and shaping of such house-*ekklesia*. They could do so because the classic division between private and public spheres was transformed in the *ekklesia* that assembled in the "house." . . . Christians were neither the first nor the only group who gathered together in house-assemblies. Religious cults, voluntary associations, professional clubs and funeral societies, including the Jewish synagogue gathered in private houses.[31]

This reconstruction Schüssler Fiorenza designates as "a hermeneutics of desire." By this I assume she voices her deepest hopes for what Christianity could have looked like according to some verses in scripture, and a plausible reading of these texts. However, she immediately turns around and warns us that "such a reconstruction in terms of a hermeneutics of desire must . . . not be misunderstood as a factual transcript of egalitarian Christian beginnings."[32]

I, on the other hand, who have no deep desires involved with the reconstruction of early Christianity, am nevertheless convinced by Schüssler Fiorenza's reconstruction. From a point of view of historical plausibility, of sociological models for marginal religious movements, and of a long history of silencing and marginalization of women, this reconstruction is at least as convincing as any other suggested by "malestream" historians and theologians in the past. In fact, it tallies well with the kind of reading I suggest for the Pharisee *havura*, which was also a private affair, its meetings conducted in private houses and its members being both men and women and both slave and free.

If Paul's claim that he was a Pharisee can be believed, it is important to understand what part of his vision he brought with him from his Pharisee experience. Paul's letters have a mixed message for women. Wrestling with given gender relations, Paul advises, exhorts, threatens, and appeases. His rhetoric has been a topic for complex feminist analyses. His appreciation of various gender situations has been assigned to various ideological and theological positions he upholds. What have feminists assigned to his Pharisee background? I take *Searching the Scriptures,* the commentary edited by Schüssler Fiorenza, as an example of how this particular issue has been discussed.

In her commentary on the Letter to the Thessalonians, Lone Fatum writes: "For Paul, the former Pharisee, illegitimate and uncontrolled sexuality was tantamount to ungodliness and pagan impurity. . . . Paul illustrates how comprehensive was the influence of traditional Jewish interpretation on his formative Christian teaching, especially relating to gender and sociosexual morality."[33] The assumption of this text is that Pharisaism had a vested interest in sexual control of women. Yet Fatum's claim is not substantiated by the citation of any source, Pharisee or otherwise. I assume she conceives of a rather loose collection of Jewish sayings and legal decisions, all deriving from the later, rabbinic literature as illustrative of "Pharisaism." Yet such an assumption takes no notice of suspicious readings of rabbinic texts, and it ignores all scholarship on the connection (or rather lack of connection) between the Pharisees and the rabbis. "Anti-Judaism" is a dirty word in feminist Christian circles. "Anti-Pharisaism" is not. The one can easily transform into the other. The Jews were not bad. The Pharisees were the villains.

Perhaps the example I have just suggested is too blatant. It is the only straightforward anti-Pharisaic statement I have found in the entire book. But a more subtle approach is also evident. Elizabeth Castelli writes in her commentary on Romans in the same volume: "Paul is beholden to a range of interpretive and ideological practices as well as modes of thought available to him as an educated Pharisee, a Greek speaking Jew, a practitioner of hermeneutics as well as rhetoric."[34] Yet, when she decides in the end which of these personas speaks for Paul of Romans, she concludes: "I wish to argue that Paul's hermeneutics is sensible from within the context of Hellenistic Judaism and his concerns are also located within this frame."[35] I have long noted that for many Christian and Diaspora Jewish feminists, one way of rehabilitating Greco-Roman Judaism, in the face of accusations of anti-Judaism, is to present the Diaspora as a showcase. Yes, they admit, it is true

that Judaism had many chauvinist failings at the time, but these were less visible in the Jews of the Diaspora and affected them less. Thus, this approach
claims, Paul's "good" Judaism is Diaspora Judaism. He could have chosen to
speak as a Pharisee, but he did not. Thus he distances himself from his
"wrong" Jewish background.

I wish to suggest the opposite. If the table fellowship of the Pharisee (Palestinian!) *havura* loomed large in Paul's vision, some of his rhetoric, and particularly what Antoinette Clark Wire designated his "rhetoric of equality,"[36]
is actually carried over from that environment. When in his First Letter to the
Corinthians Paul discusses the situation of mixed couples—Christian men
and non-Christian women, Christian women and non-Christian men—he
envisions the *haverim* (and *haverot*) and their *am-haaretz* partners. His belief
that they can stay together without compromising their allegiance to Christianity may be based on his previous experience as a Pharisee, where he had
seen such mixed couples work out their disagreements and go on living
together.

If later commentators have found Paul's idea of intermarriage bizarre, it
should come as no surprise that early Jewish commentators also found the situation described by the sectarian Tosefta bizarre. Already in the Tosefta we
find a much later sage, Rabbi Simon ben Eleazar (ca. 200 C.E.) commenting
on the halakic decision according to which a wife of a *haver* remains trustworthy even when she moves into a household of an *am-haaretz*. He states:
"(A daughter of a *haver* who is married to an *am-haaretz*) *should* take upon
herself (again) to be trustworthy." Thus he does not trust a woman married
to an *am-haaretz*. This statement he complements with a derogatory tale that
demonstrates the flighty and untrustworthy nature of women: "Once a
woman was married to a *haver* and she tied phylacteries on his arms. She then
remarried a tax-collector and would tie knots on his arms" (*t. Demai* 2:17).
Women, this story suggests, have no will of their own. The man they live with
molds their moral character. Obviously we cannot expect them to remain
loyal to the principle of the *havura* once they marry out of it. It is, thus, interesting to note that such a comment is dated to a period much later than first-
century, Second Temple Pharisaism.

The much later Yerushalmi Talmud (ca. 350 C.E.) also comments on what
is perceived to be an impossible situation: "If he is trustworthy and his wife
is not . . . it is as though he was living with a snake in the same basket. If his
wife is trustworthy and he is not . . . let him be cursed" (*y. Demai* 2:2, 22d).
Both situations the Yerushalmi deems impossible, but while the man who is

not trustworthy is religiously reprimanded, the woman who is not trustworthy is compared to a snake. These sorts of comments, together with the editing of the Mishnah, which chose to ignore completely all the relevant material on women's membership in the *havura,* are the beginning of the process of marginalization and silencing that ends with the Pharisee women becoming invisible.

My reconstruction of the Pharisee *havura* and its egalitarian ethos comes dangerously close to Elisabeth Schüssler Fiorenza's hermeneutics-of-desire reconstruction of early Christianity. Does this mean that I too am employing a hermeneutics of desire? If I am, it is completely subconscious. I have no vested interest in the Pharisees. It matters to me not at all whether they accepted women or slaves to their company or not. If everything Jesus (or rather Matthew 23) said about the Pharisees were true, I would be the last to feel betrayed.

True, I do have a vested interest in the study of Jewish women, and I am trying to reconstruct their past from available evidence. Obviously I look for women in places where social models indicate that they may be found—sects, marginal associations, noninstitutional religion. The Pharisee *havura* is one such place. I would have shed no tears had I not found them there, but since I have, I feel convinced that these traces I have uncovered are glimpses of a real past. A comparison with the Christian evidence in this context is, in my opinion, useful for the reconstruction of a Jewish past for women. I think that this Jewish past is likewise useful for a feminist reconstruction of Christian beginnings, be it within a hermeneutic of desire or otherwise.

NOTES

I wish to thank my friend and colleague Peter Zaas of Siena College, Loudonville, New York, for first drawing my attention to the phenomenon discussed here, and for the helpful conversations we then held discussing and formulating the ideas expressed in this paper. Over the years Prof. Zaas has been a constant source of inspiration for much of my work.

1. Elisabeth Schüssler Fiorenza, *In Memory of Her: A Feminist Theological Reconstruction of Christian Origins* (New York: Crossroad, 1983), 115.

2. Ibid., 105–8; see also Elisabeth Schüssler Fiorenza, *Sharing Her Word: Feminist Biblical Interpretation in Context* (Boston: Beacon, 1998), 124–29.

3. Schüssler Fiorenza, *Sharing Her Word*, 121, 77, 112–21.

4. Ibid., 76.

5. Tal Ilan, *Mine and Yours Are Hers: Retrieving Women's History from Rabbinic Literature* (Leiden: Brill, 1997), xi.

6. Schüssler Fiorenza, *Sharing Her Word*, 77.

7. Schüssler Fiorenza, *In Memory of Her*, 222–23.

8. Ibid, 236.

9. Antoinette Clark Wire sees Paul's "rhetoric of equality as a reflection of the position of the Corinthian Christian women (*The Corinthian Women Prophets: A Reconstruction through Paul's Rhetoric* [Minneapolis: Fortress, 1990], 94); she distinguishes between the rhetoric and the actual demands made on men and women, the greater demands being made on women (pp. 81–82).

[Contrast Schüssler Fiorenza's understanding of historical positivism in *Jesus and the Politics of Interpretation* (New York: Continuum, 2000), 5–6, 33–34, 91–94, esp. 56: "With the African-American feminist sociologist Patricia Hill Collins . . . I understand scientific positivism as a discourse that is constituted by the assumption that 'the tools of science,' scientific methods, and logical reasoning are able 'to represent reality, and to discover universal truth' (see Patricia Hill Collins, *Fighting Words: Black Women and the Search for Justice* [Minneapolis: University of Minnesota Press, 1998], 279)." *Eds.*]

10. Daniel R. Schwartz, "MMT, Josephus and the Pharisees," in *4QMMT: New Perspectives on Qumran Law and History*, ed. John I. Kampen and Moshe J. Bernstein (Atlanta: Scholars Press, 1996), 67–68.

11. For more on small numbers, see Joseph Sievers, "Who Were the Pharisees?" in *Hillel and Jesus: Comparative Studies of Two Major Religious Leaders*, ed. James H. Charlesworth and Loren L. Johns (Minneapolis: Fortress, 1997), 137–55.

12. Morton Smith, "Palestinian Judaism in the First Century," in *Israel: Its Role in Civilization*, ed. Moses Davis (New York: Harper, 1956), 71–78; and further on the topic see Jacob Neusner, "Josephus' Pharisees: A Complete Repertoire," in *Josephus, Judaism and Christianity*, ed. Louis H. Feldman and Gohei Hata (Detroit: Wayne State University Press, 1987), 274–92.

13. See also Steven Mason, *Flavius Josephus on the Pharisees* (Leiden: Brill, 1991), esp. 372–75.

14. Tal Ilan, "The Attraction of Aristocratic Jewish Women to Pharisaism," *Harvard Theological Review* 88 (1995): 1–33; and see now my *Integrating Women into Second Temple History* (Tübingen: Mohr, 1999), 11–42.

15. Ilan, *Integrating Women*, 37.

16. Ibid., 33.

17. See Smith, *Israel;* see also Jacob Neusner "The Fellowship (חבורה) in the Second Temple Commonwealth," *Harvard Theological Review* 53 (1969): 125–42.

18. Neusner, "Fellowship."

19. Ibid., 125.

20. A. Oppenheimer, *The Am Ha-Aretz* (Leiden: Brill 1977), 119.

21. For a good catalogue of all relevant sources, see Ellis Rivkin, "Defining the

Pharisees: The Tannaitic Sources," *Hebrew Union College Annual* 40–41 (1970): 205–49.

22. Ibid., 247–48.

23. Jacob Neusner, *The Rabbinic Traditions about the Pharisees before 70* (Leiden: Brill, 1971), vol. 3, esp. 199, 208–9, 266–67, 271–72.

24. S. Lieberman, *Tosefta ki-fshutah* V (in Hebrew) (New York: Jewish Theological Seminary, 1992), 1,335.

25. E.g., Rivkin, "Defining the Pharisees."

26. See S. J. D. Cohen, "The Significance of Yavneh: Pharisees, Rabbis, and the End of Jewish Sectarianism," *Hebrew Union College Annual* 55 (1984): 27–53; and even more extremely P. Schäfer, "Der vorrabbinische Pharisäismus," in *Paulus und das antike Judentum: Tübingen-Durham-Symposium in Gedenken an den 50. Todestag Adolf Schlatters (Mai 1938),* ed. M. Hengel and U. Heckel (Tübingen: Mohr, 1988), 125–75.

27. Judith Hauptman, "Mishnah *Gittin* as a Pietist Document" (in Hebrew), *Proceedings of the Tenth World Congress of Jewish Studies* C/1 (Jerusalem: World Congress of Jewish Studies, 1990), 23–30; eadem, "Maternal Dissent: Women and Procreation in the Mishnah," *Tikkun* 6/6 (1991): 80–81, 94–95; eadem, "Women's Voluntary Performance of Commandments from Which They Are Exempt" (in Hebrew), in *Proceedings of the Eleventh World Congress of Jewish Studies* C/1 (Jerusalem: World Congress of Jewish Studies, 1994), 161–68; eadem, "Women in Tractate Pesahim" (in Hebrew), in *Atara L'Haim: Studies in the Talmud and Medieval Rabbinic Literature in Honor of Professor Haim Zalman Dimitrovsky,* ed. Daniel Boyarin et al.; Jerusalem: Magnes Press, 2000), 63–86.

28. Ilan, *Integrating Women*, 43–81.

29. Tal Ilan, "'Daughters of Israel Weep for Rabbi Ishmael' (*m. Nedarim* 9:11): The Schools of Rabbi Aqiva and Rabbi Ishmael on Women," *Nashim: Journal of Jewish Women's Studies and Gender Issues* 4 (2001): 15–34.

30. Ilan, *Integrating Women*, 80.

31. Schüssler Fiorenza, *Sharing Her Word*, 116–18.

32. Ibid., 120.

33. Lone Fatum, "1 Thessalonians," in *Searching the Scriptures*, vol. 2, *A Feminist Commentary,* ed. Elisabeth Schüssler Fiorenza (New York: Crossroad, 1994), 258.

34. Elizabeth Castelli, "Romans," in *Searching the Scriptures,* ed. Schüssler Fiorenza, 2:284.

35. Ibid., 289.

36. Clark Wire, *Corinthian Women Prophets,* 94.

7

The Women "Priests"
of Philo's *De Vita Contemplativa*

Reconstructing the Therapeutae

Joan E. Taylor

I N THE STUDY OF WOMEN IN EARLY CHRISTIANITY, FEMINIST SCHOLARS
have made a conscious link between the reconstruction of history and present sociopolitical and theological concerns.[1] Seeing feminism as a movement
of struggle to overthrow all oppression by transforming structures of dominance, Elisabeth Schüssler Fiorenza situates her work at the heart of a radical
vision of egalitarianism and the struggle to attain that future. Among many
hermeneutical strategies, Schüssler Fiorenza identifies "slippages,"[2] which are
small kernels of reality indicating the real-life struggle of women that are
embedded in an androcentric text. These sensitize us to how early Christian
women's historical reality was different from the textual construction of that
reality, opening up possibilities of reconstructing their historical reality in
ways that do not disempower them. History can be reconstructed to indicate
that women's social position in ancient Christianity could be high: women
took leadership roles, taught, prophesied, and engaged in central functions of
religious and social importance. While early church systems and the extant
texts remain androcentric and oppressive, the church becomes one of men
and women together by means of this focus on the struggle and achievement
of women who managed to break through the patriarchal barriers around
them.

Other feminist and nonfeminist scholarship on women within nascent Christianity has focused on the issue of social status but without utilizing the same hermeneutical methodology. There is at times an underlying theological project that aims to improve the status of women within dominantly masculine church systems, which are still, in essence, considered to be "givens."[3] Such reconstructions of the early church are arrived at not by means of a radical and liberative reading of texts but by means of a construction of a "patriarchal" Judaism that forms the backdrop to the emancipatory Jesus movement and nascent church. The church is configured as being essentially more egalitarian than any other form of religion, despite the church's shortcomings, which are considered unfortunate continuations of Jewish patriarchalism.[4] Such studies have been rightly criticized by Jewish feminist historians. They critique as being intrinsically anti-Semitic any vestige of triumphalism in the reconstruction of women as "liberated" in the early church over against a construction of "patriarchal Judaism."[5] In addition, it is worth remembering that the study of the status of women in antiquity is neither a recent enterprise nor a necessarily feminist one, and can comfortably lead to an accentuation of women's marginality in both past and present. Marilyn A. Katz and Beate Wagner-Hasel have traced the origins of the study to the late eighteenth century and have argued that the entire discourse on the supposed "status" of a group categorized as "women" could and did serve certain male ideological principles connected with the eighteenth- and nineteenth-century democratic dream,[6] which originated in the writings of Jean-Jacques Rousseau,[7] and the "proper" place of women in society. A simple focus on women's status, based on a superficial reading of texts that accepts textual reality as historical reality, can lead to a reification of the oppressive structures built into the texts themselves.

In this study, I would like to show how a group of Jewish men and women can be presented in a way that indicates an equitable gender relationship and the achievement of women. In doing so, I look for slippages and deemphasized evidence in the text. While Schüssler Fiorenza's methodology was pioneered within the framework of studies of the New Testament and early Christianity, aspects of the methodology can be applied to many texts from a wide variety of religious and social perspectives. In this way, it is to be distinguished from scholarship that seeks to claim that the status of Christian women was high in a relative sense, on the basis of accepting the apparent realities of texts. Broadly understood, Schüssler Fiorenza's methodology can be applied to any text in which women have been disempowered, in order to show how the achievement of the historical women has been masked by androcentric rhetoric that creates a textual reality that means that we, as readers, do not see what the people referred to in the text in fact have seen.

Before proceeding, however, there needs to be a word about the categorizations "Jewish" and "Christian." The very reconstruction of "Jewish" women who are to be distinguished in ancient society from "Christian" women raises important issues concerning how one may formulate categories in studying antiquity that can be compared and contrasted in terms of gender, especially in the earliest stages of Christianity. Women in the ancient world participated in a broad range of cultural activities that could cross ethnic or religious boundaries. In a study of an Aramaic ostracon of an Edomite marriage contract from Maresha, dated 176 B.C.E., Esther Eshel and Amos Kloner note the very great resemblance of this marriage contract to the Jewish marriage contracts found in the Judean desert and Egyptian Demotic contracts; they propose that these similarities indicate "that different ethnic groups that inhabited Palestine and Egypt were influenced by the Aramaic common law."[8] The inheritance law of the Babatha archives, discovered in Naḥal Ḥever, is not Judaic, even though it is accepted as the legal norm by a group of Jews.[9] Such studies throw into question whether one can distinguish highly significant differences between the legal situation of women in Jewish society and surrounding cultures, whether in the Land or in the Diaspora, for cross-cultural legal systems could unite women in similar situations. Defining "cultural" difference is even more problematic. Religious texts of gender prescriptions can be ideal and reflect little social reality. Studies of women in early Christianity that have sought to define Christian women's "position" as better than that of Jewish women have often assumed absolute social, legal, and religious divisions that simply did not exist.

In the so-called Therapeutae, an egalitarian model can be found. I do not wish to present it as exceptional. I would expect that many other paradigms can be discerned within Judaism, Christianity, Greco-Roman religions, and other ancient cults and philosophies. I do not accept a construction of an overarching patriarchal Judaism that can be contrasted with a less patriarchal Christianity. I am interested in freeing the women of this particular group from the androcentric rhetoric that has prevented readers from recognizing their reality.[10]

The Therapeutae[11] are described in a single text of ca. 40 C.E. This text, *De Vita Contemplativa*, is by the prolific Alexandrian Jewish philosopher Philo. He constructs his Therapeutae—a name meaning cultic "servers," "devotees," or "attendants"[12]—to be an exemplary community of ascetic allegorizing Jewish philosophers who adopted a life focused entirely on contemplation of the Divine. At every stage, Philo is attempting to score points on their excellence and virtue; in this way, the Therapeutae are tools in Philo's rhetoric. They are not the creators of their own textual reality; their reality has been created by a third party. Like the women of early Christianity in the extant textual tradition, the entire group is the "other," molded to meet the needs of an author whose concern was to prove that this group as a whole was completely virtuous. Within this framework, the women Therapeutae appear as a second tier of "other."

Some have argued that Philo's text is so strongly focused on his goal of typifying an ideal that the group of Therapeutae he constructs is, essentially, fictional,[13] but I do not accept this notion. It seems clear that Philo was working with a real group, from which he drew out elements that would work in terms of his rhetoric. This is apparent because throughout the text Philo indicates elements that were not so helpful to him but were nevertheless apparent in the group he observed.[14] Furthermore, he also deliberately takes on some elements that are not only unhelpful but rhetorically highly problematic and tries to turn them around to use positively within his rhetorical schema, thereby directly combating potential criticism. The fact that there were women in the group he describes is one of these elements. In terms of Philo's rhetoric, the presence of women within the group caused him to adopt a defensive strategy, so that the women would be made safe and, indeed, would function as a way of scoring points.

Philo seems to have had in mind that the portrayal of the community he presents in *De Vita Contemplativa* would eclipse any description of an ideal philosophical group of the Greco-Roman world. He alludes to philosophical "heroes" of the Greek tradition (see *Contempl.* 14–17, 53–63), who turn out to be not very heroic at all, and he seems in particular to wish to eclipse the Pythagoreans and the Platonists: God is "better than a 'Good' and purer than a 'one' and older than a 'Monad'" (*Contempl.* 2).[15] Philo could not mention the women of the group without a strongly defensive line on their presence, because in extant male discourse on philosophy in antiquity, the trope "woman philosopher" was by no means always a positive one.[16] To take but a few examples from this vast literature, Cicero (*On the Nature of the Gods* 1.93) ridicules the Epicurean Leontium's reply to a work by Theophrastus, but the purpose is to undermine the Epicureans who would allow a "little whore" to write such a piece.[17] Aspasia was the subject of many comic writers' attacks on the very idea of a philosophical woman.[18] This motif is found also in Juvenal's *Satires* (6.434–36). In satiric comedies of the fourth century B.C.E. by Cratinus the Elder and Alexis, a woman who practices the philosophical regimen of Pythagoras exemplifies the sheer ridiculousness of the system (Diogenes Laertius, *Lives* 8.37). Diogenes Laertius includes a humorous tradition of the "origin" of women students of Pythagoras, which at the same time undermines the possibility that women may have chosen the philosophy seriously or independently. He states that according to a rather comic story by Hermippus, Pythagoras made a cave dwelling deep in the earth, setting his mother to guard the entrance and tell him of what happened above, and when he eventually came out he told everyone he had been down to Hades and read out a story of his experiences. The gullible men who heard this outside the cave were so affected they wailed and wept and considered him divine. In awe, they gave their wives to him (sexual implication present) in the hope that they might learn something from him, and "so they were called Pythagoreans [fem.]" (*Lives* 8.41). This story makes the women completely passive, sexual objects for Pythagoras to use and describes Pythagoras as a charlatan and sexual opportunist. It depicts the men as utter idiots and the original female Pythagoreans as no better than prostitutes, in terms of the standards of the day.

There are very many other examples that could be used, but suffice it to say that the motif of women as philosophers would probably have been introduced to promote the group under discussion and could as well have been used to undermine it. In Philo's other idealizing description—of the Essenes—there are no women (*Prob.* 75–91). If anything, the lack of women among the Essenes perfectly coheres with Philo's notions about the dangers of women in the household, which he implies were the Essenes' views also (see *Hypoth.* 11.14–18). Philo might have preferred if women were not in his ideal group of Therapeutae, but he has to include them because they were.[19]

It is perhaps rather ironic that, given the centrality of the concept of "good" in so many ancient philosophical systems, it was not so easy to present women as philosophical and "good" at the same time. There are some prototypes to which Philo may have turned. Most of the truly good women philosophers in the extant androcentric traditions of philosophy do not traverse social boundaries or challenge accepted societal understandings of gender. Despite the story summarized above, Pythagorean women are the leading examples of this type of model: the two Theanoses, Phyntis, Perictione, Myia and others. In this literature, they are fully *mathētriai*, "students" or "disciples," of Pythagoras, but this does not mean they behave in identical ways to the male disciples. The women disciples were contained within the domestic sphere as wives and mothers, even when they taught. Pleasing the husband was thought to be a special part of the correct way of life for a Pythagorean woman (Plutarch, *Moralia* 145). Modesty was a critical feature that indicated their philosophical correctness.[20] The same situation applied in Stoic philosophy. While first-century men in a Roman context knew of Stoic women who were indeed behaving in a way that was deemed not socially appropriate for women—or even offensive—the ideal Stoic woman was modest and domestic. Such is the rhetoric of Musonius Rufus when he addresses the question of the philosophical woman.[21]

In Philo's description of the community of *De Vita Contemplativa*, the women are not obviously "domesticated" in the manner of ideal female Pythagoreans or Stoic women. They appear to have abandoned the world of domesticity and procreation in order to embrace a life centered on the intellect and spirit. It is hard to believe that Philo is presenting the women of this community as the Jewish equivalent of Pythagorean women philosophers, whose ideal locus was very much within the household, or as a model that would be recognized as instantly good by Stoics, or anyone else. In leaving the household to live an ascetic life of few possessions, the women Therapeutae seem closer to the model of Hipparchia the Cynic, wife of Crates.[22] However, Hipparchia was considered an exceptional woman, a female Crates, and a very ambiguous figure for a role model. Despite her asceticism, she was sexualized in traditions concerning her: she was the epitome of a loose woman, outrageous and unique. It is highly unlikely that Philo would have commended the women Therapeutae to anyone by arguing that they were in any way like this sole Cynic woman. Rather, he seems to be very aware that the women he describes would face the criticism of being undomestic. They are a rhetorical problem.

While Philo alerts his readers early on to the presence of women in the group (*Contempl.* 2), at various points in the text he engineers things so that readers will not notice the women. For example, he writes of "superlative virtue of the men [*tōn andrōn*]" (1; cf. 78). These men leave behind their property (13) and "brothers/sisters [*adelphous*], children, *wives*, parents, numerous relatives . . ." (18). The community also uses the writings of "the men of old [*palaiōn andrōn*]" (29). When he does address the topic of the women directly, he appears to take a deep breath and deal with them very carefully. The fairly strong tradition of women within both the Pythagorean school and the Platonic academy[23] may have given him a precedent, but we do indeed feel his discomfort and apologetic tone when he introduces the women in the text:

> This common sanctuary into which they come together on seventh days is a double enclosure: one part is set apart for men, and the other [is set apart] for women. For indeed also women customarily participate in listening [like the men], having the same zeal and purpose. And the wall between the areas rises upwards from the ground up to three or four cubits in the form of breastwork, but the upper section going up to the roof is wide open. [This arrangement is] for two reasons: so that the modesty which is becoming to the female nature be preserved, and so that, by their sitting in earshot, everything is easily audible, for nothing obstructs the voice of the speaker. (*Contempl.* 32–33)

Here Philo introduces the women as students of a teacher, allowing them to have the same zeal and purpose as the men, but the very moment he has stated this he introduces a wall. In fact, he creates the image of the divided space prior to introducing the women, so that we first have the divided room, and then the women (with the same zeal and purpose as the men), and then we are drawn back to the wall once more. The entire purpose of this rhetorical construction is so that we will see these women as safely modest, hidden away from any potentially lusty looks from the men, because modesty was thought to be becoming to the female nature, and the display of modesty indicated a "good" woman. These are not the strident, immodest philosophical women some may imagine.

Later in the text, women again are presented by Philo as an element in a communal meeting.

> Women eat together [here] also. They are mostly elderly virgins. They strongly maintain the purity [of virginity/celibacy], not out of necessity, as some of the priestesses of the Greeks [do], but out of their own free will, because of a zeal and yearning for wisdom, which they are eager to live with. They take no heed of the pleasures of the body, and desire not a mortal offspring, but an immortal one, which only a soul which is loved by God is able to give birth to, by itself, because the Father has sown in it lights of intelligence which enable her to see the doctrines of wisdom. The [order of] reclining is divided, with men by themselves on the right on one side, and women on the left by themselves on the other. (*Contempl.* 68–69)

This passage also culminates in defining the men and women spatially: they are apart. These women are certainly not erotic women or courtesans. They are completely proper, modest, and chaste: models of femininity.

This is a complex section in terms of its rhetoric and allusions, and only a few matters will be explored here. Philo's assertion that the women of this group were "mostly aged virgins" (*pleistai gēraiai parthenoi*) is probably the most important rhetorical feature here. It is actually unclear whether Philo means to refer to "mostly elderly" virgins (i.e., they are all virgins, most of whom are aged), or "mostly virgins" who are elderly (i.e., they are mostly virgins, who all happen to be elderly), or both (i.e., they are mostly virgins, most of whom are also elderly). Since it would seem likely that celibacy was embraced by both men and women in this group, Philo may have had to put in "mostly" in order to include women who were not virgins but who had now decided to become celibate and also any younger women who were virgins or new celibates. As Holger Szesnat points out, Philo generally uses the word *gynai*, "women," to refer to the female members of the group, not *parthenoi*, "virgins,"[24] which might be an interesting slippage. In terms of Philo's society, there was a fundamental status shift that affected females: up until marriage they were *parthenoi*, "virgins" or "maidens." With sex/marriage, they became *gynai*, "women." Philo refers to them as *gynai* while asserting that they are *parthenoi*, which may reflect some confusion in Philo's mind about the women he was presenting. Can someone be a woman and a virgin/maiden at the same time, to Philo? Or does this language indicate that there were more married (though celibate) women in the group than Philo has led his readers to believe?

It seems that Philo's sudden insistence that readers visualize the women as elderly virgins is a smoke screen to avoid direct discussion of the tricky issue of celibacy following marriage, which seems to be the situation for at least some members of the group, both men and women. This was something in the group that Philo himself did not readily accept as "good," since he believed people should obey the commandment to multiply, as Szesnat notes.[25] We find this view of Philo indicated in his comments on the obligation to divorce a barren woman; he kindly takes pity on men who, from force of familiarity, continue to be married to their barren wives, but he has no sympathy—rather, outright condemnation—for men who married women who have previously been shown to be barren (*Spec.* 3.32–34), knowing full well they could not fulfill the obligation to multiply.

Philo writes in *Contempl.* 68–69 as if it is only the women who adopt celibacy, because they were "mostly virgins" anyway, probably because Philo believed that the obligation to multiply applied most particularly to men and not so much to women.[26] He indicates that the men had already fulfilled the commandment, since he states that they—and not the women—have left their spouses and children (*Contempl.* 18). Ross Kraemer wonders if the lack of any mention of husbands in Philo's discussion indicates that the historical women of the community had indeed never married,[27] which is certainly possible; but reading the text more rhetorically, one could also explain this as a strategy to underscore the men's fulfillment of the biblical commandment. He then becomes silent on the men's celibacy, avoiding specific discussion of this issue, and discusses the subject only in relation to the women in terms of their continuing virginity, understood here as an element of "good."

Philo can use the image of the female virgin as a positive ideal by borrowing it directly from Greco-Roman cultic practice, where virgins could play important roles. Virginity was esteemed as a means to achieve a greater access to the world of the spirit and the divine, as in the case of the Vestal Virgins in Rome, and was part of a wider rubric which Judith Gundry-Volf defines as "inspiration asceticism."[28] The Pythia at Delphi had to be a virgin in order to prophesy.[29] According to Diodorus Siculus (*Bibl.* 16.26) this is because virgin girls had their natural innocence intact and were then like the virgin goddess Artemis (who is a kind of warrior or guardian); they could then also guard the secrecy of the disclosures.[30] A woman who prophesies at the temple of Apollo in Corinth in the second century is celibate (Pausanias, *Itin. Graec.* 2.24.1), and other Apollo prophetesses are virgins (Euripides, *Troad.* 41–42; Lycophron, *Alex.* 348–64; Herodotus 1.182). Certain sibyls are virgins (Virgil, *Aen.* 3.443–45; 6.42–45; Ovid, *Metam.* 14.129–53; Lycophron, *Alex.* 1278–79; Pausanias 10.12.6). In his attempt to show that the Therapeutae exhibit greater virtue than anything found among the Greeks, Philo uses the element of virginity among the women Therapeutae to further this rhetoric. While such virginity is found among "the Greeks," it is done "out of necessity" (i.e., they are made to do it), while the women Therapeutae have chosen this state freely out of a "zeal and yearning for wisdom" (*Contempl.* 68). Another point is scored.

Philo's insistence on the women Therapeutae's unthreatening feminine modesty, his use of the women to score points in his strategy to prove that the Therapeutae are better than anything the Greeks have come up with, and his attempts to ensure that his readers do not see them as clearly as the men of the group—who are the defining set of "Therapeutae" in the text—all function to trap the historical women Philo describes into his rhetorical web. Nevertheless, Philo also lets it slip that the women of this group are powerful players who command considerable respect, especially in the final third of the treatise (64–90).

When the group comes together to eat in a special "feast" (conceptually understood, for the food is only bread and the drink is the purest water), Philo states that the junior members of this group serve the senior members as "fathers and mothers." The seniors are "their parents in common, more closely connected with them than by blood" (*Contempl.* 72). This is the basis of the extremely loving relations Philo notes, and the lack of subservience among the junior members who wait at table. He writes: "They are just like real children who are affectionately glad to be of service to fathers and mothers" (72), and "they fulfill the requirements of servants not by compulsion or by enduring orders, but, with voluntary free will, they anticipate quickly and willingly (any) requests" (71).

The identification of the elder women as mothers is important not only because it enables these women to fulfill the domestic role of a good woman in normatively gendered society but also because in much of the ancient world, as in the world today, a woman's status in a given community was connected with her being a mother. This was the case also in the Jewish community in antiquity, in which the status of a mother in family and community appears to have been quite high. The status of a mother along with a father in the ancient Israelite household is affirmed in Deuteronomy 5:16; Exodus 20:12 (cf. Lev. 19:3). A child who strikes either father or mother is liable to punishment (Exod. 21:15, 17). Proverbs 1:8 and 6:20 exhort children to listen and to adhere to the teaching of both father and mother.[31] Deborah is called "Mother in Israel," a designation of her divinely ordained leadership of the nation (Judg. 5.7).[32] In a non-Jewish context we have Tata of Aphrodisias (second century C.E.) described as being a "mother" of the city.[33] In Jewish contexts, a woman of high status or a donor who played an important leadership role in the life of the community and synagogue might be deemed "mother of the synagogue" in inscriptions (*Corpus inscriptionum judaicarum* 523, 496, 166, 639).[34] The "mothers" of the congregation are referred to also in a fragmentary text within the Dead Sea Scrolls corpus (4Q270 7.i.14). Therefore, indicating that the senior women Therapeutae were mothers was a way of enhancing their honor within the community.

While Philo's description of the relationships between the seniors and juniors is used to score points in his rhetorical schema, his concern is to show how good the members of the group are in not having slaves, and in having such loving relationships among everyone. While designating the women as "mothers," he succeeds in making them appear domestic and therefore "safe"—their status seems of less concern. He does not underscore it by stating that "both men and women are leaders in this community," even though this is implied.

Philo indicates that the hierarchy of the community is truly good, because while normatively in society status may be dependent on age, this is not the case here. Status is dependent on deeper worth, and age is irrelevant. The hierarchy of the Therapeutae is split between those who have expertise in the practices of the group, who have been part of it for a long time, and those who are new to the group and still learning various practices (*Contempl.* 67). The hierarchy is in fact between the *presbyteroi* (the elders, seniors; see 67) and the *diakonoi* (the juniors, attendants; see 75)—terms that directly parallel those of early Christian groups. Both men and women were in both strata of the hierarchy, though Philo specifically presents women only in the senior category; no junior women are shown to the reader, possibly because "young" women waiting on tables may have prompted erotic associations. Philo does not avoid indicating that gender had no bearing on matters of status, but gender is not at the forefront of his rhetoric here. It is as if Philo is saying here: "and there were women too." Still, there is no suggestion in the text that the fathers were superior to the mothers or held offices that the mothers did not hold, even if Philo or his readers might have assumed this to be the case.

So far Philo's language is traditional, and his women are characterized in a domestic, matronly way that keeps them both "good" and "safe." But in the final part of Philo's treatise they appear in a radically different light. The language of the sacred appears at various points in this part of the text to underscore the cultic dimensions of activities that are taking place here. The meal is a "sacred symposium" (*Contempl.* 71). After they have come into the room and prayed, the seniors recline in hierarchical order while the juniors stand attentive; the president gives a discourse and then stands up to sing a hymn. Philo writes:

> Then the [president] stands up and sings a hymn composed to God, either a new one of his own composition or some old one [composed] by the poets of old, for they have left behind many [songs] in many metres and melodies: hexameters, trimeters, hymns of processions, [hymns] relating to libations, [hymns] relating to the altar, for standing [in a chorus] and for [choral] dancing well measured out for turning and twisting. After him, in fact, the others according to order have a turn [at singing]. Everyone else listens in total silence, except when they need to [sing] closing lines and themes. For then all men and all women sing aloud. (*Contempl.* 80)

Philo here refers to their musical compositions as relating to cultic activities (processions, libations, altar-actions), as if the music in some way ushers in a cultic reality. The group joins in with the president in closing lines and themes, and the members sing their own songs, participating too in this powerful music, both men and women, as Philo explicitly states. After this, when all is done, the juniors bring in a table that is configured as representing the table of the shewbread in the temple.[35]

> When each person has finished a hymn, the youths bring in the above-mentioned table, upon which the most all-pure food is [set out]: [loaves] of leavened bread, along with a seasoning of salt mingled with hyssop. This [arrangement] is in reverence of the sacred table set up in the vestibule of the holy temple court. For upon this [table] are loaves and salt, without flavouring, and the bread is unleavened, and the salt in not mixed [into the bread]. (*Contempl.* 81)

This is very powerful language. Here, the bread and salt represent the holy food in the temple.[36] In fact, the book of Leviticus (24:8) states that the twelve loaves (the number indicating the twelve tribes of Israel) placed on the table are an "everlasting covenant." One is reminded of how the earliest Christians could make bread and wine represent, in various ways, the body and blood of the crucified and risen Messiah: the new covenant. Philo does not, I think, stress this conceptual cultic reality in a way that indicates it is useful for his rhetoric. It is an element he has observed that he includes in the text to explain various features of the feast without making much of it. However, if a cultic reality was actually created by the Therapeutae in their dining hall, then this has significant ramifications for the women of the group. In eating the holy food of the table of shewbread—an everlasting covenant—the group members would have held themselves to be, conceptually, the specially chosen priests, for only "Aaron and his sons" are permitted to eat the loaves. Moreover, according to Leviticus, "they will eat them inside the holy place, since for him they are a very holy portion of the food baked/burnt for YHWH" (Lev. 24:9). In eating the loaves, the Therapeutae are conceptually in the holy space of the temple sanctuary. Philo himself states:

> For it was appropriate that the simplest and purest food be allotted to the most excellent portion of the priests, as a reward for services, while others would zealously seek the same [kind of food], but hold off from the [temple loaves], in order that their betters might [rightly] have precedence. (*Contempl.* 82)

This identification of the members of the group as the most excellent portion of the priests, who have the right to eat the covenantal bread, links this action with what Philo states a little earlier on, that "just as right reason dictates abstinence from wine for *the priests* when sacrificing, so also for these [i.e., 'the most excellent portion of the priests,' viz., the Therapeutae] for a life-time" (*Contempl.* 74). He states that the Therapeutae provide their services (*leitourgia*) continually by their lifestyle and practices. The eating of the bread from the table is a reward for the services, which they offer all the time. The provision of the *leitourgia* (from which we derive the term "liturgy") indeed gives the reason for their name, *therapeutai* (masc.) and *therapeutrides* (fem.), "servers" or "attendants" of God.

This cultic language appears in the text as if it derives from what the group actually believes (i.e., the table is actually set up by the group out of reverence for the table of shewbread; it does not just happen to remind Philo of this association) and holds no rhetorical weight in Philo's argument apart from indicating that these people are more virtuous than ordinary priests (and therefore anyone else) in terms of what they eat and drink. Philo does not need to apologize for the presence of women in the conceptual category of priests here if his intended audience is Greco-Roman pagan, since women held religious offices, including the priesthood, in a number of different cults, without negative associations.[37] However, it certainly does not feature as a key element in his rhetoric of gender specifically; here the rhetorical focus is on the virtue of the group as a whole in terms of food and drink. It is more as if Philo accidentally includes the women when he has other matters in mind. Perhaps he would even prefer that his readers did not imagine them playing priestly roles. He does nothing to stress the women's presence in this particular priestly context.

If Philo is reflecting here what the group believes, then the Therapeutae see themselves as true priests in the most holy temple of God. In the sacred feast, the space of the dining hall is transformed into the holy sanctuary itself, where the chosen priests eat the bread offered to YHWH, which represents an everlasting covenant between God and Israel.[38] After eating, they then go into the middle of the room where the table is (or was) located, standing ready to sing praises to God in two choirs of perfect attendants of the Divine.

In terms of gendered space, this transformation is fascinating, given that in the material temple in Jerusalem, no woman was permitted to be in the area of the sanctuary vestibule. The temple in Jerusalem had different zones of holiness, from the lesser holiness of the outer court, in which Gentiles were allowed, to the holy of holies, where only the high priest was permitted on the Day of Atonement. Any Jew or Gentile could come into the Court of the Gentiles; any Jewish woman could enter the Court of the Women (Josephus, *War* 5.199), but at the entry to the small Court of the Israelites, she could go no further. In Exodus 38:8 a woman could minister at the door of the tent of meeting (corresponding to the sanctuary), but by the time of Herod's temple in Jerusalem women's proximity to the highest degree of holiness had been pushed back. Only Jewish men could go into the Court of the Israelites. Beyond this zone was the area where the priests undertook sacred duties and sacrifices, and no nonpriest or priest who was not serving was permitted there.[39] Women could not be priests in the Jerusalem temple, but they could see into this area from a gallery in the Court of the Women (*m. Midd.* 2:5).

The temple, or sanctuary, was divided into two areas: the vestibule and the holy of holies. As Philo notes, the table of shewbread was located in the vestibule, along with the tabernacle menorah and incense altar. The interior chamber, separated by a large curtain, was completely empty. Only the high priest would enter there once a year on the Day of Atonement. Anyone not a priest—even a Levite—who approached the artifacts of the sanctuary would die (Num. 18:3).

Spatially, the Therapeutae move into the area occupied by the conceptual table of shewbread and then stand in or before the sanctuary. At this point, having been separated from each other (*Contempl.* 69), men and women now stand together in the center of the room, in two choirs (83), apparently losing their sense of modesty. Therefore, everything changes in terms of the relationship between men and women; there are no barriers or separations. Now, inspired singing takes the Therapeutae into heights of spiritual bliss (89–90).

The careful modesty Philo has ascribed to the women breaks down completely. It is as if gender itself has been dissolved, and they form "a single choir" (85). All are singing in union and joy, communing with heavenly realities. How can this still be "good"? It is good because Philo has already done most of his rhetorical work in the text in terms of gender and in terms of establishing the character of the group as extremely ascetic (e.g., *Contempl.* 29, 31–33, 34, 66, 69). By the time we get to the dangerous issue of the group's inspired singing, we are weighted down with the impression of the whole group being completely decent, quiet, celibate, ascetic, and virtuous. We simply could not imagine the Therapeutae, at this stage, behaving in any way except in a remarkably chaste, spiritual, and contemplative fashion. Furthermore, it is good because in this final section Philo has moved into another rhetorical strategy, where he is concerned to show that the Therapeutae are the most virtuous types of ecstatics. He has already alerted the readers to the fact that these people are engaged in spiritual practices aimed at seeing heavenly realities, which he defines in terms of what is known in the Hellenistic world: they are like Bacchic revelers and Corybants (*Contempl.* 12). He states at the end that these people are "just as in the Bacchic rites . . . drinking the liquor of a god's love" (85) and that they "are drunk . . . with this beautiful drunkenness" (89). The Therapeutae are made to score another point against Greek practice: they are nothing like the wild, orgiastic ecstatics of Dionysian mysteries. This is a "sober drunkenness," a conundrum that Philo uses to bamboozle his readers into a recognition of spiritual, rather than materialistic, truth.[40]

Philo had been willing to express earlier in the text that women had the same zeal and yearning for wisdom as the men, and in the final section of his essay he is also very willing to stress that women compose music and sing like the men, and that the choir is actually made up of one part men and the other part women, using the model of Israel's song(s) after the crossing of the sea (Exod. 15), when Moses led the men and Miriam led the women (*Contempl.* 85, 87–88). However, the cultic language is left randomly strewn around the text without any comment from Philo affirming that "women too formed the most excellent portion of the priests." This omission is interesting, given what he otherwise affirms; and modern readers, led along by Philo's rhetorical emphases and "deemphases," have not noticed the inclusion of women in this conceptual category.

In shifting his rhetorical interests first to food and drink, for example, or to ecstasy, Philo did not emphasize what he had described: women who understood themselves to be priests, whose inspired singing led them into the heart of heavenly realities. Reading for the women, and laying aside their entrapment in Philo's rhetoric, it seems apparent that nothing was out of bounds. The barriers and separations that Philo had carefully noted earlier for the sake of modesty have no bearing on what is of ultimate importance. One is reminded, strikingly, of the apostle Paul's statement in Galatians 3:28, where what divides people socially in the material world can be dispensed with in Christ: "There is not male and female, for you are one in Christ Jesus." Here, all are one in the wisdom that allows the Therapeutae access to the Divine.[41]

When we consider that the senior women of the Therapeutae were understood to be (conceptually) priests in a cultic service, Philo's earlier comments designed to make them safe and good appear even more starkly rhetorical than at first sight. Philo's introduction of these women in a box that keeps them away from men and his presentation of them as passive listeners are contrasted with this later presentation of their active participation in the group's sacred rites: eating and drinking sacred food, standing in the sanctuary, singing their own songs, being ecstatically inspired. This latter section also highlights what he has stated earlier about the group as a whole being true disciples of Moses (63), who study scripture alone in their little huts, compose music, and contemplate (25-29). The women are fully included in the category of the mindful servers (*therapeutai/therapeutrides*) of God at all times, and are therefore identified with the most excellent portion of the priests.

Thus, while Philo presents these women as passive listeners in the room where the group goes for instruction from the most senior member, nothing he states would preclude a woman from holding the highest office in the community, that of the *presbytatos*, "the most senior person" (31) or *prohedros*, "president"' (79–80). Philo clearly presents this person as male throughout the text, but this office is held by someone who is "most experienced in the doctrines" (31). This means that, while Philo may have observed a male president or may have assumed one, the office need not necessarily always have been held by a male. The masculine forms of the words here do not indicate that the holder of the office had to be male, as there are numerous instances of women holding titles that occur in the masculine form in Greek.[42] If women and men were separated in communal gatherings for the purposes of removing temptation, apart from when people reached an inspired state, this does not mean that women were placed in a position inferior to men; it simply means that the group as a whole took steps to avoid lustful thoughts, which would be consistent with their general ultra-ascetic line. Nevertheless, a woman could speak from the women's section of the divided hall and be heard by all, just as easily as a man could speak and be heard by all. It is we, the readers, who can make an imaginary design in our heads that might place the women in this meeting in a marginal place: even Philo does not in fact do this, despite his rhetoric of "passivity" and "modesty."

Philo himself can present a model of female teacher. In another treatise, Philo states that he went for instruction to a wise woman named Skepsis, meaning "consideration," who personifies insight gained through the allegorical exegesis of scripture (*Fug.* 55, 58). Scholars usually pass over this personification as merely that, but the image must have been based on real models of female teachers known to Philo—otherwise it would have appeared odd. There is positive evidence of Pythagorean female philosophers

—writers and teachers—in Alexandria at this time;[43] and nothing would prevent women from being teachers in the Jewish community, especially if their locus for teaching was the home, as in the case of the Pythagoreans. It is not intrinsically improbable that the Jewish Therapeutae had women teachers as well as men, given the Alexandrian context of the group. No barriers can be placed around the women Therapeutae that would exclude them from any functions in the community.

About 380 years after Philo wrote his treatise on the Therapeutae, Eusebius, bishop of Caesarea, made excerpts from it for his monumental *Ecclesiastical History* (17). By this time, the group was unlike any group of Jews known to Eusebius, and he took pains to argue that Philo had in fact used Christians in his presentation. Eusebius picked up anything from the text that supported his contention and quoted Philo's comments about women in *De Vita Contemplativa* 32–33 to prove the point that it is Christians who are discussed—the "segregation of men and women living in the same place" being something "still practiced among us" (*Hist. eccl.* 2.17), a real clincher. But Eusebius was wrong. As is quite clear from the imagery of the table of shewbread and the identification of the Therapeutae as "disciples of Moses" (63–64), Philo is not describing Christians. He shows us an example of a type of Jewish group that would, like Philo himself, exert some influence on Christianity, even though the chain of influence is still poorly understood. I have argued elsewhere that this small group Philo described was not isolated and was part of a much wider Jewish school of allegorical exegesis in Alexandria, into which the seed of Christianity was planted.[44] One cannot help but consider the parallel of the inspired women[45] in the church of Corinth, whose lack of modesty during prayer and prophecy so exercised the apostle Paul (1 Cor. 11:1–16),[46] some fourteen years or so after Philo wrote his treatise on the Therapeutae. It is precisely at Corinth that we find a direct connection with Alexandria, through the missionizing of Apollos (Acts 18:25; 1 Cor. 1:10–12; 3:4–10, 22; 4:6; 16:12, cf. Titus 3:13), a man with whom Paul did not necessarily agree.[47] To what extent did Apollos carry Alexandrian practices to the Christians of Corinth? Did he know the Therapeutae, like Philo, or provide models for the Corinthian church to follow based on what he had already seen or experienced within Judaism? However we may answer such questions, it seems clear that in both Corinth and Alexandria women engaged in similar enterprises—finding meaning in spiritual practices, enjoying opportunities for leadership in religious groups, and communing with the Divine—in ways that break down the barriers that texts may erect.

NOTES

1. For example: Elisabeth Schüssler Fiorenza, *In Memory of Her: A Feminist Theological Reconstruction of Christian Origins* (New York: Crossroad, 1983); eadem, *But She Said: Feminist Practices of Biblical Interpretation* (Boston: Beacon, 1985); eadem, *Discipleship of Equals: A Critical Feminist Ekklēsia-logy of Liberation* (New York: Crossroad, 1993); eadem, *Jesus: Miriam's Child, Sophia's Prophet: Critical Issues in Feminist Christology* (New York: Continuum, 1994); Luise Schottroff, *Let the Oppressed Go Free: Feminist Perspectives on the New Testament* (Louisville: Westminster John Knox Press, 1993); eadem, *Lydia's Impatient Sisters: A Feminist Social History of Early Christianity* (Louisville: Westminster John Knox Press, 1995).

2. Schüssler Fiorenza, *Jesus: Miriam's Child*, 29.

3. E.g., Ben Witherington III, *Women in the Ministry of Jesus: A Study of Jesus' Attitudes to Women and Their Roles as Reflected in His Earthly Life* (Cambridge: Cambridge University Press, 1984); idem, *Women in the Earliest Churches* (Cambridge: Cambridge University Press, 1988); Leonard Swidler, *Yeshua: A Model for Moderns* (Kansas City: Sheed & Ward, 1988).

4. For an identification of this and critique, see Schüssler Fiorenza, *But She Said*, 22–23.

5. For a critique of how investigations of the historical Jesus play into the construction of a nonliberative Judaism, see Amy-Jill Levine, "Second Temple Judaism, Jesus and Women: Yeast of Eden," *Biblical Interpretation* 2 (1994): 8–33.

6. Marilyn A. Katz, "Ideology and 'the Status of Women,'" in *Women in Antiquity: New Assessments*, ed. Richard Hawley and Barbara Levick (London/New York: Routledge, 1995), 21–43; eadem, "Ideology and 'the Status' of Women in Ancient Greece," in *History and Feminist Theory*, ed. Ann-Louise Shapiro, History and Theory 31 (Middletown, Conn: Wesleyan University Press, 1992), 86–92; Beate Wagner-Hasel, "Das Private wird politisch," in *Weiblichkeit in geschichtlicher Perspektive: Fallstudien und reflexionen zu Grundproblemen der historischen Frauenforschung*, ed. U. A. J. Becher and J. Rüsen (Frankfurt am Main: Suhrkamp, 1988); eadem, "Frauenleben in orientalischer Abgeschlossenheit? Zur Geschichte und Nutzanwendung eines Topos," *Der altsprachliche Unterricht* 2 (1989): 18–29.

7. Jean-Jacques Rousseau uses classical Athens as the paradigm for the incorporation of women into the ideal state (*The Social Contract* [1762], trans. Maurice Cranston [Baltimore: Penguin, 1978], 64–65; see Katz, "Ideology," 34). For Rousseau, women were both secluded from the public realm and respected on account of this.

8. Esther Eshel and Amos Kloner, "An Aramaic Ostracon of an Edomite Marriage Contract from Maresha, Dated 176 B.C.E.," *Israel Exploration Journal* 46 (1996): 1–22.

9. See Hannah M. Cotton and Jonas C. Greenfield, "Babatha's Property and the

Law of Succession in the Babatha Archive," *Zeitschrift für Papyrologie und Epigraphik* 104 (1994): 211–24.

10. For important studies that have made a contributions to seeing the women of the group more lucidly, see Ross S. Kraemer, "Monastic Jewish Women in Greco-Roman Egypt: Philo Judaeus on the Therapeutrides," *Signs* 14 (1989): 342–70; Holger Szesnat, "'Mostly Aged Virgins': Philo and the Presence of the Therapeu-trides at Lake Mareotis," *Neotestamentica* 32 (1998): 191–201; idem, "'Pretty Boys' in Philo's *De Vita Contemplativa*," *Studia Philonica Annual* 10 (1998): 87–107; see also idem, "Philo and Female Homoeroticism: Philo's Use of *gunandros* and Recent Work on Tribades," *Journal for the Study of Judaism* 30 (1999): 140–47.

11. I use here the customary Latin form of the name, which is found in the Greek text as *therapeutai* (masc.) and *therapeutrides* (fem.). In order to highlight the women, I call them "women Therapeutae," using the conventional term, rather than the Greek *therapeutrides*.

12. See J. E. Taylor and P. R. Davies, "The So-Called 'Therapeutae' of *De Vita Contemplativa*: Identity and Character," *Harvard Theological Review* 91, no. 1 (1998): 3–24, here 4–10.

13. Troels Engberg-Pedersen, "Philo's *De Vita Contemplativa* as a Philosopher's Dream," *Journal for the Study of Judaism* 30 (1999): 40–64; see esp. 48.

14. David Hay, "Things Philo Said and Did Not Say about the Therapeutae," in *Society of Biblical Literature 1992 Seminar Papers* (Atlanta: Scholars Press, 1992), 673–83.

15. Ibid., 678.

16. This point is made by Richard Hawley, "The Problem of Women Philoso-phers in Ancient Greece," in *Women in Ancient Societies: 'An Illusion of the Night,'* ed. Leonie Archer, Susan Fischler, and Maria Wyke (Basingstoke: Macmillan, 1994). For compilations of material on women philosophers in antiquity, see *A History of Women Philosophers: Ancient Women Philosophers 600 B.C.–500 A.D.*, ed. Mary Ellen Waithe (Dordrecht/Boston/Lancaster: Martinus Nijhoff, 1987); and for a seventeenth-century view, see Gilles Ménage, *Historia Mulierum Philosopharum (History of Women Philosophers)*, ed. and trans. Beatrice H. Zedler (Lanham, Md.: University Press of America, 1984).

17. Hawley, "Women Philosophers," 80.

18. Clement of Alexandria, *Strom.* 4.122.3; Plutarch, *Pericles* 24.6. See Madeleine Henry, *"Prisoner of History": Aspasia of Miletus and Her Biographical Tradition* (New York: Oxford University Press, 1995).

19. Hay, "Things Philo Said," 674; Szesnat, "Virgins," 196.

20. Clement of Alexandria, *Strom.* 4.121.2; Diogenes Laertius, *Lives* 8.43; Theodoret, *Therapeutike* 12.73; Plutarch, *Moralia* 142D.

21. See Hawley, "Women Philosophers," 75. For the Greek text of Musonius with English translations, see Cora E. Lutz, *Musonius Rufus: The Roman Socrates* (New Haven: Yale University Press, 1947); see the discussion on women on pp. 39–49.

22. Diogenes Laertius, *Lives* 96–98; see also Epictetus, *Discourses* 3.22.76; Theodoret, *Therapeutike* 12.49; Clement of Alexandria, *Strom.* 4.121.6; Antipater of Sidon, *Anthology* 3.12.52; Suidas, "Hipparchia," in *Patrologiae cursus completus: Series Graeca,* ed. J.-P. Migne (Paris, 1857–), 117:1275.

23. Waithe, *Women Philosophers,* 68–71; Hawley, "Women Philosophers," 73–74; cf. Diogenes Laertius, *Lives* 3.1; 4.2; Plato, *Ep.* 12.

24. Szesnat, "Aged Virgins," 196.

25. Ibid., 193 (cf. Philo, *Praem.* 108–9).

26. For it being men's obligation to multiply in particular, see *m. Yevamot* 6:6, which also gives R. Yohanan b. Baroka's dissenting opinion that women were also obligated.

27. Kraemer, "Monastic Jewish Women," 352–53.

28. Judith Gundry-Volf, "Celibate Pneumatics and Social Power: On the Motivations for Sexual Asceticism in Corinth," *Union Seminary Quarterly Review* 48 (1994): 105–26.

29. So Plutarch, *Def. Or.* 51, cf. idem, *Pyth. Or.* 22. See for this and what follows Gundry-Volf, "Celibate Pneumatics," 110–11, following E. Fehrle, *Die kultische Keuschheit im Altertum* (Giessen: Töpelmann, 1910), 76–97.

30. See Gundry-Volf, "Celibate Pneumatics," 122 n. 30.

31. For discussion of "mothers" in Israel, see Carol Meyers, *Discovering Eve: Ancient Israelite Women in Context* (New York/Oxford: Oxford University Press, 1988), 150–52.

32. Ibid., 159–60. Meyers also notes that the northern Israelite city of Abel is called "a mother in Israel" (2 Sam. 20:19), and she conjectures that it may have been an oracular center. It was where a wise woman resolves a crisis concerning David's general Joab (2 Sam. 14:1–24). See also Rachel Adler, "'A Mother in Israel': Aspects of the Mother-Role in Jewish Myth," in *Beyond Androcentrism,* ed. Rita M. Gross (Missoula, Mont.: Scholars Press, 1977), 237–55, here 246–49; Cheryl Exum, "Mother in Israel: A Familiar Story Reconsidered," in *Feminist Interpretation of the Bible,* ed. Letty M. Russell (Oxford: Blackwell, 1985), 73–85.

33. Ross S. Kraemer, *Her Share of the Blessings: Women's Religions among Pagans, Jews and Christians in the Greco-Roman Period* (New York/London: Oxford University Press, 1992), 86, 120–21; see also *Corpus inscriptionum judicarum* 100; 738.

34. See Bernadette J. Brooten, *Women Leaders in the Ancient Synagogue: Inscriptional Evidence and Background Issues* (Brown Judaic Studies 36; Chico, Calif.: Scholars Press, 1982), 63–70.

35. See Exod. 25:23–30; 35:13; 37:10–16; 39:36; Lev. 24:5–9; cf. Num. 4:7; 1 Kgs. 7:48; 2 Chr. 3:19; 13:11; 29:18. The loaves on the table are a permanent offering to God and were made by Levites (1 Chr. 9:31; 23:28–29).

36. In the Masoretic Text there is only bread on the table, but the Septuagint adds salt; see also Philo, *Mos.* 2.104.

37. For a survey, see Kraemer, *Her Share,* 80–92.

38. Even the celibacy of the group is relevant here, for in 1 Sam. 21:2–7, Ahimelech the priest gives David the loaves to eat, "as long as the men have kept themselves from women."

39. For a detailed discussion of the temple layout and its operations, see E. P. Sanders, *Judaism: Practice and Belief 63 BCE–66 CE* (London: SCM, 1992), 47–76.

40. See Hans Lewy, *Sobria Ebrietas: Untersuchungen zur Geschichte der antiken Mystik* (Giessen: Töpelmann, 1929), who examined every instance of this concept in Philo's work. I am also grateful to Shelly Matthews for sending me the paper she read at the Society of Biblical Literature meeting in November 1998 that discussed "honorable drunkenness" in *De Vita Contemplativa*.

41. See also, and quite remarkably: "But you are a chosen race, a kingdom of priests, a holy nation, a people to be a personal possession to sing the praises of God who called you out of the darkness and into his wonderful light" (1 Pet. 2:9; cf. Isa. 43:20–21 LXX).

42. For example, Iulia Crispina is an *episkopos* (P. Yadin 20); Phoebe is a *diakonos* (Rom. 16:1); a woman serves in public office as *logistēs*, *prohedros* (as here) and even "father of the city" in P. Oxy. 36.2780. For more examples, see Kraemer, *Her Share*, 84–86.

43. See Sarah Pomeroy, *Women in Hellenistic Egypt from Alexander to Cleopatra* (New York: Schocken, 1984), 61–71.

44. See Joan E. Taylor, "Virgin Mothers: Philo on the Women Therapeutae," *Journal for the Study of the Pseudepigrapha* 12 (2001): 37–63; eadem, *Jewish Women Philosophers of First-Century Alexandria* (Oxford: Clarendon, 2003).

45. Or woman—the reference in the text is singular.

46. The literature on this question is vast. For the classic discussion by Elisabeth Schüssler Fiorenza, see *In Memory of Her*, 226–30. See also Antoinette Clark Wire, *The Corinthian Women Prophets: A Reconstruction through Paul's Rhetoric* (Minneapolis: Fortress, 1990), 116–34.

47. See Wire, *Corinthian Women Prophets*, 209–11.

8

The Happy Holy Family
in the Jesus Film Genre

Adele Reinhartz

ELISABETH SCHÜSSLER FIORENZA HAS TAUGHT ME MUCH. FROM HER written and spoken words, and from her actions, I have learned to look beyond the canon and the written word and to incorporate into my academic work a variety of experiences and considerations that have traditionally been deemed irrelevant to the serious study of scripture. Above all, I, like many of her readers, have learned to exercise the hermeneutics of suspicion and to value the hermeneutics of creativity.

These lessons not only affect my research and teaching but also come to mind, unexpectedly, during moments of leisure. One such moment occurred as I watched a touching domestic scene from a 1966 Italian black-and-white movie: A rugged-looking man surveys a nearly deserted beach. The camera cuts to a beautiful young woman spreading a blanket on the sand and then focuses at length on her earnest and loving face and eyes. She smiles slowly. The camera cuts back to the man. He meets her gaze and smiles back. The camera then turns to a small child of perhaps two or three years of age as he walks cheerfully away from a group of playing children. The boy strides toward the camera and then breaks into a run. The man holds out his hands to the child and the boy runs toward him. The man picks him up tenderly. The camera work as well as the facial expressions and gestures of the three characters imply their family connection as mother, father, and son. The soundtrack is a soothing symphonic score; there is no dialogue. The scene is an everyday one, but it conveys the strength of their love for one another and their enjoyment of one another's company. Particularly moving is the image of the child basking in the warmth of his family, the sun, and the beach. The son's tiny toga, worn over a pair of short pants and (apparently) diapers, is the only sign that the sequence may be set in the distant past. Otherwise the scene is a timeless tribute to familial love and devotion.

Touching, to be sure. But the scene takes on a different level of significance altogether once it is placed in the context of the film as a whole. Despite the camera's lingering gaze upon the faces of the man and the woman, the real focus of the scene is the little boy, whose story is the subject of the film. The film is Pier Paolo Pasolini's *The Gospel According to St. Matthew* (1966). The child is Jesus; the adults are Mary and Joseph. As its name implies, this film is an adaptation of the First Gospel; its narrative structure and dialogue are taken entirely from the Gospel of Matthew. In this context, the scene is all the more striking, as it depicts an occasion that does not appear in Matthew, nor, indeed, in any of the canonical or noncanonical Gospels. Its purpose is visually to declare the devotion and love that united Jesus to Mary and Joseph and to portray the happiness that he experienced in the bosom of his family. This scene affirms more eloquently than any words can the human element in Jesus' messianic identity.

The arena of film may seem far from the texts and concerns that come to the fore in Elisabeth's own writings in the field of biblical hermeneutics. Yet as a mode of cultural expression, film provides a fertile ground for the hermeneutics of suspicion, for paying attention to the ways in which contemporary concerns and sensibilities shape exegesis, and for considering the cultural afterlife of biblical women and their menfolk. In this paper, I will look at the depictions of Jesus' family relationships in film. In doing so, I will concentrate primarily on the cinematic expansions of and additions to the canonical texts. Most of the family-related expansions in the Jesus films express a theme that we might call "The Happy Holy Family," in which, as in Pasolini's beach scene, emphasis is on the love and harmony among Jesus, Mary, and Joseph. I will argue that these additions serve two functions. One is to resolve the tensions inherent in the Gospel accounts. The second is to convey, indirectly and implicitly, the filmmakers' christologies, that is, their understanding of Jesus as the Messiah whose nature is both human and divine. Fundamental to both of these functions is a set of commonplace assumptions regarding family life, human development, and social relationships.

Before describing and analyzing these cinematic additions, it will be useful to review the canonical portrayal of Jesus' family relationships. This survey is not intended to address the historical question of what Jesus' family was "really" like but rather to consider the texts that are the primary sources for the cinematic retellings of Jesus' story. Most filmmakers, even those who focus primarily on one Gospel, take a harmony of the Gospels as their starting point. For this reason, it will be useful to look at the composite story— its events and its emotional undertones—with which filmmakers would be familiar.

JESUS AND HIS FAMILY IN THE GOSPELS AND ACTS

Childhood

The Gospels vary with respect to their emphasis on Jesus' familial relationships, as evidenced by the amount of "airtime" they devote to this element of Jesus' story. The Gospels of Mark and John evince no interest at all in Jesus' early life. Both Luke and Matthew include an infancy narrative, though the details differ considerably. Matthew's infancy narrative (Matthew 1-2) begins with a genealogy tracing Jesus' ancestry back to Abraham, then continues with the angel's announcement that Mary would give birth to a son. The family is visited by the wise men and then by an angel who warns them that they must escape to Egypt because Herod plans to slaughter all the young children out of fear that someone will usurp the crown. After Herod's death, the family returns to Nazareth to live. The narrative then leaps forward to Jesus' baptism at the hands of John the Baptist and Jesus' subsequent ministry (Matthew 3). Luke's version (Luke 1–2) begins not with Mary and Joseph but with another couple, Zechariah and Elizabeth, and the conception of John the Baptist, who in this version is a blood relative of Jesus. Mary experiences the annunciation, and she then goes to visit Elizabeth, whereupon the two babies recognize each other *in utero.* Because of a census requirement, Mary and Joseph travel to Bethlehem, where Jesus is born in a stable and is visited by shepherds who are guided there by angels.

Matthew's interest in the young Jesus ends with the family's return to Galilee, but Luke continues on with Jesus' circumcision and naming according to Jewish tradition (2:21) and the family's trip to Jerusalem for Mary's purification after childbirth and the presentation of Jesus to the Lord as required by Jewish law (2:22–23). The next event is yet another trip to the temple, twelve years later, this time for the Passover and perhaps, though this is not stated, for Jesus' coming of age (2:40–42). But Luke is interested not only in marking these rites of passage in Jesus' early life but also in contemplating the role of Mary and Joseph. Mary treasures in her heart all that she hears about her son (2:19). Both of his parents are amazed at what was being said about him by Simeon, who enigmatically prophesies Jesus' future and intimates Mary's future sorrow by referring to the sword that will pierce her heart (2:33–35). Mary and Joseph experience natural parental anxiety when their son fails to return with them from the temple. The Gospel of Luke describes their relief at finding him in the temple among the teachers, and also their anger at the anxiety he has caused them. Jesus, like many another teenager, knows how to deflect their anger. He tells them that they should have known he would be in "his Father's" house. As the narrator informs us, they did not understand his meaning. Jesus then returned with them to Nazareth (2:51) and lived with them in obedience; his mother, again, "treasured all these things in her heart." Emphasis in these stories is on the uniqueness of this particular child and of the circumstances of his conception and birth, as well as on his future significance for humankind. Implicit in both of these accounts, however, is what we take as the natural joy of parents at the birth of a child and the care they take for their infants' safety and well-being.

Adult Life

Little is said about the relationship between the adult Jesus and his parents. Nowhere is it stated that Jesus visited his childhood house, though he does come to Nazareth and teaches in the synagogue (Matt. 13:54); however, both John and the Synoptic tradition hint at some contacts. In the Fourth Gospel, Jesus' mother draws his attention to the fact that the wine has run out at the Cana wedding that they are both attending. Jesus' initial response is somewhat surprising: "Woman, what concern is that to you and to me? My hour has not yet come" (John 2:4). He then proceeds to provide superior wine, for which he is praised by the steward: "Everyone serves the good wine first, and then the inferior wine after the guests have become drunk. But you have kept the good wine until now" (2:10). Although the precise meaning and import of Jesus' statement in John 2:4 are difficult to determine, his words nevertheless imply some distance between Jesus and his mother. Also troubling is the relationship between Jesus and his brothers. John 7:3–8 implies some tension. His brothers urge him to go up to Judea "so that your disciples also may see the works you are doing; for no one who wants to be widely known acts in secret. If you do these things, show yourself to the world." The narrator comments that "not even his brothers believed in him." Jesus replies, "My time has not yet come, but your time is always here. The world cannot hate you, but it hates me because I testify against it that its works are evil. Go to the festival yourselves. I am not going to this festival, for my time has not yet fully come." This, too, implies distance between himself and his family, who seem not to understand who he really is.

The Synoptic Gospels depict an occasion upon which Jesus denies his familial connections to his mother and siblings. According to Mark 3:31–35 and parallels, "his mother and his brothers came; and standing outside, they sent to him and called him. A crowd was sitting around him; and they said to him, 'Your mother and your brothers and sisters are outside, asking for you.' And he replied, 'Who are my mother and my brothers?' And looking at those who sat around him, he said, 'Here are my mother and my brothers! Whoever does the will of God is my brother and sister and mother.'" Jesus does not sever the connection to his family so much as redefine the notion of family itself. Family ties are no longer to be grounded in biology or genealogy but are to be based on common relationship with God, that is, "doing the will of God." The family's reaction to or feelings about Jesus' behavior are not recorded, but it is not difficult to imagine the hurt and puzzlement that might result from his words.

Both of these stories imply a rupture or at least some tension in Jesus' adult relationship with his mother and siblings. But the presence of Jesus' mother at the foot of the cross, according to John 19:25 and perhaps the Synoptics (see Mark 15:40; Matt. 27:56; Luke 23:49), implies an ongoing relationship or at least some knowledge on her part of his activities and his fate. These stories allow us also to imagine her anguish.

The picture that emerges from the canonical Gospels is of Jesus as a man who begins his life in a close, nuclear family circle. As an adult he leaves his family to strike out on his own, but maintains some level of contact with some family members, or perhaps only his mother. They in turn follow his activities from a distance but are not directly involved. Acts 1:14 mentions that Jesus' mother and brothers were among the group that included the apostles who were staying together after Jesus' death and praying constantly. This may imply but does not require some level of involvement in his ministry.

This portrait may or may not be historically accurate, though it is not implausible. It does, however, testify to the ways in which the early believers put together Jesus' family life and also the tensions that they saw as inherent in his identity as both human and divine. As a human being, he is born into a family and linked socially with them, and as a Jewish human being, he owes honor and respect to his parents. As the Messiah and Son of God (see John 20:30-31), however, his all-consuming relationship must be with God and hence must at least potentially override his obligations to and connections with his biological family.

This tension is not only hinted at in the narratives about Jesus' life but also is made explicit in some of the sayings associated with Jesus in the Synoptic Gospels. In his discussions of Jewish law, the Synoptic Jesus often adjures his audience to observe the fifth commandment, to honor father and mother. In Mark 7:10–13, Jesus declares that any action that violates the fifth commandment makes void the word of God: "For Moses said, 'Honor your father and your mother'; and, 'Whoever speaks evil of father or mother must surely die. But you say that if anyone tells father or mother, 'Whatever support you might have had from me is Corban' (that is, an offering to God)—then you no longer permit doing anything for a father or mother, thus making void the word of God through your tradition that you have handed on. And you do many things like this.'" In Mark 10:19, the commandment to honor father and mother is listed along with several other commandments of the Decalogue, to which Jesus urges obedience: "You shall not murder; You shall not commit adultery; You shall not steal; You shall not bear false witness; You shall not defraud; Honor your father and mother."

One might argue, however, that Jesus himself violates this commandment when he redefines family relationships in terms of allegiance to God, thus giving expression and priority to the need to honor God above any human relationships. Some passages state even more explicitly that following Jesus can or perhaps must require the severing of familial ties. According to Matthew 10:35–38, Jesus says that he has "come to set a man against his father, and a daughter against her mother, and a daughter-in-law against her mother-in-law; and one's foes will be members of one's own household. Whoever loves father or mother more than me is not worthy of me; and whoever loves son or daughter more than me is not worthy of me; and whoever does not take up the cross and follow me is not worthy of me." The point is also made in Matthew 19:29, in which Jesus praises those who leave their homes behind: "And everyone who has left houses or brothers or sisters or father or mother or children or fields for my name's sake will receive a hundredfold, and will inherit eternal life." Mark's version of this passage (Mark 10:28–30) contains a more sinister note, that in leaving behind family one also leaves behind safety but inherits eternal life: "Peter began to say to him, 'Look, we have left everything and followed you.' Jesus said, 'Truly I tell you, there is no one who has left house or brothers or sisters or mother or father or children or fields, for my sake and for the sake of the good news, who will not receive a hundredfold now in this age—houses, brothers and sisters, mothers and children, and fields, with persecutions—and in the age to come eternal life.'"

Luke's Jesus views family dissension as an inevitable product of his ministry: "Do you think that I have come to bring peace to the earth? No, I tell you, but rather division! From now on five in one household will be divided, three against two and two against three; they will be divided: father against son and son against father, mother against daughter and daughter against mother, mother-in-law against her daughter-in-law and daughter-in-law against mother-in-law" (Luke 12:51–53). Indeed, hatred is required. The Lukan Jesus states categorically: "Whoever comes to me and does not hate father and mother, wife and children, brothers and sisters, yes, and even life itself, cannot be my disciple" (Luke 14:26).

Those around Jesus, however, continued to define him by his familial relationships, as in Matthew 13:55 when the crowds in Nazareth ask among themselves, "Is not this the carpenter's son? Is not his mother called Mary? And are not his brothers James and Joseph and Simon and Judas?"

THE HAPPY HOLY FAMILY ON FILM

Filmmakers who wish to adapt the Gospel stories must therefore make some strategic decisions. They have the option of preserving the ambivalent canonical picture of Jesus' family life. This choice is made by Pasolini, who not only depicts the Happy Holy Family at the beach, but also dwells on the pain of Jesus' mother when Jesus rejects his ties to her. Alternatively, filmmakers may decide to resolve the indeterminacies by filling the gaps left by the canonical texts, by omitting elements they view as discordant and/or by bringing all of the family scenes into a coherent picture. In what follows, I will focus on those who choose to fill the gaps. I will argue that in doing so they are also making a theological statement with respect to christology and finding a way to resolve the tensions inherent in the Gospels' portrayal of Jesus as both human and divine.

The Happy Holy Family theme appears most clearly in the narratives that are added to the canonical framework and is expressed in dialogue and plot as well as by visual elements such as gestures, facial expressions, and *mise-en-*

scène, including groupings of characters relative to each other and within the frame. The additions cluster in four main areas: Jesus' childhood, Jesus' adult relationship to his mother, Jesus' mother as his disciple and/or helper, and expansion of or focus on Mary's role at the foot of the cross.

Jesus' Childhood

Pasolini's beach scene is unique among the major Jesus films in that it shows the Happy Holy Family at play. Most other additions to Jesus' early life focus on Jesus' parents as his teachers in early childhood. The early silent film *From the Manger to the Cross* (1912) has a section entitled "Period of Youth" that effectively inserts a number of scenes into Luke 2:40–45. At the outset of the scene, we see the Happy Holy Family at home. Joseph is in the right center of the frame. Occupying much of the left side of the frame are Mary and Jesus, who appears to be six or seven years of age. Mary is seated, with her arm around Jesus, and both are looking intently at a scroll that she has stretched out between them. She appears to be reading to him or with him, and explaining as she goes. Jesus nods his head in understanding. Joseph stops working, leans on his workbench and listens too. Mother and son look fondly and intently at each other. Joseph turns back to his work. Thereupon follows an intertitle stating that the child grew strong in wisdom (Luke 2:40). This intertitle is the transition to the next episode, in which Jesus, now strong not only in wisdom but in body as well, carries a big jug out of the house, followed by Mary. The gestures make it clear that he is helping her with her daily work. Another quotation, from Luke 12:42, follows, regarding their trip to Jerusalem for the Passover. The journey is shown. Despite his size and strength, Jesus rides on the donkey, with his mother walking along beside him and his father out ahead. As in the Lukan narrative, Jesus is left behind when his parents leave, and the film spends several minutes expanding on the parents' distress at his disappearance and their joy at finding him back at the temple. We see the threesome walking away from the temple, Mary with her arm around her son, Jesus looking up lovingly at her face, and Joseph walking along beside Jesus on the other side. In the final scene of this sequence, the young teenage Jesus is carrying a wooden board on his shoulders. This image resonates in two ways. First, it indicates his obedience to his parents, in that he becomes a carpenter like his father. Second, it foreshadows his passion, when he will carry the cross in precisely this manner. The entire sequence entitled "The Period of his Youth" emphasizes the love within the Holy Family and draws on conventions and stereotypes that we see in other films of this era: emphasis on the mother–child bond, the father's role as defined primarily by his profession and his caring for his wife and male child, and tenderness as a characteristic of family relations. The emphasis is also on the nuclear family as a social grouping somewhat isolated and separate from other social units. These elements appear, for example, in the "Modern Story" of D. W. Griffith's *Intolerance*. This film weaves together four stories from four historical periods. The main story, called "The Modern Story," concerns a man, a woman, and their son, and their unfortunate victimization by the forces of intolerance. These same traits are present as the father tries to earn a living despite the general strike, the wife tries to care for her son, and they all react with one another tenderly.

These features, however, are not exclusive to American films from the silent era. They are present to an even greater extent in an Italian film by Roberto Rossellini, *The Messiah*, made some sixty years later. This film portrays Mary as Jesus' teacher and also depicts Joseph as mentoring him in the more practical details of life. This film expands upon the family trip to the temple at Passover time and conflates it with Jesus' coming of age as implied in Luke 2:40–45. We come upon Jesus' mother just outside the tent that the family has set up in the area of the temple compound. She is dressing the young Jesus, tenderly but briskly. Meanwhile she speaks to him intently: "This is a very important day for you. For the first time in your life you will be allowed into the house of the Eternal, to be blessed in his name."

She puts his hat on his head and continues, "For the first time you will dedicate a sacrifice to Him."

She places the prayer shawl (*tallith*) around his shoulders: "Here, this is your *tallith*. Do you know what a *tallith* is? A thousand years ago our people were slaves in Egypt until the joyous day Moses our father, blessed be his name forever, liberated them. And for forty years with the rain and the sun beating down our people walked and walked having as their sole protection a white shawl made from sheep's wool. Since then, every man in Israel has his *tallith*."

Throughout this recitation she continues to fuss over his clothing and to speak to him fervently. "As of today you also are a man. And having become a man, with your head covered by your tallith, you will be able to speak with doctors and teachers who have studied the Holy Law. Because from now on you belong to the Law, my son, as you know, and the Law belongs to you."

She hugs him and kisses him. This is clearly a momentous occasion. A young man, apparently Joseph, arrives, and the child goes off with him.

Joseph places his arm around Jesus' shoulder and explains how to acquire a lamb for the Passover sacrifice. We see a closeup of Jesus' face as they prepare to offer the sacrifice. Jesus watches intently as the lamb is slaughtered, hung up, and disemboweled. The entire scene foreshadows Jesus' sacrifice of his own life at a future Passover feast. The scene then moves to a dramatization of Jesus teaching in the temple, his parents' search, and their joyous reunion. These segments portray the primary function of Joseph and Mary as teaching Jesus about his heritage and preparing him to take his place within the traditional Jewish world into which he was born. In addition to portraying their love for one another, the scenes also educate the movie audience about Jesus' Jewish context and his place within it.

From the Manger and the Cross and *The Messiah* come from different eras and film traditions, yet in both cases the treatment of Jesus' relationship to his parents is similar. Both emphasize the teaching role, give more or less equal time to Mary and Joseph, and assign them to specific spheres of life. This pattern may reflect the filmmakers' assessment of gender roles in the ancient world and/or the persistence of such roles into the twentieth century in the United States and Italy. The films also reflect the specific interests of the filmmakers, for example, the screenwriter of *From the Manger and the Cross* was Gene Gauntier, who also played the role of Mary and may have had an ideological and professional interest in augmenting her role. Rossellini often had very positive female characters in his films. In this film, the figure of Mary takes over some of the narrative and emotive roles that in other films are associated with Jesus.[1]

The parents' teaching function is also prominent in Franco Zeffirelli's made-for-television series *Jesus of Nazareth* (1977). In contrast to the silent *From the Manger to the Cross* and Rossellini's *Messiah*, however, Zeffirelli's representation of Jesus' mother and father is hierarchical, patriarchal, and stereotypical. The Happy Holy Family theme comes to expression in a scene in which the family is seen praying together, a dramatization of the cliché that the family that prays together stays together. Joseph recites the *Shema,* "Hear, O Israel, the eternal our God the eternal is one. They all bow. Mary has her hand on the child's shoulder. Here, as in many scenes throughout the Jesus film genre, there is greater proximity between Jesus and his mother than between Jesus and his father.

Immediately after this scene, we see Joseph teaching a group of the children including Jesus. Joseph conveys not only the principles of carpentry but also their deeper meaning: "Our work has a second meaning in God's eyes.

As we use a ruler to make straight lines, God gave us rules to keep our lives straight. . . . God gives the wood and man with his skill and invention that God gave him is always finding new uses, sometimes wonderful uses for it . . . wheel, plough, ladder." The young Jesus (blond, blue-eyed), looks pensive as Joseph explains that "a ladder can sometimes reach from earth to heaven." Joseph may have Jacob's ladder in mind (Gen. 28:12), but Jesus, like any other young child, takes him quite literally and climbs up a tall ladder nearby while his father's back is turned. We see the beauty of the land that the child surveys, and watch as his father's eyes, catching him on his way up the ladder, express first panic and then joy.

Jesus' mother is absent from this teaching event. We see her in the scene that follows, set in the synagogue on the occasion of Jesus' coming of age ceremony, or bar mitzvah, in the synagogue. She peers at Jesus from behind the separation (mehitzah) in the synagogue as he reads from the Torah in the men's section and is praised by the rabbi. As in Rossellini's film, Joseph is portrayed as instructing Jesus on the choice of a sacrificial lamb. As they proceed up to Jerusalem, Joseph tells Jesus to look at the city, and the camera provides us with an extreme closeup of his intent gaze, as if to imply that he knows what will happen to him in this place in the future. Later, Joseph places a pure white lamb on Jesus' shoulders and kneels down to tell him: "This is a lamb without blemish," and smiles at him. This brief moment not only reflects the joy at Jesus' coming of age but also foreshadows his passion, when he himself will be the sacrificial lamb. Mary is prominent throughout the film, particularly in the early segments, which portray the betrothal, annunciation, and infancy. But she does not emerge from the role of the pure and passive spiritual beauty: she remains in her place both literally and figuratively behind the mehitzah, or barrier, that separates the genders.

These various additions to the canonical representation of Jesus' early life stress a number of points: the intense love between Jesus and his parents; the close proximity of the mother, and the hint that this relationship is more intense than that between Jesus and Joseph; the normalcy of Jesus' childhood in the nuclear family; and his learning a trade from his father and other skills, such as his place in Judaism and his knowledge of Jewish tradition, from his mother. Jesus is shown as an obedient, loving, helpful child at all points except when his allegiance to his "real" father, that is, God, causes distress and temporarily disrupts the harmony of his earthly family.

This portrayal has christological implications. The fact that Jesus is closer to his mother than to his father coheres with the notion, already present in

the infancy narratives of Matthew and Luke, that while Mary is truly his biological mother, it is God and not Joseph who is Jesus' "real" father. The other
elements emphasize his humanity, but show that it fulfilled the twentieth-
century ideal of a nuclear family, bonded by intense love, in which it is the
role of the parents to teach the children in their own separate spheres (home/
culture vs. profession) and the children's duty to obey, honor, and return their
parents' loving concern. Thus, in the christology of Hollywood, Jesus' early
life hints at his future role and his divine paternity, but in all everyday respects
he is much the same as any lucky child raised by his parents whose sole purpose in life is to love him, teach him, and ensure his well-being.

THE ADULT JESUS
AND HIS RELATIONSHIP TO HIS MOTHER

In scenes that are added to fill out the adult Jesus' relationship to his mother,
the christological balance is reversed. Jesus' primary relationship now is with
God, whose will he obeys and in whose service he wanders, collects followers, heals, and teaches. Implicit in these films is the question of how Jesus' fil-
ial allegiance to God affects his human family relations. The canonical Gospels
suggest that family ties all but fall by the wayside as Jesus carries out his divine
mission. This pattern is also evident in a number of Jesus films, such as
Pasolini's *Gospel According to St. Matthew*, in which Mary's anguish and distress at her son's denial of family ties are obvious in her facial expressions.
Martin Scorsese's *Last Temptation of Christ* not only portrays Jesus' troubling
words of rejection but lingers on this scene. As Jesus is walking along with his
disciples, healing the lame and the sick, his mother catches up to him and
says, "Son, come back with me, please."

Jesus says to her in genuine puzzlement, "Who are you?"

She is shocked that he does not recognize her. She answers, "Your mother."

Jesus says, "I don't have a mother. I don't have any family, but I have a
father, in heaven."

"Don't say that to me," she moans.

He repeats, "Who are you, I mean really?" He treats her gently but dis-
tantly; he kisses her on the forehead and walks on.

She breaks down in tears. A woman who had witnessed the exchange
approaches and says, "Mary, why are you crying? Didn't you see them? When
he spoke to you there were thousands of blue wings behind him, armies of
angels . . . thousands."

Mary replies, "I'd be happier if there weren't." This scene raises but does not resolve the question of why she is crying. It might seem at first glance that she is crying because of his refusal, or perhaps his inability, to recognize her. But the final exchange suggests that in fact her tears come from her knowledge of the fate that awaits him.

Other films omit this sequence and instead portray an ongoing loving relationship between Jesus and his mother. In doing so they do not critique the high christology which focuses on Jesus as God's son but rather attempt to keep Mary in the picture while acknowledging the priority of Jesus' relationship with God. Joseph is completely out of the picture, having faded away without a trace, except in Zeffirelli's magnum opus which leaves no gap unfilled. Zeffirelli has a lengthy deathbed scene in which the dying Joseph is tended by his loving wife. He worries about Mary being left alone and then says, "We have always known that it was not for us that Jesus came to earth. If only he could have stayed a little longer. God's will be done." His last words are those that Jesus will later say upon the cross: "Into thy hand I commend my spirit" (Luke 23:46).

Three basic trends can be seen in the cinematic treatment of the adult relationship. One views Mary as a follower or disciple of Jesus, perhaps inspired by Acts 1:14. This view is also plausible in light of the information about Jesus' identity to which Mary is privy from the moment the angel appeared to her in the annunciation scenes in Matthew and Luke. In Cecil B. DeMille's silent film *From the Manger to the Cross*, Mary's faith in her son's messianic identity can be surmised from a scene early in the film in which Mary leads a blind girl to Jesus for healing. That Mary followed Jesus is implied also by a scene in Nicholas Ray's *King of Kings*, which begins with a voice-over narration: "For many months Jesus preached in Judea . . . he angered the scribes and Pharisees, who thought how they might kill him, and numbered his days and knowing the sum thereof, Jesus came to spend time with his mother." Meanwhile we see Mary joyfully rushing toward him with her water jug. The two greet and kiss each other joyfully. He takes the jug from her and follows her into the house. She seems rather agitated, however. As Jesus sets about fixing a chair, she paces the room and winds wool onto a skein. The music contributes to this mood of anxious anticipation. In come Peter and John, who tell Jesus, "We have done all that you asked. It is time we leave for Jerusalem."

Jesus tells her, "The chair will have to wait until I return."

She replies, "The chair will never be mended." An intense look passes between them. Mary walks purposefully, sets down the skein, and declares, "I am going with you." Here it is not clear whether she is prompted primarily by faith or by maternal love and the desire to protect him or at least to share his fate.

This theme is developed at greatest length by Rossellini, whose film stresses that Mary not only accompanied Jesus but also was actively involved in his teaching mission. The beginning of this partnership seems to be the moment that Jesus is chased out of the synagogue (implied in Matt. 13:57). She catches up with him; they walk along together. Later we see that she is a teacher about the kingdom of God, in the fishing community on the shores of the Sea of Galilee where they all seem to work. We observe Jesus teaching as he does some carpentry work; then the camera turns to Mary. She is working, perhaps baking, and talking about the kingdom of heaven to a young child who is sitting on her lap. "When everyone remembers to love, this will be the kingdom of God and fulfilment of the Law."

The child asks, "How will this kingdom of heaven be?"

She responds, "Beautiful . . . " Her leadership role is also implied in the fact that when some members feel they must leave, in order to protect the children from the Roman soldiers, they apologize to Mary, who, we know, will never leave her son's side. "Mary, forgive us, the children . . . ," they say.

A second widespread element, evident in the scene from Scorsese's film described above, is the fear of the mother for her son—the sword that will pierce her soul (Luke 2:35). In the silent film *INRI* (1923), Mary wanders around in the wilderness in search of her adult son, who has departed for Jerusalem. Late at night, she comes upon a group of shepherds sitting by the fire. She tells them her story and they invite her to sit with them and eat. She says, "I seek Jesus of Nazareth. Know ye aught of him?" They tell her that "he is lodged even now within the city gates." We presume, though we are not told, that the city is Jerusalem. One adds, "He comes from God, he is the Messiah." Despite the late hour, and despite the protests of the shepherds, she leaves immediately to continue her search, for, as she says, she cannot rest until she finds him. Some time later, she does find him in Jerusalem. She stands at the back of the crowd that is watching and listening as he teaches his disciples. Unnoticed, she edges closer, leans against the pillar, watches, and listens. The camera cuts back and forth between her and Jesus until Jesus notices her. They exchange glances; she holds out her arms; he rises slowly and walks into her arms; they embrace warmly. He does not put his arms around her, but leans his head into her breast, as a young child might do. She clutches his hand and says: "Those who cling to thee now will desert thee in the hour of need. Yet will I be with thee." In this case the mother's devotion is seen not so much as a product of her faith in his messianic identity, which is taken for granted, but as her desperate need to be with him in his time of need, thereby fulfilling her role as his mother.

A similar scene appears in DeMille's *King of Kings*. Mary is waiting outside the room where the disciples have been having their "last supper" with Jesus. As the men leave the room, the atmosphere is ominous and solemn. She says, "O my beloved Son, wilt thou not return to Nazareth with me? Here, I fear thine enemies." Mother and son embrace lovingly, but Jesus leaves, as do the others, while she has her back turned to them, very sad. The camera lingers on the empty room, the laden table, with a glowing wine goblet in its center. A dove, associated early in the film with Mary, flies around the goblet, to the accompaniment of sad and solemn music. In this film too, Mary's belief is taken for granted, but she is not among those who accompany him, and she is motivated in her behavior by a natural fear for the fate that awaits him.

Fear for her son also motivates the Mary of George Stevens's *Greatest Story Ever Told*. Here Jesus visits his mother, and they greet each other warmly. Lazarus, though ill, comes to see Jesus along with his sisters Mary and Martha. He warns Jesus of the danger that he will be arrested imminently. Jesus takes tender leave of his mother. She doesn't say anything, but they exchange glances as he leaves. The scene implies their sense that they will never see each other again. Mother reaches out her hands to Lazarus and siblings. Poignant music is in the background throughout.

A third, tragic moment of family togetherness is the crucifixion. Mary reappears at the cross in the majority of the Jesus films. Often the camera lingers on her suffering face as she watches him die on the cross, and then again in the "Pietà" scene in which she cradles the dead Jesus in her arms after he is taken down from the cross. The role of the mother is emphasized, for example, by Nicholas Ray in *King of Kings*. Ray's scene is based on John 19:25, in which Jesus gives his mother over to the care of the Beloved Disciple with the words "Woman, behold your son." In Ray's rendition, the Beloved Disciple is absent from the scene; the camera work indicates that these words direct Mary to behold her son Jesus as he is dying on the cross. In Scorsese's *Last Temptation of Christ*, Jesus calls for his mother and for Mary Magdalene from the cross. Most interesting, again, is Rossellini's *Messiah*. This film omits the conventional procession of Jesus with the cross, during which he stumbles, and instead focuses on Mary's running through the streets of Jerusalem, following the cross to Golgotha, and stumbling twice. In this way Rossellini implies, as he does when he shows her teaching, that Mary truly participates fully in the mission and death of her son.

In adulthood, the Happy Holy Family has changed; Joseph has disappeared, to make way for God as the Father. Nor is it entirely happy, in the sense of being carefree. But it remains a loving family focused on Jesus. It still presents a hierarchical relationship, but it is not one based on age or gender but rather on what Elisabeth Schüssler Fiorenza has called kyriarchy. All is focused on Jesus. In becoming his disciple, his mother also subordinates herself to him. In this way, filmmakers resolve the christological tensions inherent in the view that Jesus is both human and divine.

On the whole, films tend to uphold the theological status quo: hence the tendency to affirm Jesus' identity as Son of God and his mother's status as follower. Many factors contribute to this theological conservatism: the filmmakers' frequently expressed wish to affirm faith, formal and informal censorship, and audience considerations. But there are some films that subvert, mock, or challenge the status quo in various ways.

Luis Buñuel's film *The Milky Way* depicts the adventures of two pilgrims on their way to Santiago de Compostela in Spain. It includes "flashbacks" to the story of Jesus that provide a hilarious spoof of the theme of the Happy Holy Family and, in particular, the piously harmonious relationship between mother and son. In one scene, Mary admires her son the carpenter because of his handsome beard. A second, lengthier scene is a pastiche of the Wedding at Cana and the Last Supper. Jesus is shown running down the path. A man reports: "Master, the guests have arrived. Your mother and brothers await you." Jesus answers, "Here are my mother and brother." This leads us to expect that, as in the Synoptic Gospels, Jesus will now redefine his notion of family. But no, after a brief interlude, the camera returns to the feast, which is now identified as a wedding, and we see Jesus eating and talking and laughing. His mother is close by, telling those around her about her feelings upon discovering that she was pregnant by the Holy Spirit. "At first I didn't believe, then I was very happy." As in the work of some classical artists in this film, Jesus' mother does not age, either physically or emotionally—as her rather immature behavior implies. She remains the teenage girl who is awestruck by the famous son to whom she gave birth. Buñuel's targets here are the clichés and conventions of the art and film tradition as well as Mariology in the Catholic Church.

That the Happy Holy Family was indeed holy—in other words, that Jesus' mother was a virgin impregnated by God or the Holy Spirit—is accepted in most of the Jesus films, many of which portray the angel's annunciation to Mary and/or Joseph in one form or another. This notion is critiqued, however, in the 1989 Canadian film by Denys Arcand, *Jesus of Montreal*. This film follows a small acting troupe as they prepare and perform a passion play on the grounds of St. Joseph's Oratory, a Catholic shrine atop Mont Royal in Montreal. The passion play includes a documentary-like narration in which Arcand presents a view of Jesus' life that is at odds both with the Gospel accounts and with historical-Jesus research. Arcand picks up on the rabbinic derision of the Christian belief in Mary's virginity. He has his actors declare: "Paradoxically, Jesus wasn't Christian but Jewish. He was circumcised and observed Jewish Law. . . . The Jews claimed that Jesus was a false prophet, born of fornication. They called him Yeshu Ben Panthera, 'the son of Panthera.' We've discovered an order to transfer a soldier from Capernaum in 6 A.D. His name was Panthera. Jews always referred to a man as 'his father's son.' Unless he was illegitimate. When Jesus returned to his village, the villagers cried out, 'Is not this the carpenter? The son of Mary?'" The contradiction of Mary's virginity fits into the more general effort of this film to diminish Jesus' uniqueness as well as his divinity.

The circumstances under which the Messiah was born come to the fore also in Monty Python's *Life of Brian*. To be sure, this film is not a Jesus film as such. Jesus appears briefly as a character, but his representation is always very distanced, respectful, and clichéd. Its main character, Brian, is a figure whose life parallels that of Jesus to an extraordinary degree, but in a much more colorful and comical way. Because it is a "Brian movie" rather than a "Jesus movie," the film can have some fun with the Jesus tradition and its cinematic forms through its portrayal of the life of Brian. Brian is very concerned with his genealogy and Jewish identity. One day he comes home to the abode he shares with his mother to find that she is preparing to "entertain" a Roman soldier. As an anti-Roman revolutionary, Brian is naturally very upset about this. His response forces his mother to reveal the secret of his paternity to him. She tells Brian: "Your father isn't Mr. Cohen. . . . He was a Roman, Brian, he was a centurion in the Roman army. Nautius Maximus. . . . The next time you go on about the bloody Romans, don't forget you're one of them." Brian responds in somewhat childish anger, "I'm not a Roman, I never will be! I'm a kike, a yid, a hebie, a hook-nose, I'm kosher, mum, I'm a red sea pedestrian and proud of it." He stalks off. This scene is not to be taken as a serious challenge to Jesus' divine paternity. It derives its humor at least in part from Brian's emphatic application to himself of every anti-Semitic epithet in the book. But on this issue, as throughout, the film presents an alternative biography that uses not only ancient sources and contemporary life-of-Jesus research but also imagination and a wacky sense of humor.[2]

Finally, the issue of christology and the question of whether Jesus' identity as Son of God was known to him or to those around him are suggested in Scorsese's *Last Temptation of Christ*. Like the Monty Python troupe, Scorsese is careful at the outset to clarify that his film is not intended as a historical study or an adapation of the Gospels per se. Rather, it is based on the novel *The Last Temptation of Christ*, by Nikos Kazantzakis. This disclaimer seems intended to allow Scorsese the freedom to explore sensitive issues without raising the ire of conservative Christians—though this strategy did not in fact work.[3] Like Python's Brian, Scorsese's Jesus lives with his mother well into adulthood. She is concerned about him, particularly about the dangers involved in his collaboration with the Romans, for whom he builds and sets up crosses for crucifixion. One day, as Jesus is helping with a particularly tragic case, she arrives on the crucifixion field and asks him to come with her. He refuses to do so. That night he has a nightmare. We see him writhing on the ground, as she tries to wake him up. He moans, "God loves me, I know he loves me, I want him to stop. I can't take the pain, the voices . . . I want to crucify every one of his messiahs. I want him to hate me. . . ."

At breakfast the next morning, she asks him, "You're sure it's God, you're sure it's not the devil?"

He responds, "I'm not sure."

She continues, "The devil . . . the devil can be cast out."

Jesus counters, "But what if it is God? You can't cast out God, can you?" He packs provisions and leaves. Throughout this film, Jesus is never sure whether the impulses that prompt him and that rule his life are from God or the devil. This ambivalence comes to the fore also in the temptation scenes, where he receives a number of apparitions who claim to come from God but in fact are the manifestations of the devil. It occurs also in the final dream sequence, where Jesus is taken down from the cross by a red-headed girl who claims to be his guardian angel sent by God to forestall the final sacrifice of his life. In the end, this angel turns out to be the most dangerous manifestation of the devil.

CONCLUSIONS

The Jesus films are not strict adaptations of their source texts, nor are they theological treatises. The pieces that they add to the Gospel accounts testify, however, to the essential tensions between Jesus' human and divine dimensions. The human aspects are highlighted in the Happy Holy Family motif, in the scenes of Jesus' contented childhood in the bosom of his family and in his loving adult relationship with his mother. Implicit in this treatment are a number of conventional assumptions of modern Western society: the connection between childhood experiences and adult identity and the notion that one of the marks of a good and mature adult is the quality of her or his relationship with parents and other family members. As a perfect human being, Jesus must have had a happy childhood, and he must have retained a lifelong, loving relationship with his mother.

From the point of view of the Christian Scriptures and subsequent Christianity, of course, Jesus is preeminently not the son of Mary and certainly not of Joseph, but rather of God. Therefore, his relationship with God comes first and overrides all human relationships. This aspect of Jesus' identity is extraordinarily difficult to capture on film. Most Jesus films refer to Jesus as Son of God but fail to portray Jesus' divine connections convincingly, if at all, until the final scenes of the crucifixion and resurrection.

The theme of the Happy Holy Family therefore contributes primarily to a low christology by implying that Jesus, like all human beings, is a product of family life. Jesus' mother plays a particularly important role in this regard. One might imagine that the cinema's interest in Mary could be explained on the basis of her important role in Catholicism. But, on the whole, her film presence serves a christological purpose, insofar as it helps to flesh out (so to speak) Jesus' personality and experiences and to transform him simultaneously into a role model and a focus of faith.

No one would argue that the directors and producers of Jesus films are New Testament exegetes, just as it is plain that they are not theologians. Applying the hermeneutics of suspicion to their work reveals the extent to which the Jesus films do not reflect a critical stance toward the Gospels but rather play upon modern Western conventions, beliefs, and attitudes. At the same time, however, their creativity in itself points to genuine tensions and ambiguities within the New Testament as well as within Christian theology and, in doing so, enhances our critical hermeneutical work itself.

NOTES

1. Peter Brunette, *Robert Rossellini* (Berkeley: University of California Press, 1996), 346.

2. Rabbinic sources for this claim include *b. Shabbat* 104b and *b. Sanhedrin* 67a;

there are also many other places where this idea can be found. The notion that the Jews believed Jesus' father to have been Panthera appears also in early Christian sources, e.g., *Acts of Pilate* 2.3–6; Origen, *Against Celsus*, book 1, chs. xxviii, xxii. See also Jane Schaberg, *The Illegitimacy of Jesus: A Feminist Theological Interpretation of the Infancy Narratives* (San Francisco: Harper & Row, 1987).

3. For an account of the uproar that greeted the release of Scorsese's film, see Michael Medved, *Hollywood Vs. America: Popular Culture and the War on Traditional Values* (San Francisco: HarperCollins, 1992).

9

Wisdom's Deviant Ways

Tina Pippin

THEORIES OF DEVIANT BEHAVIORS

IN AN IMAGINATIVE MOVE, ELISABETH SCHÜSSLER FIORENZA SUGGESTS a way to engage the story of the "wo/man anointing Jesus." She rereads the versions of this story as part of her agenda for a "hermeneutics of creative imagination." Schüssler Fiorenza defines this method as one that

> seeks to generate utopian visions that have not yet been realized, to "dream" a different world of justice and well-being. The space of imagination is that of freedom, a space in which boundaries are crossed, possibilities are explored, and time becomes relativized. What we cannot imagine will not take place. The imagination is a space of memory and possibility where situations can be re-experienced and desires re-embodied.[1]

Schüssler Fiorenza imagines a role-play to interpret the story in Mark 14:3–9, Luke 7:36–50, Matthew 26:6–13, and John 12:1–8. Her playful reading calls for interviewing the characters and writer of each Gospel and playing the parts of different characters (those in the story and imagined in the margins, such as "the poor" and "the granddaughter of the woman").[2] This clever pedagogical exercise is a way to engage students in the dance of Wisdom, and to imagine justice-readings and the "*ekklēsia* of wo/men." For Schüssler Fiorenza, this dance is necessary to break through the bonds of patriarchal interpretation and make new meanings by exploring the gaps in the text. She encourages us "to make present Divine Wisdom in the 'blank spaces' between the biblical wo/men and our own lives. Hence, every enactment is different."[3] In these ways, "wisdom ways," wo/men readers can engage in transformative play that links the reading of biblical texts with lived experience (past, present, and future).

This hermeneutic is a part of Schüssler Fiorenza's agenda for feminist biblical interpretation for those who seek to remain within faith communities. Her political agenda is clear and is grounded in her work conversing with third world women and in her strong antiviolence campaign (strong in both theory and commitment). The importance of this hermeneutic was made clearer to me at a session on her book *Wisdom Ways* at the annual meeting of the Society of Biblical Literature in Toronto in 2002. This book provided the framework of a session of the Academic Teaching and Biblical Studies Section entitled "Pedagogy and Practice: Using *Wisdom Ways* in the Classroom." Three respondents, Jane Schaberg, David Barr, and Katie Cannon, spoke about the usefulness of the pedagogical exercises in various classroom settings (church-related university, state university, and seminary, respectively). Schaberg spoke about why readings are and must be political. Cannon related her experiences of teaching for transformation by using creative imagination as a source for ethics. Both women respondents used the exercises in the book with classes out of their commitment to feminist and womanist pedagogies. The book reinforced the need to trust students more and share power and authority in the classroom. Schüssler Fiorenza notes that at the root of biblical authority is "the original Latin meaning of *augere/auctoritas* as enhancing, nurturing, and enriching creativity."[4] Schaberg and Cannon shared a commitment to a pedagogy that not only sees the approach to biblical authority as a power-sharing activity but also extends this basic notion of authority to the classroom. In such pedagogy of engagement, real-life contexts come into direct conversations with biblical texts. Barr took a different approach, defending malestream biblical studies against such unravelings. Schüssler Fiorenza responded by upholding a critical pedagogy that puts the students (not the textbook) in the center. She called for an "embodied scholarship" in which students and teachers find their own voices: "You can't do the work of justice if you don't have a voice." This session revealed the ongoing divisions in biblical studies—the malestream "Voice" and the voices of the broad range of readers/interpreters of the Bible.

I would like to push the theoretical underpinnings of this debate further. Schüssler Fiorenza remains a reconstructionist, making meaning in communities of wo/men within a framework of socioliterary and historical-critical methods, while I like to push against those boundaries and explore postmodern territories. I continue to want to explore the possibilities of deconstructing biblical texts. Structures such as faith, etymologies, Roman society, and authorship spin off into different territories across the centuries and cultures. Schüssler Fiorenza's approach to the story of the woman anointing Jesus is an important entry into a dialogical way of reading texts; the realities of wo/men's lives converge with the biblical text. The politics of wo/men's lives, both biblical and contemporary, are central. I think postmodern critical theories can add to this justice-oriented discourse. Postmodernism is another step in the dance/s.

This biblical story of the woman anointing Jesus exists in multiple worlds: in art, in cultures, in knowledges, and in politics. I will visit only a few of these worlds in this reading, and I want to throw into chaos such reconstructionist beliefs as Schüssler Fiorenza's: "The unnamed woman who names Jesus with a sign-action in Mark's gospel is the paradigm of a true disciple."[5] Does this mean that this woman, as opposed to the male disciples, is the one who really understands the outcome of Jesus' life by preparing him for burial/kingship? Maybe, but I don't think the narrative is so straightforward, no matter where she anoints him. Or as a paradigm of true discipleship is this woman showing that women really did have a dominant place and role in the leadership of the early church, and her story, not Judas's, needs to be lifted up and out of this anointing narrative? While I'm sure this is one possible and important reading, I'm not so sure we can ever know "origins." And I'm especially uneasy about locking in a view that we can ever know this woman's motives or intentions. Schüssler Fiorenza is encouraging me to explore the gaps, and I accept this invitation, while rejecting a search for the god-of-the-gaps (or goddess-of-the-gaps).

While I grant the importance of reading each story individually and respecting the integrity of the Gospel writers, as Schüssler Fiorenza shows with her creative exercise with this story, I see in this "story" a collusion of the individual Gospel passages into a sort of diatesseron, a unitary text. The story is present in all four canonical Gospels, yet it merges in the retellings to one story. This blending is not smooth but rather chaotic; un/named wo/man,[6] a sinner or not, anointing head or feet. Rather than focus on one of the Gospels, I want to explore this tangle of texts.

A FEW DEVIANT READINGS

This story of the un/named woman anointing Jesus resounds with echoes. I hear echoes of (in no particular order): head, hair, feet, food, ointment, the disenfranchisement of the poor, erotic touch, (in)hospitality, burial preparation, life, luxury, political anointing, *christos* (anointed one), death, scent, wisdom, *logos,* danger, purity. This story in its various tellings says a lot about Jesus, about Wisdom, about strange and potentially dangerous women, about how the community is to care for the poor. I want to focus on a few parts of the pictures these tellings create.

First, the woman's hair. Although only mentioned by Luke and John, her hair is a dominant echo, and one that sounds danger. There are echoes through the nineteenth century in which, according to Bram Dijkstra, "women's hair was fetishized . . . [as] the perfect example of the process of 'cultural entrapment.'" Long hair could represent a "symbolic lasso." Woman's hair could be Medusa's snakes, poisonous, "tempting tentacles" that men must avoid.[7] Dijkstra relates this heady/hairy threat, "Hair was not the only lure with which woman attempted to drag the male soul seekers back down to earth. Every feature of her material being could serve, and every legend and historical incident was combed for new suggestions of woman's perverse ability to unseat the male from his lofty spiritual promontory."[8] Even Jesus is not safe from such potentially dangerous tresses.

Whenever dangerous women's hair is evoked, Medusa comes to mind. Mieke Bal, in her head-hunting exercise in reading the book of Judith, finds Michelangelo da Caravaggio's *Medusa's Head* (1600–1601). The painting shows Medusa just before Perseus beheads her; apparently she is gazing in the mirror he holds before her. Bal studies the juxtaposition and confusion of paintings of Perseus with the head of Medusa and Judith holding the head of Holofernes. The standard Freudian line is, of course, that beheading and castration are linked. Bal relates, "Which gender kills becomes totally confused."[9] In Bal's reading, is male or female beheading or being beheaded? The famous pairs are Perseus/Medusa, Jael/Sisera, Delilah/Sampson, David/Goliath, Judith/Holofernes, Salome/Herod(itas)/John the Baptist, and (now I add) un/named wo/man/Jesus. The scorecard on women who mess with men's heads in the Bible warns that such encounters do not usually end well for the men. The women are bearers of the news of death; they have the power to bring death, either by their own hands or through instructions to others. In Matthew and Mark the unnamed woman comes in and begins messing with Jesus' head. Is no one nervous about the possibilities? Perhaps yet another death "by the hand of a woman" (Jdt. 13:15)? The Gospel writers immediately cut to a discourse about the expense of the ointment/perfume and the poor. But let us go back to that entrance and head/hair mussing. There is intertextual weight here; this woman is armed (but there is no visible sword or hammer and tent peg, only the alabastar jar) and dangerous. Is she a murderer, a prostitute, or merely (!) an embalmer? Jesus' head (and feet) remain intact and sweeter smelling by the end of this story.

But death has entered in an excessive way; expensive perfume, costing almost a year's pay for a day laborer, is used to prepare Jesus for burial. Not just his head, but his whole body is included in the death pronouncement. The woman speaks only through her action of touch, but what is she saying? That Jesus is king, Messiah, a corpse? The head is fetishized but also the feet; both point (for Freud) to possible castration. Artemisia Gentileschi (1593–1651) painted a series on Judith over several years. In her first representation of Judith cutting off the head with the help of her maid (*Judith Slaying Holofernes* [1612–13]), Gentileschi painted a violent scene of castration; Holofernes' arms look like thighs and his head is blurry. In her 1620 remake of this painting, the artist steps back slightly, thinning Holofernes' arms and showing a part of his right thigh and knee. Mieke Bal calls this visual experience "an act of miss-seeing, of the same order as miss-taking arms for thighs, women for men."[10] So perhaps I am miss-seeing this un/named woman entering the house where Jesus is; she is not Judith/Jael entering the tent. She holds a jar of perfumed ointment, not a sword. This woman is not scary; we know what she comes to do; she merely prepares the body for the upcoming crucifixion by committing the political act of anointing the head. Besides, she only uses her loose hair to wipe Jesus' feet; there is no chaos or danger caused by her hair in the stories where she anoints Jesus' head. Maybe I am the one who is head hunting, expecting Judith to step in from the white pages of the text. Judith, like the un/named woman, was a woman of great faith (and seductive deception?). Judith's famous (murderous) act came out of that faith. Or is Jael or Delilah or Salome lurking in these intertextual spaces? When I open the New Testament again, will the text remain the same (as if it ever remains the same!), or will I find that the un/named wo/man has a sword or scissors, poised to cut off Jesus' power? Or will I be too late—the woman beating the Roman soldiers to the punch—a head rolling my way? Will it be Jesus' head or the head of Medusa? Or was it Medusa who stepped into the text, her snakes nipping at Jesus' toes, and in one brief instance turning all the men to stone? There is shape-shifting going on here, as Bal asks about the representations of "Judith": "Could she/it be the representation of an alternative story of origin, not one where the one gender's wholeness must be safeguarded by the other's fragmentation, but one where fragmentation is endorsed to prevent 'wholeness' from being pressed into service as an excuse for the fierce safeguarding of separation?"[11] I want to turn Bal's question around: How can a story that is seen as linking, through the prophetic, political act of the un/named woman's anointing, to Jesus' death be also a(nother) story about cutting him off from his disciples, his teaching, his life? In Mark's Gospel the plot to kill Jesus directly precedes the anointing. What better "way to arrest Jesus by stealth and kill him" (Mark 14:1) than by the hands of a woman? Enter a strange woman with something in her hand . . .

Is the anointing a foretext for his cross and burial, as traditional readings hold? Or is this act a foreplay of what could potentially be the ultimate erotic derailment (*sans* sword) of Jesus' mission? Robin Morgan notes, in her critique of Joseph Campbell's idea of the hero, that in Campbell's schema the hero must beware of such generous offerings. The mere presence of the female spells danger, especially if she steps out of her patriarchally defined place:

> But now she appears as a *being unto herself.* Now she is not present solely as a source of support for *him.* And now she is dangerous. Now she is the temptress, the Medusa, the Wild Woman of Russian folklore, the Jezebel, the Magdalen, the witch. If, before, she existed (in his eyes) as a boon to be used and discarded, now she exists (in his eyes) as a threat to be fled from or conquered. She is object; he is subject. She is noun; he is verb.[12]

For Campbell, "The hero of yesterday becomes the tyrant of tomorrow, unless he crucifies *himself* today" and transcends what this woman represents.[13] Is this Markan (and parallels) scene what Gail Streete calls "the return and revenge of the Strange Woman?"[14] Or is she Wisdom, full of eschatological knowledge? Is she a trickster/demon or a prophet? Or all of these? Streete states that "the woman is the mirror in which Jesus as strange Wisdom is reflected."[15] The lines between the strange and wise woman are fluid. The Strange Woman, whoever she was, became "a being unto herself" in the guise of Mary of Bethany or Mary of Magdala–or (repentant) prostitutes everywhere. The story cannot hold her. As Streete says, Jesus "protects Wise and Strange Woman from the assailants," and the memory of her deed is held up so that what she has done will be told in remembrance of her" (Mark 14:9).[16] Jesus may serve as protector in this scene, but this woman enters and exits the narrative as "a being unto herself," yet intertextual echoes continue to drift around her.

So how to sort out the relations of male/female, wisdom/folly/*logos,* and so on? The traditional German dialectical thought of my training is not helpful any more. In her study of John's Prologue, Alison Jasper draws on Hildegard of Bingen, who made the connections of Word/Logos with female wisdom and flesh. Women embody and sustain the Word. In medieval mystical performance, women could also devour the Word/Flesh through the phenomenon of *inedia*, surviving on the eucharistic bread and wine (see also Carolyn Bynum on this topic). Hildegard's theology was that of the Word acknowledging the flesh as a "delightful garment and a beautiful adornment." Jasper asks: "Does Hildegard's sapiential theology go some way towards articulating a heterogeneous *jouissance* that may deconstruct a divine economy constructed within the (masculine) symbolic order of the Christian churches simply to serve the needs and anxieties of men?[17] Hildegard resurrected the pleasure concepts and relinked the Word–Wisdom connection pulled apart by Augustine.

Perhaps Nikos Kazantzakis (and following him, Martin Scorsese) in *The Last Temptation of Christ* was onto something other than the usual form of humanizing Jesus by connecting him with (unfulfilled) sexual desires and the temptation these entail. These desires could potentially drag Jesus to earth permanently, as in D. H. Lawrence's portrayal of a Jesus who survives the crucifixion to recuperate and join with a priestess of Isis.[18] The priestess wants to anoint Jesus' crucifixion scars and also the rest of his body. She is Isis; she considers Jesus her Osiris. Jesus relates the story of his first anointing by a woman, and the priestess asks, "Did you let her serve you with the corpse of her love?" Jesus replies, "I asked them all [the disciples] to serve me with the corpse of their love. And in the end I offered them only the corpse of my love. This is my body—take and eat—my corpse—."[19] What Jesus realizes is that he previously engaged others with a disembodied love. For Lawrence, it is sexual experience that "resurrects" Jesus—all under the gaze of a pagan goddess in her temple. In other words, Jesus' bodily resurrection is a raising up to life and sexual desire, with emphasis not on the spirit but on the flesh, blood, and body.

Or back to hair: the hair could be a pointer—to the feet of Jesus (in Luke and John), toenails, calluses, and all—or the head (in Mark and Matthew), hair, face, and neck—that is the *body* of Jesus.[20] Jesus' body—his physical presence—in the room becomes central, and the other bodies, the strange woman, Judas, and others, revolve around this body. Literary critic Peter Brooks notes that bodies can be unveiled, transgressive, and spiritual. In terms of the body of Jesus he observes:

> Then there is the central Christian story of the Incarnation, of the word made flesh, repeated every time the Eucharist is celebrated. The insistence on the

bodiliness of Christ is an endless source of narrative within the Christian tradition, since the adventures of the flesh on the way to the redemption of mankind [*sic*] provide a series of emblematic moments where spiritual significances are embodied. From the early Middle Ages through the Renaissance, writers in the West necessarily see sign and meaning in terms of embodiment and spirit. . . . In Shakespeare, for instance, the body is omnipresent as both metaphor and physical presence, be it the anointed body of the king or the sweating, decaying body of Falstaff, and the organization of human society is regularly described in terms of a body, whole or sick.[21]

So the church as the body of Christ by the time of Augustine is to uphold this focus on the spiritual body. But the Gospels drag us down to earth—the smell of the expensive, perfumed oil, the loose hair wiping the feet.

Norman Mailer turns to his own peculiar fantasies in his first-person novel of Jesus' life, *The Gospel According to the Son*:

> But this spikenard had power over me. Its aroma entered my ears as well as my nose, and I heard the Song of Songs. First came the voice of the Bride. She said: "While the king sat at his table, my spikenard sent forth its fragrance."

The disciples object to the woman's action based on their focus on the poor. But Jesus is swayed by her act:

> Nor was I without a sentiment of peace as she gave this homage to my ankles and toes (as if blessing the miles we had walked).

Then Jesus admits further:

> Now I was of two minds. The love that had come from this woman's hands had given me a moment of happiness; so at this instant I did not feel like a friend of the poor.
>
> So for the first time, I knew how the rich feel . . . yet from the other side of my mouth, I had, if only for an instant, been scornful of the poor.
>
> Did I speak with a forked tongue so that I might reach out to all? The perfume of the spikenard was in my nose, and I had an image of beautiful temples. They would be erected for me. I could see how I wanted to be all things to all men. Each could take from me a separate wisdom.[22]

But these are Mailer's heterosexual fantasies. If Jesus is Word/Wisdom, could there not be a queer reading of these stories? In her recent book on Mary Magdalene, Jane Schaberg refers to Susannah Heschel's article "Jesus as Theological Transvestite,"[23] to raise questions about a queer reading of Jesus and Mary Magdalene. There is gender performance in scenes such as these. Schaberg raises the issue of a queer Jesus: "Not a 'real man,' he represents

Sophia as a wo/man."[24] Does Jesus also represent the Strange Woman as wo/man?

I think that Fatima Mernissi is right about how Western men—and women—read the harem and the women in it: as mindless sex objects. But not so in the Orient, argues Mernissi; the woman's intelligence is key.[25] And these stories of head/feet anointing do not come from the West; the woman imparts wisdom as she imparts perfumed oil and kisses. We see this woman and search for her profession, her sin, her hair, her wastefulness/appropriate use of money (depending on your perspective).

I am reminded here of the scene in the film *Jesus Christ Superstar* in which Mary Magdalene enacts this Gospel story. To be honest, Judas's objections make a lot of sense to me, and I find myself siding more with him than with Mary Magdalene. Mailer has Jesus thinking: "Yet I was obliged to forgive Judas. For indeed, had I not scorned the poor?"[26] I think Jesus does dismiss the poor in this story. "For you'll always have the poor with you" is a problematic dismissal of deep historic structural abuses.

Although these concerns for the poor are ancient, they still grate against the eschatological discourse of the Gospel texts. In setting a nice framework of these actions in Mark, Elizabeth Struthers Malbon in her book *In the Company of Jesus* makes the point that the woman comes into the house and gives up money for Jesus, while Judas leaves the house, giving up Jesus for money. The gift of the women represents self-denial. Malbon finds a parallel with the story of the widow in Mark 12:41–44 in that each story frames the eschatological discourse of the Markan Jesus).[27] Jesus, like the temple, will soon be gone. Streete (and Malbon and others) have helped me reread this story in new, more honest ways. Schüssler Fiorenza observes in this process of feminist "meaning making":

> Jewish hermeneutics has imagined that the Shekhinah, the Divine Presence, dwells in the blank spaces between the letters of the word. The process of storytelling or role-playing, or imagination, so to speak, seeks to make present Divine Wisdom in the "blank spaces" between the biblical wo/men and our own lives . . . [in] a catalytic process that liberates us from the false images that we have made.[28]

Schüssler Fiorenza has imagined the presence of Wisdom in the blank spaces of this story and in so doing has pushed me to reimagine these texts, these images, these characters, these voices. And every time I open these texts, I begin to imagine things. Something or someone in the text is different, and I begin to question my previous reading/s: Has the furniture been moved?

Are there more people in the room (perhaps Gentileschi, Mailer, Lawrence, Scorsese—or is it also Jael, Delilah, David, Judith, Salome)? Are the look on Jesus' face and tone of his voice more revealing? Is the wo/man's entrance a little more intrusive this time around, her touch more disconcerting? And am I more suspiciously, and a bit anxiously, glancing at the object in her hand?

NOTES

1. Elisabeth Schüssler Fiorenza, *Wisdom Ways: Introducing Feminist Biblical Interpretation* (Maryknoll, N.Y.: Orbis Books, 2001), 179. See also her discussion in *In Memory of Her: A Feminist Theological Reconstruction of Christian Origins* (New York: Crossroad, 1983), xiii–xiv. Elisabeth was the external reader of my dissertation on the Gospel of John and has continued to be an important conversation partner on this topic.

2. Schüssler Fiorenza, *Wisdom Ways*, 182.

3. Ibid., 179.

4. Ibid., 49.

5. Schüssler Fiorenza, *In Memory of Her*, xiv.

6. The woman is named only in John's Gospel, as Mary of Bethany. Since she is both unnamed and named (as various Marys), I am using the designation un/named. And since I argue that the gender lines are blurred, I will sometimes use the designation un/named wo/man to refer to her.

7. Bram Dijkstra, *Idols of Perversity: Fantasies of Feminine Evil in Fin-de-Siècle Culture* (New York: Oxford University Press, 1986), 229, 230–31.

8. Ibid., 231.

9. Mieke Bal, "Head Hunting: Judith on the Cutting Edge of Knowledge," in *Feminist Companion to Esther, Judith and Susanna,* ed. Athalya Brenner (Sheffield: Sheffield Academic Press, 1995), 258.

10. Bal, "Head Hunting," 274. Elisabeth Moltmann-Wendel points to the h(a)unting nature of the head touching by commenting that, "in body language, a woman towering head and shoulders above Jesus, and performing a masculine, prophetic action on him, did not quite correspond with the Christian ideal of women" (*The Women Around Jesus: Reflections on Authentic Personhood* [New York: Crossroad, 1982], 101).

11. Bal, "Head Hunting," 285.

12. Robin Morgan, *The Demon Lover: On the Sexuality of Terrorism* (New York: W. W. Norton), 69.

13. Quoted in Morgan, *Demon Lover*, 70.

14. See Gail Corrington Streete, *The Strange Woman: Power and Sex in the Bible* (Louisville: Westminster John Knox Press, 1997), 140–43. I am also referring to an

unpublished paper, "The Return of the Strange Woman: Mark 14:3–9 and Parallels," presented at meeting of the New Testament Section of the Southeast Society of Biblical Literature in March 2003 in Chattanooga, Tennessee, to which Elizabeth Malbon and I served as respondents.

15. Streete, "Return of the Strange Woman."

16. Ibid.

17. Alison Jasper, *The Shining Garment of the Text: Gendered Readings of John's Prologue* (Sheffield: Sheffield Academic Press, 1998), 84.

18. D. H. Lawrence, *The Man Who Died* (New York: Knopf, 1928). When Jesus leaves the tomb, he takes up with a peasant couple who give him shelter for a while: "They smelled with terror the scent of rich perfumes that came from him, from his body" (p. 16).

19. Ibid., 89–90.

20. See Stephen Moore's chapter on the body of Jesus, "Dissection: How Jesus' Risen Body Became a Cadaver," in his *God's Gym: Divine Male Bodies of the Bible* (New York/London: Routledge, 1996).

21. Peter Brooks, *Body Works: Objects of Desire in Modern Narrative* (Cambridge, Mass.: Harvard University Press, 1993), 4.

22. Norman Mailer, *The Gospel According to the Son* (New York: Random House, 1997), 193, 194.

23. Susannah Heschel, "Jesus as Theological Transvestite," in *Judaism Since Gender,* ed. Miriam Peskowitz and Laura Levitt (New York/London: Routledge, 1997).

24. Jane Schaberg, *The Resurrection of Mary Magdalene: Legends, Apocrypha, and the Christian Testament* (New York: Continuum, 2002), 103.

25. Fatema [Fatima] Mernissi, *Scheherazade Goes West: Different Cultures, Different Harems* (New York: Washington Square Press, 2001), chap. 13, "The Western Women's Harem."

26. Mailer, *Gospel According to the Son*, 195.

27. Elizabeth Struthers Malbon, *In the Company of Jesus: Characters in Mark's Gospel* (Louisville: Westminster John Knox Press, 2000), 53–57.

28. Schüssler Fiorenza, *Wisdom Ways*, 183.

10

Boundary Transgression and the Extreme Point in Acts 10:1–11:18

Ute E. Eisen

T HE CONTEXT OF MY REMARKS IS THAT OF NARRATOLOGICAL ANALYSIS
and interpretation of texts. Narratology (or better: narratologies) use(s)
categories to analyze the ways narratives create meaning. Every story can be
told in an infinite number of ways. Raymond Queneau demonstrates this
vividly in his 1947 book *Exercises de style*,[1] where he tells a story in ninety-
nine variants. Even the New Testament presents some very clear examples of
different narrations of the same story. The four Gospels all tell the same story
of Jesus of Nazareth, each in its own way. In each of these Gospels the world
is depicted somewhat differently, which shows us that narrating is also the
projection of a world. The world that is told, that is represented, is always a
designed, projected world. The focus of narrative analysis is this depicted
world; it attempts to grasp it in its structures and ways of functioning, to
describe it and unlock its meaning.

The framework within which my theories operate is classical narratology,
whose fundamental works appeared in the 1970s and 1980s,[2] but which has
experienced a considerable number of modifications since then. Especially in
the last several years, the discussion of theories of narratology has experienced
such an interdisciplinary differentiation that it is almost impossible to command the whole field.[3] David Herman writes:

Translated by Linda Maloney.

Among the many recent articles and books that have promoted a rethinking of classical narratological models are those written from a feminist perspective . . . those written from linguistic, sociolinguistic and psycholinguistic perspectives . . . those written from a cognitive perspective . . . those written from a logico-philosophical perspective based on the concept of possible worlds . . . those written from a rhetorical perspective . . . and those written from a post-modernist perspective that stresses the ludic, nonformalizable, and anti-totalizing forces and effects of narrative. . . .[4]

The works Herman mentions as representing feminist modifications (Susan S. Lanser, *Fictions of Authority;* Kathy Mezeis, *Ambiguous Discourse;* and Robyn R. Warhol, *Gendered Interventions*)[5] are only the tip of the iceberg of feminist narratology. In addition to the great number of studies on narratology that have appeared, one should mention as one of the founding mothers of classical narratology the highly creative Dutch literary scholar Mieke Bal, who has also contributed feminist literary-critical studies of the First Testament.[6]

Out of the plethora of narrative-theoretical questions, I have chosen a central concept, that of "events," which I would like to explore, presenting first the model suggested by the Estonian literary and cultural semiotician Jurij M. Lotman, then its development by Karl N. Renner, and finally its application to Acts 10:1–11:18.

JURIJ M. LOTMAN'S THEORY
OF BOUNDARY TRANSGRESSION

In the eighth chapter of his principal work, *The Structure of the Artistic Text* (1977), Lotman developed an independent concept of the event.[7] The previous concept of an event regarded the smallest unit of an action as an event. According to this definition, narrative segments such as "Cornelius had a vision," "he saw an angel of God," "it spoke to him," and so on (Acts 10:3) are events.[8] In contrast, Lotman's concept of event is less attached to the narrative microlevel; instead, he developed criteria for defining as events within the multitude of incidents in a narrative act only those that are of central importance for the happening. The sum of these events, in Lotman's sense, constitutes the *sujet* of a narrative. He is thus working within the dimension of the space of the depicted world, and in this context with the concept of the boundary. The depicted world is, according to Lotman, a semantic space defined by a congeries of semantic features that only this space possesses in this combination. This reference to features leads to a division of the whole space into disjunctive partial spaces that, in their totality, constitute the static basic order of the narrated world, against whose background action can occur. The central topological feature of a semantic space is its boundary, which also marks off partial spaces and is posited as impassable. The figures in the narrative are connected to particular spaces. An event happens when a figure in the depicted world is displaced across the boundary of a semantic field, that is, a limited space. Then a boundary transgression takes place.

The background for Lotman's theory is his conviction that artistic works —and in this sense literary texts are no different from pictures, buildings, or films—are secondary, model-building systems, and that as semiotic systems they project a specific view of the world. These designs for the world, according to Lotman, follow the iconic principle—that "in the majority of cases visible spatial objects serve as the denotata of verbal signs. . . ."[9] In light of this significance of spatial categories in modeling the world, Lotman has shown that spaces in literary texts therefore in many ways assume semantic functions beyond their mere task of forming a backdrop for the actions of the figures. Lotman formulates:

> While serving as the principle of organization and disposition of the personae within the artistic continuum, the structure of the *topos* emerges as the language for expressing other, non-spatial relations in the text. This determines the special modeling role of space within a text.[10]

This point of view can be illustrated also by the fact that nonspatial matters are frequently expressed through spatial metaphors, for example, "left" and "right" for political positions, or "above" and "below" for social relationships.

Lotman develops his concept of event against this background, and in this context he unfolds his theory of the transgression of boundaries. It implies a two-step analysis. First the depicted world is to be conceived at the textual level, still *sujet*-less, that is, eventless. The depicted space is grasped and defined in terms of a group of features. In the process of analysis, boundaries become perceptible, and those boundaries divide the space into disjunctive partial spaces. The boundaries are characterized by their impassability. The sum of the partial spaces and their semantics constitute the static fundamental order of the depicted world in which the action takes place. In the process of analysis, each element of the text (both objects and figures) must be assigned to a semantic space. Clues for the definition of the "semantic space" of the topological system are often found in the topographical, that is, the geographical relationships within a text. However, topography is not always the basis for the topology. Topology is a more abstract reality in comparison to topography and may be inferred from axes such as vertical versus horizontal, or oppositions such as inner and outer, open and closed, alone or together, and so on.

In a second step, our analysis should be directed to the movements of figures within the depicted world and its order, that is, the dynamic narrative action in the "eventfull" (*sujet*-full) layer of the text. As soon as a figure moves across a boundary within the fundamental order of the depicted world and its borders, the narrative becomes eventfull (*sujet*-full). An event is thus always an offense against the norms of the order of the depicted world in which boundaries are posited as impassable.

We may in principle distinguish two groups of event types: restitutive and revolutionary transgressions of boundaries. Restitutive transgression can take the following forms:

1. *Retraction of the transgression: return to the initial space.* A figure moves into the counterspace, thus damaging the existing order, and then returns to the space from which it departed. There is a brief "disturbance of the balance"[11] at the moment when the heroine is in the counterspace, but she returns to her point of departure and thus the previous balance, the given order of the spaces, is restored. This can be illustrated by an advertising spot for so-called K heels:

> She's quitting her job. The secretary marches angrily through the office door, slaps her letter against her ex-boss's tie, and leaves. Then it happens: the heel of her shoe gets caught in the doorsill. Snide grins. But the heel holds solid, her departure is saved, and the heroine achieves an especially effective exit.[12]

The heroine enters the counterspace, the office of her former boss, and disturbs the order of the space. The counterspace bears multiple markers: the protagonist storms through a door into the office without knocking and slaps her letter of resignation on her ex-boss's chest. Moreover, in doing this she stands out as a woman in a world in which men are the bosses. She massively disrupts the order of the counterspace, but after doing so she returns to her previous space. The order of the counterspace was damaged, but it, together with that of the initial space, is restored.

2. The second variant of the restitutive type is *departure into a new space;* that is, the hero accepts the condition of the space he has entered. The order of the previous space is replaced by that of the new space. Here is an example from an advertising spot for a Panasonic camera:

> Father comes home drunk from a business dinner. His family is waiting for him at home. Mother films his entrance with their new Panasonic video camera. Suddenly, he is sober.[13]

Here the door of the apartment is the boundary between business and family. There are different orders in the two spaces. With the change of space the man's behavior suddenly changes; he accommodates himself to the norms of the family. The damage to order is repaired and order is restored.

3. In contrast to restitutive transgression of boundaries, revolutionary transgression is differently shaped. There is a *transformation of order or an elimination of order or destruction of space:* These variants of boundary transgression are also called *meta-events.*

The order of semantic spaces is changed by this kind of boundary transgression, and the basic order of the depicted world is transformed. Boundaries shift, are removed, constitute themselves anew. There is no longer any conflict between the heroine and the semantic space. The following advertising spot for adhesive stickers may illustrate this:

> A teacher, of the old-maid type, is visiting a museum with her class, and has to pass a roomful of nudes. She makes the class wait until she has applied black adhesive strips to all the indecent spots. The boys tumble through the room like a bunch of dummies, but two smart girls drop out of the group and take a closer look at the interesting nudes—which is all the easier because taking off the stickers is as easy as putting them on.[14]

Here the protagonists rearrange the order in the space, and doubly so. The teacher changes the order by covering particular parts of the nudes. The young women alter that order by taking off the stickers, but they are also able to put them back on. The order of the space is altered and reconstituted in a new way.

KARL NIKOLAUS RENNER'S RULE
OF THE EXTREME POINT

Karl Nikolaus Renner has suggested an expansion of Lotman's theory of transgression of boundaries: the rule of the *extreme point.*[15] He thus attempts to model the internal structure of spaces and the movements of the figures within limited spaces, points neglected by Lotman.

Renner's rule of the extreme point begins with the concept that semantic spaces are ordered according to internal structure and frequently according to hierarchical elements, that is, extreme points. This last can be a topographical center or the summit of a mountain, the bow of the Titanic or political and social structures such as the office of a president or the position of the *paterfamilias*. According to Renner, it is striking that the figures do not wander aimlessly within their limited spaces; instead, their movements are frequently ordered toward such extreme points. Aiming at the extreme point can fulfill two functions: arrival at the extreme point becomes either a turning point or the end point of the event.

Extreme points become turning points when the directions of movement change and there is either return to the initial space or a transformation of order. In the example of the "K" heels, we have a case in which the extreme point, the boss's desk against the back wall of the office (where, in addition, the hierarchically topmost figure in the space is located) is the turning point of the movements of the secretary who is quitting; she then returns to the space from which she departed.

Extreme points become end points when the movements of the figures stop there. An advertising spot for fireplaces may serve as an example:

> A fireplace with fire burning, an empty room. The door opens and, one after another, a dog, a cat, and a mouse enter and settle down peacefully in front of the cozy fire without attacking each other. That is how pleasant the atmosphere of a real fireplace is.[16]

The structure of the space is presented in such a way that the fireplace is the focus, the center of the room. The animals' route leads to the fireplace, which here constitutes an extreme point, and there it ends. Thus, in every respect the extreme point is the end point of their movements—for the animals who enter this peaceful space behave differently than expected, namely, contrary to their nature, equally peaceful. They adopt the condition of this peaceful space. Renner also calls the extreme point the *focus of the event*.

Thus, Renner's reception of Lotman's theory of transgression of boundaries results in a modification: he reformulates and expands Lotman's concept of event as the disturbance of an order: an event happens when the boundaries (Lotman) and thus the order (Renner) of the depicted world are disturbed. From the side of the protagonists this leads to a return to the initial space or to acceptance of the order of the counterspace or—and then it is a *meta-event*—to the transformation of the order of the depicted world.

Boundary Transgression
and the Extreme Point in Acts 10:1–11:18

The story of Peter and Cornelius (Acts 10:1–11:18)[17] can be briefly sketched. It is told in four scenes taking place on four days within an indeterminate period of time, possibly one to two weeks:[18]

First Scene (Acts 10:1–8): At the ninth hour the centurion Cornelius has a vision in his house in Caesarea and is instructed by an angel to have Peter brought from Joppa (10:1–6). He sends three of his people to Joppa (10:7–8).

Second Scene (Acts 10:9–23a): The next day, at the sixth hour, Peter goes up to the roof of the house of Simon the tanner in Joppa; there, in ecstasy, he sees heaven opened and three times a vessel descending from heaven filled with the greatest variety of animals. A voice instructs Peter to kill and eat them, something he emphatically refuses to do. At the same time Cornelius's envoys arrive, and after they have reported Cornelius's vision, they are received by Peter into the tanner's house.

Third Scene (Acts 10:23b–48): Peter's departure on the next day, together with brothers and sisters from Joppa and Cornelius's envoys (10:23b) is very compactly summarized. The scene itself begins—on the fourth day, according to narrative time—with the arrival of Peter and his company at Cornelius's house in Caesarea. The house is already filled with Cornelius's family and close friends (10:24, 27, 44). When Peter is about to enter, Cornelius throws himself at his feet; Peter rejects this (10:25–26). Only after this encounter does Peter enter the house, justifying this step (which is not permitted to him as a Jew) by a summary reference to his vision (10:27–29). Then Cornelius tells his vision (10:30–33). A speech by Peter follows (10:34–43). At the same moment, the Holy Spirit descends on all the hearers and is poured out upon them (10:44–46). Peter decides to baptize these Gentiles, who are filled with the Holy Spirit (10:47–48). He is entreated to remain a few days in Cornelius's house (10:48).

Fourth Scene (Acts 11:1–18): Days later. In a summary note it is reported that the apostles and believers in Jerusalem learn that the Gentiles, too, have accepted the word of God (11:1). When Peter comes to Jerusalem, he is accused of having entered the house of non-Jews and eaten with them (11:2–3). Peter gives an account of the events in Joppa and Caesarea (11:4–

17). His report closes with a summary note telling of the agreement of the brothers and sisters in Jerusalem (11:18).

The world depicted in this narrative sequence is characterized by two striking axes, vertical and horizontal. On the horizontal axis three cities are particularly significant: Caesarea, Joppa, and Jerusalem. The figures in the narrative are oriented to these cities, and they acquire significance through particular groups of features.

Caesarea is a city that, as its name already indicates, was founded in honor of the Roman emperor. (It was built under Herod the Great.) It was thus part of the pagan *Imperium Romanum* and since 6 C.E. had been the seat of the Roman procurator. Its belonging to the *Imperium Romanum* is emphasized also by the characterization of Cornelius as a centurion. Cornelius is introduced as centurion of the Italian cohort, which at the same time semanticizes the city as a base for Roman troops. It was not such a base at the time of the narrative, however, although it may have been one beginning in 69 C.E.[19] Cornelius, as his extended Latin name tells us, is a Roman and, as a Roman officer, a member of a Gentile nation. These features are all in contrast to Judaism, yet he is portrayed sympathetically by the narrator—from a Jewish perspective—as devout and generous toward the people of God, that is, as a sympathizer of the Jewish faith and people (10:2, 4, 22, 31).[20] However, that does not alter Cornelius's life context, which stands in opposition to Judaism, something that is further underscored by the geopolitical situation of Caesarea in Samaria.

Joppa, in contrast, was a Jewish port city in Judea after 145 B.C.E. (1 Macc 12:33; 13:11) and thus constitutes a geopolitical opposition to Caesarea. Moreover, in 66 C.E. Joppa was one of the centers of the Jewish revolt against the Roman occupation. Joppa thus stands in sharp contrast to Roman Caesarea and the pagan *Imperium Romanum*.[21]

When Peter is called to Joppa, there is already a group of Jews in the city who believe in Christ, centered on the disciple Tabitha, a Jewish woman emphatically identified as having devoted herself to the poor (9:36; cf. 9:39). Her charitable work is described in the same vocabulary that will later be used to characterize Cornelius (9:36; 10:2). Giving alms is to be understood in Tabitha's case, as in that of Cornelius, in the larger context of the exercise of justice.[22] Peter's raising of Tabitha from death (9:36–41) brings many more people to the faith, as is summarily told in 9:42. Thus, Joppa is the semantic place of Jews who believe in Christ and exercise justice. Peter is staying there in the house of Simon the tanner.

The third geographical pillar of the narrative is Jerusalem. Like Joppa, Jerusalem is a Jewish city; moreover, it is the center of Judaism and at the same time the place of the culmination of the events surrounding Jesus of Nazareth and the point of departure for the witness given by Jesus' disciples (Acts 1:8). Acts tells how the group of Jesus' apostles is reconstituted in Jerusalem with the election of Matthias; here all his disciples receive the Holy Spirit and begin to spread the message about Jesus as the Christ (Acts 2ff.). In Jerusalem, since Jesus' ascension, what may be called the central office of Christian believers has existed; here decisions are made about the norms for the group, its organization, and so on (see Acts 5; 6; 15). It is thus only natural that Peter should go up to Jerusalem to give a report on the events in Caesarea (11:1–18). In accordance with the geographical and geopolitical order, the depicted world is divided into the space of the Jews, the Jews who believe in Christ in Joppa and Jerusalem, and the (different) Gentiles in Caesarea and in the house of Cornelius. With regard to the much-discussed question of the relationship between Jews and Christians in Acts,[23] it is important for this narrative sequence that a boundary cannot here be determined between Jews and Jews who believe in Christ. The boundary is clearly laid between Jews and Gentiles.

Within this triangle of cities, the house of the Gentile Cornelius constitutes the focal point of the event. Peter and his company, all figures from the Jewish initial space, enter the counterspace of Caesarea (*eisēlthen eis tēn kaisareian*) (10:24). There they find the house of Cornelius. At this point there is a scenic intermezzo that prepares for Peter's monumental crossover. As the Jew Peter is about to enter the house of a Gentile (*hōs de egeneto tou eiselthein ton Petron*) (10:25), Cornelius meets him and throws himself at Peter's feet. At the doorstep of the house of the pagan Cornelius, the Jew Peter is venerated by Cornelius as if he were a god. Peter raises Cornelius up and explicitly rejects this veneration by emphasizing that he is only a human being. Only after this short episode does Peter finally enter (*eisēlthen*) the house (10:27). Here Cornelius has gathered his relatives and closest friends, which is clearly emphasized (10:24, 27). Those assembled in Cornelius's house are members of Cornelius's own nation and can be interpreted, *pars pro toto,* as non-Jewish people: Gentiles. Thus the house of Cornelius becomes the extreme point of Caesarea, which is semanticized as Roman and Gentile. The transgression of the impermeable boundary of the space takes place as the Jew Peter enters the house of the Gentile Cornelius—and Peter is not alone. The Jewish believers in Christ from Joppa are with him; they cross the boundary with him and later serve as witnesses in Jerusalem.

The size of the groups associated with the conversion of the Roman Cornelius distinguishes this narrative from the first story of the conversion of a Gentile in Acts 8. There the God-fearing court official from Ethiopia, while traveling through Samaria, is converted and baptized by the evangelist Philip (Acts 8:26–39). Philip and the Ethiopian are alone on the road in a lonely place (this is emphasized; see Acts 8:26). In contrast, Cornelius's conversion by Peter affects a large group of people and is narrated as a boundary transgression by Peter. It is explicitly so characterized by Peter when he says: "You yourselves know that it is unlawful (*athemiton estin*) for a Jew (*andri ioudaiō*) to associate with (*kollasthai*) or to visit (*proserchesthai*) a foreigner (*allophylō*); but God has shown me that I should not call anyone profane or unclean (*koinon ē akatharton*)" (10:28).

Thus is the norm formulated that will be violated by Peter's crossing of the boundary. Entering the house of a foreigner, that is, a member of a foreign nation, is excluded by this norm as something forbidden to Jews. This rigid norm[24] is sharpened by the next statement, which describes foreign people, in opposition to Jews, as common or unclean. Within the narrative sequence this ordering of the depicted world in stark contrasts is repeatedly brought to the fore, varied, and ultimately transformed.

In Peter's vision he is called upon to slaughter and eat unclean animals, something that as a Jew he must resolutely refuse to do, as demanded by the order of the depicted world (10:13–15). This order, based on the opposition between clean and unclean, is challenged by the scene in Peter's vision, but it remains intact because Peter refuses to establish the new order that is demanded of him. But this changes in the subsequent scene: when Peter enters the house of the Gentile Cornelius, who is regarded as unclean, the order of things whereby Jews are to avoid what is unclean is massively attacked. Peter's transgression of this boundary accomplishes a transformation of the order of the depicted world when he, as a Jew, accepts "that I should not call anyone profane or unclean (*koinon ē akatharton*)" (10:28).

In the fourth scene in Jerusalem, then, it is not the news that the Gentiles have also accepted the word of God that causes outrage. What awakens resistance is Peter's transgression of boundaries, his entry into the house of a non-Jew. That is the real offense against order that is the subject of controversy. It is addressed in two different ways. Peter is reproached, first, because he, a Jew, entered the house of uncircumcised men (*eiselthes pros andras akrobystian echontas*) and, second, because he ate with them (*synephages autois*) (11:3). With this the offense against norms that Peter himself spoke of in Cornelius's house (10:28) is repeated, with variation. The repetition emphasizes that

Peter's boundary transgression—his entry, as a Jew, into the house of non-Jews and his eating with them—is the *meta-event* in this narrative sequence. The consequence of this boundary transgression is a transformation of the order of the depicted world: from now on, for Jews who believe in Christ, the boundary between what is Jewish and the Gentiles, who until this point have been regarded as unclean, has been removed. The sharply drawn parallel narrative of the conversion and baptism of Lydia, the God-fearing dealer of purple goods, and the matter-of-fact entry and exit of Paul and his companions into and out of her house is an example of this fact (Acts 16:13–15, 40).

The transformation of the order of things as presented in Acts 10:1–11:18 contains an additional refinement. In a further presentation, in Peter's speech in Cornelius's house, told from Peter's perspective, we read at the very beginning (10:34–35): "I truly understand that God shows no partiality (*prosōpolēmptēs*), but in every nation (*en panti ethnei*) anyone who fears God (*phoboumenos auton*) and does what is right (*ergazomenos dikaiosynēn*) is acceptable to God" (10:34–35). Thus a shift has occurred. In the transformed order the fundamental difference between the people of Israel and the other nations has been removed; what counts in the new order is not belonging to this or that nation, but fear of God and righteous action. Against this background it is clear that the repeated description of Cornelius as devout, God-fearing, and a person who is generous in giving alms (10:1–2, 4, 22, 31) is not mere ornamentation. Within this narrative sequence the character of Cornelius as a God-fearing and generous Gentile is a precondition for his vision. The narrator causes the angel himself to express this causality (10:4), and it is also presented in Peter's speech (10:35).

In addition to this horizontal axis, the vertical axis of the narrative sequence is also sharply delineated. It presents the opposition between heaven and earth, the divine and human spheres. Figures and objects from heaven cross the boundary between heaven and earth, the human realm. This is explicitly the case on three occasions. In the first scene, the angel's appearance in Cornelius's house represents a first boundary transgression between heaven and earth and constitutes an *event* in Lotman's sense. Angels are beings that belong to the heavens, and this angel is additionally characterized in the narrator's discourse as an angel of God (10:3) and thus unmistakably belonging to God's space. The case of the second boundary crossing between heaven and earth, the descent of the "sheet" in Peter's vision (10:11) is analogous. It is accompanied by a massive violation of order. The Jew Peter, who lives according to Torah, is asked to slaughter and eat unclean animals. This boundary transgression also has event character. Both transgressions of boundary are, however, retracted, because the figure (angel) and object (sheet) return to the place from which they came. It is said of the angel that Cornelius sees him enter (*eiselthonta pros auton*) (10:3), but he also departs (*apēlthen ho angelos*) (10:7). Of the "sheet" it is said that Peter sees the heaven opened (*ton ouranon aneōgmenon*), and this container descending to earth (*kai katabainon skeuos ti hōs othonēn megalēn tessarsin archais kathiemenon epi tēs gēs*) (10:11), and that this happened three times. But this vessel is also taken up again into heaven (*anelēmphthē to skeuos eis ton ouranon*) (10:16). As events that emphasize the axis heaven–earth, these happenings function here as prelude. They lead to the *meta-event* and lend it divine authorization.

It is different with the descent of the Spirit in the third scene. The Spirit is also associated with the heavenly world through the epithet "holy." In the third scene, the Spirit descends on the hearers (*epepesen to pneuma to hagion epi pantas tous akouontas ton logon*) (10:44), and soon afterward the Holy Spirit is poured out even upon the Gentiles (*epi ta ethnē hē dōrea tou pneumatos tou hagiou ekkechytai*) (10:45). Nothing is said about a return to the place of origin. The descent of the Spirit can thus be interpreted as the divine sealing of Peter's boundary transgression and thus as a way of expressing the transformation of the order of things. The order of the Christ group, as it had been analogously constituted through the event of Pentecost (Acts 2), is now established among the Gentiles. In the Peter–Cornelius sequence only certain paradigmatic bits and pieces are narrated: namely, the ability to speak in tongues and to praise God (*lalountōn glōssais kai megalynontōn ton theon*) (10:46). Reception of baptism is proleptically referred to (10:48). With the outpouring of the Spirit the *meta-event* of Peter's boundary transgression and the transformation of the order of things that occurs as a result, which is told as something coming from heaven and thus from God (and prepared for by Peter's vision), is now sanctioned on that basis.[25]

The result to be affirmed is that an analysis of the text in terms of Lotman's theory of boundary transgression puts us in a position to explicate the central event in the narrative sequence in a methodical manner. In this narrative that event is not, as appears at first glance, the conversion of Cornelius but rather the "conversion" of Peter. His movement across the boundary of the counter-space of the Gentiles, coded as forbidden, is the central event in this narrative sequence; and staying in the house of a non-Jewish person is the turning point for Peter the Jew. He returns to the center of his Jewish place of origin and transforms its order. The boundary between the place of origin (the people of God) and the counterspace (the Gentiles) has become permeable. A few verses later in the narrative, the group-name "Christians" is introduced (Acts 11:26). The Jewish group of "Christians" forms within Judaism—certainly not outside of it[26]—and acquires a profile. This ultimately leads to conflict within the Jewish people, with groups that cannot accept this transformation of order. But that is another story.

———

Elisabeth Schüssler Fiorenza's vita is also characterized by the crossing and transgression of boundaries. She crossed the boundaries of her place of origin, Europe, and she has transgressed boundaries as a Roman Catholic woman. She has established herself as a Catholic exegete in North American universities, which when she began her work were still primarily dominated by men. But she did not lose herself in this male-dominated counterspace. Elisabeth's boundary transgression is, instead, a *meta-event*. It led to a transformation of the order of things, an enormously effective transformation of the order of the space of the university and of the church. She has sustained women's joy in theology and given them self-confidence; she has encouraged both women and men to lift up their voices and not allow themselves to be silenced. For this I, together with many others, owe her immense gratitude.

NOTES

1. Paris: Gallimard, 36th ed., 1959.

2. These include Gérard Genette, *Figures III (Poétiques)* (Paris: Editions du Seuil, 1972; partial English translation, *Narrative Discourse* [Ithaca, N.Y.: Cornell University Press, 1980]); idem, *Nouveau Discours du Récit (Poétique)* (Paris: Editions du Seuil, 1983); Mieke Bal, *Narratology: Introduction to the Theory of Narrative,* trans. C. van Boheemen (2nd ed.; Toronto: University of Toronto Press, 1997); Seymour Chatman, *Story and Discourse: Narrative Structure in Fiction and Film* (Ithaca, N.Y.: Cornell University Press, 1978); Gerald Prince, *Narratology: The Form and Functioning of Narrative* (Berlin/New York/Amsterdam: Mouton, 1982); Shlomith Rimmon-Kenan, *Narrative Fiction: Contemporary Poetics* (London/New York: Routledge, 1983).

3. See the review of research by Ansgar von Nünning, "Towards a Cultural and Historical Narratology: A Survey of Diachronic Approaches, Concepts, and Research Projects," in *Anglistentag 1999 Mainz: Proceedings of the Conference of the German Association of University Teachers of English 21*, ed. B. Reitz and S. Rieuwerts (Trier: Wissenschaftlicher Verlag Trier, 2000), 345–73.

4. David Herman, "Introduction," in *Narratologies: New Perspectives on Narrative Analysis*, ed. David Herman, Theory and Interpretation of Narrative Series (Columbus: Ohio State University Press, 1999), 27.

5. Susan S. Lanser, *Fictions of Authority: Women Writers and Narrative Voice* (Ithaca, N.Y.: Cornell University Press, 1992); *Ambiguous Discourse: Feminist Narratology and British Women Writers*, ed. Kathy Mezei (Chapel Hill: University of North Carolina Press, 1996); Robyn R. Warhol, *Gendered Interventions: Narrative Discourse in the Victorian Novel* (New Brunswick, N.J.: Rutgers University Press, 1989).

6. To mention only Mieke Bal's most important works: *Narratology; Lethal Love: Feminist Literary Readings of Biblical Love Stories* (Bloomington/Indianapolis: Indiana University Press, 1987); *Murder and Difference: Gender, Genre, and Scholarship on Sisera's Death*, trans. M. Gumpert (Bloomington/Indianapolis: Indiana University Press, 1988); *Death and Dissymmetry: The Politics of Coherence in Judges* (Chicago: University of Chicago Press, 1988); *On Story-Telling: Essays in Narratology*, ed. David Jobling (Sonoma, Calif.: Polebridge Press, 1991).

7. Jurij M. Lotman, *The Structure of the Artistic Text*, trans. from the Russian by Ronald Vroon, Michigan Slavic Contributions 7 (Ann Arbor: University of Michigan Press, 1977), 209–84. His theory of boundary transgression was developed and modified by Karl N. Renner, *Der Findling: Eine Erzählung von Heinrich von Kleist und ein Film von George Moorse: Prinzipien einer adäquaten Wiedergabe narrativer Strukturen*, Münchner Germanistische Beiträge 31 (Munich: Wilhelm Fink Verlag, 1983). For an example of its application to drama, see Hans Krah, *"Gelöste Bindungen/bedingte Lösungen": Untersuchungen zum Drama im ersten Drittel des 19. Jahrhunderts* (Passau: Wissenschaftsverlag Rothe, 1996), 90–170, 274–305; idem, "'Zeichen, die wir deuten müßten': Raumenentwurf, Zeiterfahrung und Selbstfindung in Hans Henny Jahns *Der staubige Regenbogen* (1959)," in *Forum Homosexualität und Literatur* 39 (2001): 5–25; and on films and narrative texts, see idem, *Die Narration vom Ende: Weltuntergangsszenarien in Literatur und Film nach 1945*, Habilitationsschrift am Institut für Literaturwissenschaft in Kiel 2000, forthcoming.

8. See, e.g., the influential definition by the Russian formalist Boris Tomashevski, *Theorie der Literatur: Poetik*, trans. U. Werner from the text of the 6th ed. [Moscow/Leningrad, 1931], edited and introduced by K.-D. Seeman (Wiesbaden: Otto Harrassowitz, 1985), 211ff.

9. Lotman continues: "We might perform a sort of mental experiment: let us imagine some extremely generalized concept, some sort of all, totally lacking concrete attributes, and try to determine its features for ourselves. It will not be difficult to

ascertain that for the majority of people these features will have a spatial character; 'boundlessness' (i.e. relation to the purely spatial category of boundary; in addition the word 'boundlessness' in the everyday meaning it has for most people, is merely a synonym for something very large, an enormous expanse of something), the ability to have parts. The very concept of universality, as a number of experiments have shown, has an abstract spatial character for most people" (*Structure,* 217).

10. Ibid., 231–32.

11. Tzvetan Todorov describes the narrative structure of a story as a succession of "balance–disturbance of the balance–restored, new balance" ("Grammatik und Erzählgrammatik," in *Poetik der Prosa,* Ars poetica, Studien 16 (Frankfurt am Main: Athenäum, 1972), 115–25, esp. 117, 124.

12. Karl N. Renner, "Räume–Grenzen–Handlungen: Die Grenzüberschreitungstheorie als Analyseinstrument von Texten und Filmen" (paper presented at the Ringvorlesung "Grenzen erfahren . . . ," Johannes Gutenberg-Universität Mainz, 14 December 1998), 1–21, here 11 <http://www.journalistik.uni-mainz.de/grenz.htm>.

13. Ibid., 12.

14. Ibid.

15. For this and what follows, see Karl N. Renner, "Zu den Brennpunkten des Geschehens: Erweiterung der Grenzüberschreitungstheorie: Die Extrempunktregel," *diskurs film: Münchner Beiträge zur Filmphilologie* 1 (1986): 115–30; idem, "Räume–Grenzen–Handlungen" (see n. 12 above).

16. Renner, "Räume–Grenzen," 15.

17. The following literary-critical studies of Acts 10:1–11:18, narratological in the broadest sense, but with very different emphases, have been published in *Recherches de science religieuse* 58 (1970): Roland Barthes, "L'analyse structurale du recit: A propos d'Acts X–XI" (pp. 17–37); Louis Marin, "Essai d'analyse structurale d'Actes 10,1–11,18" (pp. 39–61); Edgar Haulotte, "Fondation d'une Communauté de Type Universal: Actes 10,1–11,18" (pp. 63–100); see also Claude Chabrol, "Analyse du 'texte' de la Passion," in *Languages: Sémiotique Narrative: Récits Bibliques,* ed. C. Chabrol and L. Marin (Paris: Didier, 1971), 75–96; Joseph Courtes, "Actes 10, 1–11, 18 comme système de représentations mythiques," in *Exégèse et Herméneutique,* ed. X. Léon Dufour (Paris: Editions du Seuil, 1971), 205–11; Robert W. Funk, *The Poetics of Biblical Narrative* (Sonoma, Calif.: Polebridge Press, 1988), 150–56 passim; Robert C. Tannehill, *The Acts of the Apostles,* vol. 2 of *The Narrative Unity of Luke-Acts: A Literary Interpretation* (Minneapolis: Fortress, 1990), 128–45; Ronald D. Witherup, "Cornelius Over and Over and Over Again: 'Functional Redundancy' in the Acts of the Apostles," *Journal for the Study of the New Testament* 49 (1993): 45–66; William S. Kurz, "Effects of Variant Narrators in Acts 10–11," *New Testament Studies* 43 (1997): 570–86; Günter Wasserberg, *Aus Israels Mitte–Heil für die Welt: Eine narrativ-exegetische Studie zur Theologie des Lukas,* Beihefte zur Zeitschrift für die neutestamentliche Wissenschaft 92 (Berlin/New York: Walter de

Gruyter, 1998), 273–305; Daniel Marguerat and Yvan Bourquin, *How to Read Bible Stories: An Introduction to Narrative Criticism,* trans. John Bowden (London: S.C.M. Press, 1999, 80 passim.

18. In my methodological approach, the question of the historical background of the narrative sequence is not vital; the historicity of the circumstances described is neither verified nor questioned. That question simply does not occur here; a different methodology would be required to address it. The following analysis is directed primarily to the narrated time, the narrated space, and the narrated figures, and analyzes what, within this projected world, is "eventful" in Lotman's sense. At certain points it seems to me worthwhile to refer to historical contexts, and here especially to additional literature, in order to indicate how the manner of narrating has sharply reduced the historical complexity.

19. See Jacob Jervell, *Die Apostelgeschichte: Übersetzt und erklärt,* Kritisch-exegetischer Kommentar über das Neue Testament 3 (17th ed.; Göttingen: Vandenhoeck & Ruprecht, 1998), 303.

20. For the "God-fearers" in Acts, see most recently the discussion in Wasserberg, *Israels Mitte,* 44ff.; on the whole problem of a precise definition of this group, see Bernd Wander, *Gottesfürchtige und Sympathisanten: Studien zum heidnischen Umfeld von Diasporasynagogen,* Wissenschaftliche Untersuchungen zum Neuen Testament (Tübingen: Mohr-Siebeck, 1998).

21. See Ivoni Richter Reimer, *Women in the Acts of the Apostles: A Feminist-Liberation Perspective,* trans. Linda M. Maloney (Minneapolis: Fortress, 1995), 33–34.

22. See below, and extensively on this subject Richter Reimer, *Women in Acts,* 36–41; on Tabitha, see especially the whole of ch. 2, "The Miraculous Story of the Disciple Tabitha (9:36–43)" (pp. 31–69).

23. See most recently Matthias Blum, "Antijudaismus im lukanischen Doppelwerk?" in *"Nun steht aber diese Sache im Evangelium . . .": Zur Frage nach den Anfängen des christlichen Antijudaismus,* ed. Rainer Kampling (Paderborn: Ferdinand Schöningh, 1999), 107–49.

24. For the complexity of Jewish life in the first half of the first century in Palestine, see Emil Schürer, *The History of the Jewish People in the Age of Jesus Christ (175 B.C.–A.D. 135),* 4 vols., rev. and ed. by Geza Vermes, Fergus Millar, and Maxwell Black (Edinburgh: T & T Clark, 1973–1987); as well as Martin Hengel, *Judaism and Hellenism: Studies in Their Encounter in Palestine during the Early Hellenistic Period,* trans. John Bowden (Philadelphia: Fortress, 1974).

25. The strongly developed vertical axis is also emphasized within the human sphere by the opposition between above and below. It is seen in Peter's going up to the roof of the house of Simon the tanner in order to pray, that is, in order to be closer to the sphere of heaven, which is semanticized as divine (*anebē Petros epi to dōma*) (10:9), or also in Cornelius's *proskynēsis,* when he throws himself at Peter's feet and

thus shows him the honor that belongs to God (10:25). Peter, who raises Cornelius to his feet (*ēgeiren auton*) (10:26), interprets this downward movement explicitly as divine worship, which he decisively rejects (*anastēthi; kai egō autos anthrōpos eimi*) (10:26). Finally, Peter goes up (*anebē*) to Jerusalem, the city of God and of Judaism, in order to have the transformation of the order of things sanctioned there.

26. The much-disputed question of the relationship between Jews and Christians in Acts can be answered unequivocally for Acts 10:1–11:18: believers in Christ belong absolutely and entirely to Judaism (for this problem, see also n. 23 above).

11

Slavery and Gender

Sheila Briggs

———————

SLAVERY: AN INSTITUTION
BETWEEN ANCIENT AND MODERN IDEOLOGY

CHRISTIANITY CAN CLAIM THE DUBIOUS HONOR OF HAVING flourished in two large—if not in fact the two largest—slave societies in human history: the Roman Empire and the American South. So, on the one hand, one might argue that Christianity is the ideological thread running between the ancient and modern institutions of slavery. Yet, on the other hand, one should not be misled by the continuity of Christianity into thinking that it faithfully reproduces among its conservative believers an unchanging theological argument for slavery or that it contains, for its radical adherents, an original critique of slavery that could only become more devastating to the institution with time and the advent of modern democracy. To understand Christianity in this way is to misunderstand the relationship of ideology to material reality. The source of such a misunderstanding is the naturalization and reification of categories of human identity, especially gender. The supposed consistency of Christian ideology (whether as a socially conservative ethics or as a theology of freedom) is borrowed from a perceived stability of human nature and distinctions, exemplified by gender. Always lurking behind modern debates about ancient slavery and early Christianity are contemporary politics of gender and the ontological presuppositions on which they are based.

The modern justification of slavery both combined and distinguished the categories of race and class. Already in colonial America of the seventeenth century there arose a legal distinction between white and black unfree laborers as between those subject to temporary indenture and those in permanent bondage. With the rise of democracy and the replacement of aristocratic by bourgeois elites, class status as a condition fixed by birth became an untenable proposition. This led to opposition to slavery among even many theologically and socially conservative Christians, such as William Paley and William Wilberforce in England. A condition as inherently brutal and degrading as slavery could hardly be justified as a person's "station in life." Indeed, social reformers in nineteenth-century England, America, and elsewhere often protested the mistreatment of the working classes as illegitimate by making the comparison to black slavery. At the same time as class was becoming denaturalized in modern Western societies, gender was being radically recast not as the higher and lower grades of an essentially identical human nature but as the fundamental distinction in humanity between feminine and masculine natures. Increasingly, race was cast as the other fundamental distinction among human beings. Defenders of slavery redefined it as an inherent condition of race instead of class. This reconstruction of race as analogous to gender and not to class was further promoted by the ideological needs of the massive expansion of European colonialism in the nineteenth century. Europeans had to be innately superior to all other races so that they could justify the subjugation of peoples and cultures who, even by their own standards, possessed civilizations even more ancient than their own. Indians and Chinese as well as Africans were assigned a human identity that was fundamentally different from and inferior to the humanity of those of European descent.

Gender had become and to a large extent remains the essential ploy in any rhetorical strategy to limit equality. How often do we hear even today that equality does not mean sameness, that men and women (and by analogy other human groups) can be equal without being the same, and that therefore differences in social roles and functions—and even the distribution of resources (e.g., the wage gap between white male workers and others)—are simply the cumulative result of individual choices based on differences in temperament and values between the sexes (and also by analogy between other human groups). Contemporary debates about ancient slavery and early Christianity not only bring to the surface discomfort about race in a society of formal racial equality but extensive racism; they also provoke deep anxieties about gender in a society of formal equality of the sexes but persistent patriarchal practices. If gender and race are no more natural and fixed permutations of human nature than class, then at least the conservative traditions of Christianity have played a crucial role in stabilizing racial and gender hierarchies in a modern world that is otherwise inhospitable to the notion of fixed social status. Modern conservative Christianity has disconnected the New Testament injunctions to wives and slaves from their historical location as Greco-Roman constructs of human inequality and put them successfully to work in the utterly transformed context of modern anti-egalitarian discourse.

FROM DEFENDING SLAVERY TO DEFENDING PAUL

The statements about women and slaves in the New Testament writings have been matters of deep concern to Christians, who still form the majority of those engaged in the scholarly study of these texts. For most of the twentieth century, progressive Christian New Testament scholars undertook a double strategy. First, they emphasized the historical context of the New Testament writings. Paul's and other New Testament writers' words could not be taken at face value and applied in any literal way to other situations. They were the culturally and socially conditioned views of early Christians and as such possessed no normative value. Second, this historicist approach was supplemented by the appeal to a normative emancipatory core that, although seldom explicitly expressed in relation to social justice, was nonetheless the center of the early Christian kerygma as the proclamation of the gospel of freedom. Galatians 3:28 was the preeminent articulation of Christian freedom as transforming social reality, and all other New Testament texts were to be read in its light and subordinated to it in interpretation. In the postwar period and into the 1980s this strategy reshaped how scripture was applied to questions of ethics and polity inside the churches and to Christian participation in the formation of broader social policy. Two waves of feminism and the failure of racist social systems in Nazi Germany, the United States, and South Africa undercut Christian social conservatism at least in the mainstream churches. The defense of social hierarchy by appealing to scriptural authority, especially that of the apostle Paul, was no longer seen by most New Testament scholars and Christian theologians as a viable enterprise.

The publication of Elisabeth Schüssler Fiorenza's *In Memory of Her* in 1983 changed the terms of the debate by prioritizing hermeneutics over historical reconstruction in feminist biblical interpretation. She redefined the relationship of early Christian (and later Christian women) to the New

Testament texts as one of tension and contestation. New Testament writings were no longer historical documents that, if examined with skill and without patriarchal prejudice, would yield knowledge about women's full participation and leadership within early Christianity. The feminist problem of the New Testament was not one of lack or neglect of historical evidence about women. The New Testament writings were *constituted* as the ideological suppression of women in the Christian communities. The normative emancipatory core was to be found not in the texts but in the resistance of women to the ideology of the texts, which were caught in the discursive bind of preserving what they sought to eradicate in the very act of suppression. Earlier social conservatives had sought to justify slavery or other forms of social hierarchy through appeals to scriptural, especially Pauline, authority. Their liberal opponents had sought to wrest that authority from them and deploy it for emancipatory projects. After *In Memory of Her*, progressive interpreters often reversed their task. Reintegrating an emancipatory agenda into the Pauline texts was now essential for defending Paul.[1]

Slavery creates severe problems for feminist and other progressive biblical interpreters who wish to defend Paul. Even excluding the New Testament *Haustafeln* (household codes) and the post-Pauline tradition, there are two places in the authentic Pauline corpus where gender, sexuality, and slavery are juxtaposed in Paul's rhetoric: Galatians 3–4 and 1 Corinthians 6–7.[2] These two larger text complexes and the Letter to Philemon make it difficult to disengage Paul's Christian theology from its sociorhetorical context—Greco-Roman slaveholding patriarchy. Even in terms of conventional historical reconstruction and philological analysis such an undertaking seems a Sisyphean task. When we evaluate attempts to defend Paul against the biblical hermeneutics that Schüssler Fiorenza has developed since *In Memory of Her*, we can see that such defenses of Paul are serious distractions from something far more important: the conceiving of historical inquiry in such a way that it no longer reinscribes the silences imposed by the texts on the weak and the powerless.

NEITHER MALE NOR FEMALE?
GALATIANS, GENDER, AND SLAVERY

The juxtaposition of gender and slavery in Galatians 3–4 should make it difficult to separate the question of the status of women in early Christian communities from that of slaves. Therefore, if one understands Galatians 3:28 as a pre-Pauline baptismal formula with social implications for those who were initiated into the early Christian community, then this must have had import for how early Christians dealt with the social relationships of slavery as well as those of gender. Interpreting this passage, Schüssler Fiorenza remarks in *In Memory of Her:*

> While the baptismal declaration in Gal 3:28 offered a new religious vision to women and slaves, it denied all male religious prerogatives in the Christian community based on gender roles. . . . It is often argued that it was impossible for the tiny Christian group to abolish the institution of slavery and other social hierarchies. That might have been the case or it might not. However, what is often overlooked is that the relinquishment of religious male prerogatives within the Christian community was possible and that such a relinquishment included the abolition of social privileges as well.[3]

Whatever one considers to be the character and extent of the social implications of Galatians 3:28, one must assume that the effects were similar for both slaves and women. Not to make this assumption requires one to presuppose that gender and slavery operated in very different ways and created very different hierarchies in the construction of ancient identity. Yet this is problematic in and of itself. There may have been no simple homology between how gender and slavery encoded identities and social hierarchies, but they were also not discrete social, cultural, and linguistic processes. To be a woman was always to be a slave or a free woman, to be a slave was always to be either a male or a female slave. All these configurations of identity (as well as other markers of lower status) were defined as incomplete or defective. They marked persons as those to be dominated through the exercise of political, economic, psychological, sexual, and other forms of power. If Galatians 3:28 indicates that baptism redistributes religious or spiritual power, then one must ask how it affects other power relationships. If in Christ no one dominates another nor is she or he dominated by another, then is the paradigm of domination, which underlies all social hierarchies, undercut? A simplistic historicist answer that social egalitarianism is a product of the Enlightenment and that no one in the ancient world envisaged the abolition of slavery is insufficient. History does not run like a train schedule with fixed points spread out in linear development. Like the physical universe of which it is a part, human history is marked by nonlinear events and conditions that are not predetermined by and predictable through a precisely definable set of preconditions. The real historical question is not whether social egalitarianism was possible in the ancient Mediterranean world of the first century but how it was more or less successfully resisted. In terms of early Christianity this question becomes, How was the radical rupture with a paradigm of domination contained by New Testament writings? Linked to this investigation is another one. If we have shifted the terms of historical inquiry from whether New Testament authors could envisage social egalitarianism to how they were able to resist its becoming part of their discourse, then we can search for the silent residues of that which they refused, the ghostly remnants of what they rendered unthinkable and therefore preserved as an invisible shadow of their own thought.

Elisabeth Schüssler Fiorenza's later work provides us with important pointers to the conceptual frameworks that we need to adopt and how we are concretely to apply them to the relationship of gender and slavery in early Christianity and to the exegesis of Galatians 3:28. Even in her earlier works, Schüssler Fiorenza paid careful attention to the patriarchal household. Her recognition of it as a primary material and ideological site for the production of identity and social power has allowed her to develop an ever more complex understanding of the social matrices in which gender relationships are embedded and evolve.[4] She has also drawn consistently on feminist political and social theory to elucidate the ideological trajectory from the ancient Greco-Roman household to forms of family in later Christian societies. One of the most obvious results of the theoretical sophistication of her analysis is that she places the terms "androcentric" and "patriarchy" within the conceptual framework of the newly coined ones, "kyriocentric" and "kyriarchy." She rightly sees that patriarchy has become divorced from its original meaning as "rule of the fathers" and is now synonymous with male domination of women. But the patriarchal household was never just a narrowly defined gender system. The *paterfamilias* ruled not only over his wife and children but also over slaves and other dependents in the household. Hence the long-term effects of the patriarchal household, which in a variety of forms survived in the West until industrialization, should not be measured only in terms of gender.[5] As we will see, Schüssler Fiorenza is able to see that a slave woman in antiquity was not simply a woman who was additionally or simultaneously oppressed as a slave. The slave woman occupied a distinct social location within the patriarchal household, the gendered character of which was not interchangeable with that of the freeborn wife. The gender system (patriarchy in the modern sense) was integrated through the ancient household into a comprehensive structure of domination (designated "kyriarchy" by Schüssler

Fiorenza). The injunctions to slave owners and slaves inscribed gender relations just as much as those to husbands and wives. The privileges of freeborn wives were just as much those of gender as they were of class. The legacy of the patriarchal household is to be found not only in the modern family but also in the modern state.[6] Although the feminist problem of the modern family may seem to be that its division of roles and responsibilities reproduces inequality between the sexes, in fact it is an obstacle to radical democracy because it socializes its members into relationships of domination and subordination. It is also not the case that we simply mimic gender inequality in other social relationships. Rather there is a circular movement in which different sets of social hierarchies mold one another.

Alongside the significance that Schüssler Fiorenza attaches to the patriarchal household, we also see her moving away from any essentialist notion of gender. Indeed, as she has deepened her analysis of kyriarchy as the dominant form of social organization, encompassing the family, state, and all social institutions, she has come to understand gender not as the inherent character of human beings but as the identity that always emerges as specific to a certain social location. Continuous throughout her work is the opposition between two fundamentally different forms of Christian community, one based on the patriarchal household and the other a radical egalitarian and emancipatory movement (the *ekklēsia* of women). The final chapter of *In Memory of Her* considers the status of slaves in the Christian community to be linked to that of women, but still explicates the "patriarchalization of church and ministry" primarily in terms of gender (see, e.g., the section entitled "The Genderization of Ecclesial Office"). Similarly, the *ekklēsia* of women is described almost exclusively in gender terms, and its transhistorical dimension reinforces rather than dilutes an essentialist conception of gender.[7] Roughly a decade later Schüssler Fiorenza already has a fully articulated anti-essentialist understanding of gender which places it in a broader system of domination. Certainly, she has been influenced by her critical engagement of feminist poststructuralist thought even though she faults it for staying within a patriarchal symbolic universe.[8]

An anti-essentialist conception of gender, which locates it historically in a kyriarchal social order, where it is entwined with slavery, especially in the context of the ancient household, is the precondition for a more adequate interpretation of Galatians 3:28 within its broader text complex. Schüssler Fiorenza offers us such an interpretation in *Rhetoric and Ethic*.[9] She makes use of the materialist feminist critique of ideology found in the work of Rosemary

Hennessy to uncover how biblical exegesis often leaves unexamined its own assumptions about what gender is. It takes as commonsense and universal the Western construction of gender, which has existed only since the Enlightenment and which posits that men and women are constituted as two inherently different pyscho-biological sexes. In consequence, Galatians 3:28 is anachronistically read as overcoming gender duality.[10] In contrast, Schüssler Fiorenza is able to ask the key question that must be answered as the initial step in and prior to further historical reconstruction of Galatians 3:28.

> In order to understand and translate Gal. 3:26–29, one needs to ask, for instance, whether the expressions "Jew/Greek, slave/free" mean only men or whether they include wo/men so that wo/men as a matter of course belong to these groups.[11]

Schüssler Fiorenza acknowledges that "neither male nor female" would seem redundant if the previous two categories were already seen as gendered by those who first created the baptismal formula. She, therefore, sees Galatians 3:28c as referring specifically to the gender relations of patriarchal marriage. To judge the merit of this suggestion it is helpful to investigate more closely the premodern construction of gender.

In the ancient world, human nature was conceived of as a hierarchically ordered unity.[12] Hence the different social locations of human beings were thought of as polarities *internal* to this order. The modern idea that sexes or races are "separate but equal" would seem incoherent within this ancient frame of reference because by definition those who are different cannot be equal. Women were seen as inferior to men not because they did not share the same humanity as men but because in them humanity lacked the excellence it achieved in the male sex. Yet this lack of excellence was essential to the hierarchical order of the cosmos and human life within it. Without lack of excellence there could be no inequality; without inequality there could be no hierarchy; and without hierarchy there could be no order in the cosmos, the city, or the household. The *humanity* of women is not denied, but it is assigned a specific location in the hierarchy of being, which is simultaneously a hierarchy of purpose sustaining the collective life of human beings. The distinction of sex serves the purpose of procreation, and patriarchal marriage exceeds the breeding of animals and slaves, which augments only the property of the household, because it produces heirs and therefore reproduces the social hierarchy of the household. Thus, the distinction "male and female" in antiquity did not denote two radically different psycho-biological versions of humanity but the hierarchical ordering of the human race to achieve the purpose of procreation and through marriage the continuity of the social order.

Schüssler Fiorenza may be both right and wrong in seeing Galatians 3:28c as referring to patriarchal marriage. She is right in that the sex distinction achieved its highest purpose in marriage, the reproduction of the social order through legitimate heirs. Yet the sex distinction served a procreative function also among the slaves, which was ordered to, admittedly, a lesser good, the increase of the household's property through the birth of new slaves. Galatians 3:28c may well have seen the sex distinction being abolished among the slave as well as the free since procreation was no longer necessary in the Christian community. This is not to claim that the baptismal formula originated in a community practicing sexual asceticism. Procreation had lost its purpose in Christian communities in the middle decades of the first century because the impending reign of God made the physical and ideological reproduction of the household redundant. Furthermore, behind the situation of the baptismal formula in the Pauline text there may have lain not the renunciation of sex but the disavowal of the hierarchical order. It is this possibility of resisting kyriarchy that Schüssler Fiorenza chooses to reconstruct as the meaning of the formula standing in tension with the Pauline text.[13]

Slaves were obviously also situated in the hierarchical unity of human nature and the hierarchical order of the cosmos, city, and household. One can make statements about slavery that are parallel to the ones just made about gender. The humanity of slaves is not denied, but their inferiority maintains a hierarchical order and serves a purpose within it. Yet the distinction between slave and free serves no single and easily defined purpose such as procreation. The labor of slaves had practical utility, but in the Greco-Roman world of the first century the tasks and roles assigned to slaves were very diverse indeed and often not distinguished from those of the nonelite free. On the ideological level, slavery was intrinsic to the very notion of freedom itself. Yet enslavement was often portrayed as an arbitrary fate in Greek romances and Roman comedies, an attitude that was reinforced by the actual conquest and enslavement of millions of people during the expansion of the Roman Empire.[14] The distinction between slave and free became even more precarious when its gendered character was revealed. In their introduction to a collection of essays exploring the intersection of slavery and gender in antiquity, Sandra Joshel and Sheila Murnaghan remark:

> Gender and slavery are not independent phenomena that operate in parallel ways but intersecting variables in a process that we have labeled "differential

equations" whereby women and slaves are assimilated only to be distinguished, compared but never quite identified. . . . Throughout Greco-Roman culture the most urgent issues are addressed through the permutations that result when gender and slavery are crossed with one another: the free woman, the female slave, the male slave, the free man.[15]

Gender always implies and is constructed through sexuality, and the inferiority of slaves marked them for sexual exploitation.[16] Male as well as female slaves were sexually vulnerable, and the sexual subjection of slaves of both sexes was critical to the boundary between slavery and freedom because it indicated the free person's honor and the slave's lack of honor.[17] In the ancient world, honor, like virtue, was not a gender-neutral concept. A free woman's honor was dependent on the preservation of her chastity.[18] The male slave's lack of honor was certainly inscribed by the fact that he could be penetrated like a woman. His masculinity was compromised because, instead of fulfilling the male role of penetrator, he could find himself in the female role of the penetrated. But how did penetration of a slave woman, which also denoted her dishonor, affect her femininity, or, put in the terms of the anxiety of the freeborn of antiquity, in what way was the penetration of a slave woman different from the subordination of a free woman in sexual intercourse? In the differentiation of the two classes of women, chastity played the crucial role. If one is considering elite women, then the freeborn woman was sexually available only in marriage (and, of course, sexually limited to marriage unless she wanted to brave social censure and legal penalties). However, free women of humble origins could not aspire to marriage with a man of high social status, and in such cases concubinage was the legally recognized form of the sexual relationship. Here the boundary between slave and free became blurred, since a freedwoman could also enter into marriage and into the legally recognized form of concubinage, not to mention all the informal forms of concubinage in which a man would take a slave woman as his permanent sexual partner and treat her in many respects as a wife or legal concubine.[19] Free men who did not belong to the highest social ranks could manumit a female slave and marry her. The stark contrast between the free woman's honor and chastity and the slave woman's lack of honor and sexual availability was constructed on the model of the elite woman's legal and social status compared to that of a female slave.[20]

Although ideologically dominant, this construct did not always coincide with the experience of freeborn women of the lower classes, who would have seen and in many cases resented a far less defined boundary between their status and that of female slaves and freedwomen. This is not to say that sexuality provided a path to upward social mobility for many female slaves; enslaved women were infinitely more often made prostitutes than they were made wives. Nonetheless, the idea of the slave woman as the sexual (and potentially social) competitor of the free woman exercised considerable influence on the ancient imagination. Ancient literature, like literature about the American Old South, abounds in examples of jealous wives who harshly treat the female slaves whom they view as sexual rivals. The actual reality was probably very different. In many cases neither the free wife nor the female slave would have wanted the sexual attention of the husband. What was really in jeopardy was not the sexual partnership between husband and wife but an unambiguous articulation of the free wife's social status.

Whenever slavery and gender intersected in the social hierarchy, there was the risk of dissonance in the categories of identity it established. Although this carried the potential of disrupting the social and symbolic order, resistance was hindered also because solidarity between subordinated groups was undermined by their competition. Freedwomen as well as freeborn women worried about their husbands' sexual liaisons with female slaves. Similar dismay might be provoked by their husbands' sexual use of male slaves. Even greater fear was occasioned by the prospect of free women having sex with male slaves, which was criminalized under Roman law but was so unthinkable to the patriarchal imagination that accusations were rare.[21] Sexuality was deployed, on the one hand, to maintain the hierarchical social order through the contrast of the free wife's chastity and honor to the female slave's sexual degradation, and through the demolition of the male slave's masculinity through sexual penetration. On the other hand, this inscription of social hierarchy through the legally unconstrained access of free men to slaves simultaneously threatened what it reinforced.[22] The problem of distinguishing between the sexual subjection of the free wife, the female slave, and the male slave was never adequately resolved, and thus a source of conflict among the subordinated and within the social order persisted.

Turning back to Galatians 3:28 in the light of the uneasy but necessary connection of slavery to gender, we can now detect how the three pairings Jew/Greek, slave/free, and male/female are related to one another. Despite their syntactic equivalence, there is a disjuncture between the first polarity of Jew/Greek and the second and third polarities slave/free and male/female. This goes against the grain of the usual interpretation of this verse, which appeals to the repetition of the first two pairs and omission of the third in later Pauline and Deutero-Pauline contexts (1 Cor. 12:13. and Col. 3:11) . If anything, it would seem that the pair male/female is qualitatively different from the other pairs. I would counter, however, that this conventional interpretation describes the trajectory of the baptismal formula in Pauline thought and does not answer how these categories of identity were related to one another in the original baptismal formula. When one reads Galatians 3:28 as a series of three parallel statements, then the distinction between Jew and Greek is one of religious or ethnic privilege and division; between slave and free it is class privilege and division; and between male and female the distinction is one of gender privilege and division. Now it is quite clear who holds privilege and who is subordinated in the groups slave/free and male/female throughout the ancient Mediterranean world and beyond. However, Jews held no such universal religious or ethnic privilege in the Greco-Roman world. On the contrary, they were frequently persecuted and despised.[23] Shortly before Galatians was written, many Alexandrian Jews had been killed in a pogrom in 38 C.E., and the following century saw the mass destruction of Jewish populations in disastrous conflicts in Palestine, Egypt, and elsewhere. The assumption that Galatians 3:28a is a statement about Jewish religious privilege and superiority is entirely dependent on its context of the anti-Judaizing polemic of Paul's letter.[24]

Taken on its own, the baptismal formula speaks of three differences among human beings in the Greco-Roman world, having the one common denominator that they can lead to conflict. Understanding it in this way, we can gain a fresh perspective on the meaning of the baptized being described as "one in Christ Jesus" in Galatians 3:28d. This "oneness" has been interpreted either as ontological sameness or as equality (whether spiritual, social, or both). The arguments for ontological sameness put their weight on the male/female distinction, seeing some form of androgyny in which either there is ontological unification of the sexes or the female is absorbed and transformed into the male.[25] The arguments for equality start from the social inequality of slave/free and male/female and then assimilate the Jew/Greek distinction by claiming that this refers to the religious inequality of Jew and Gentile. Instead, I am proposing that an analogy is being drawn between the communal strife of Jew and Greek and the conflictual relationships inherent in the patriarchal dual system of slavery and gender. The original baptismal formula proclaimed "oneness" in Christ as the overcoming of hostility. Although internal dissension between Jew and Greek in the Christian community could have been the motivation for the inclusion of 3:28a in the original baptismal formula, it is not its necessary presupposition. Any Christian community composed of Jews and Gentiles would have had its internal cohesion threatened by mounting animosity toward Jews in the broader society of the first century. Civic life was a site of communal struggle between Jews and Greeks in ways similar to the patriarchal household as a site of conflict between the *paterfamilias* and his subordinates and among the latter. The household was frequently viewed as a microcosm of the city, and civic strife was often seen as being reflected in the household. One characteristic that Jews, slaves, and women shared was that, in the Greco-Roman world, they could all be seen as disloyal—Jews to city and empire, slaves to masters, and wives to husbands.[26] The original formulation of Galatians 3:28 was replacing the city and the household as sources of identity and conflict with Christ as the source of a new identity and harmony.

Although Paul's deployment of Galatians 3:28 in the polemic of his letter obscures its prior meaning of Christian baptism as overcoming hostility, we find that the original sense reemerges when Paul uses another version of the baptismal formula in 1 Corinthians 12:13. Paul is concerned in 1 Corinthians 12 that the different gifts and activities in the Christian community not lead to dissension. Here Paul relates "oneness" in Christ neither to ontological (or functional) sameness nor to social or spiritual equality. Christians are not identical to one another in the roles they play within the community, nor is there an equality of function. A significant difference between 1 Corinthians 12:12–13 and Galatians 3:27–28 is that the Corinthian passage identifies oneness with inclusion in the body of Christ: "we were baptized into one body—Jews or Greeks, slaves or free." Paul thinks of the body as hierarchically organized, the physical human body being a metaphor for the organization of the church as Christ's body. The justification of social hierarchy through comparison to the well-functioning human body occurred frequently in antiquity.[27] Paul, however, balances the call for hierarchical unity with an emphasis on the respect and honor due to its inferior members— "those members of the body that we think less honorable we clothe with greater honor, and our less respectable members are treated with greater respect" (1 Cor. 12:23). Is Paul recognizing here that hierarchical orders tend to subvert the harmony they claim to achieve by provoking resentment and resistance in the subordinated? If this is the case, then the further question arises of whether the original baptismal formula itself envisaged Christians being initiated into a hierarchy that overcame hostility among its members by affording even the most subordinated some measure of honor.

Yet perhaps this is the wrong question, at least at the outset, to pose. More likely is it that this baptismal formula generated a range of responses among early Christians, of which the Pauline texts are only one. Paul does not invest it with any emancipatory and egalitarian meaning, and this is more the case in Galatians than in 1 Corinthians. Taking the larger complex of Galatians 3–4, the overall argument of Paul is to demonstrate that Christians are the true descendants of Abraham. Integral to that argument is the Hagar–Sarah allegory in Galatians 4:21–31, which draws its metaphors from the patriarchal dual system of slavery and gender. Sarah and Hagar are pitted against each other within a patriarchal household. Sarah is in the most vulnerable position of a free woman, a childless wife. Deprived of her primary function in the patriarchal household, the ability to give birth to her husband's heir, she must endure her slave becoming her husband's concubine and thus producing for him an heir. Paul retells the Genesis story to stress the conflict between mistress and slave, the rivalry between Hagar's and Sarah's sons, and the absolute superiority of the free woman and her child to the slave woman and her offspring. Paul describes Hagar as "bearing children for slavery" (4:24), who, although they are the physical descendants of Abraham, will not be his heirs (4:30). If, as I have argued, Galatians 3:28b–c is foremost about overcoming the hostility inherent in the patriarchal dual system of slavery and gender, then Paul's development of the Hagar–Sarah allegory is fundamentally at odds with its basic import. If one wants to go further, as I would, and claim that an emancipatory and egalitarian understanding of the baptismal formula was possible and present in early Christianity, then Paul is opposed to that as well.

Such a conclusion has recently been attacked by Brigitte Kahl, who wants to "challenge the common notion of Paul's overall 'conservatism' regarding gender issues and slavery."[28] Her central argument is that Galatians as a whole problematizes masculinity, the male body as a marker of religious identity and superiority (circumcision), and patrilineal kinship. In contrast to this, she sees motherhood becoming symbolically dominant in the letter and calls Galatians 4 "the 'mother-chapter' of Paul," but prefers to leave the slave/free contrast in the Hagar–Sarah allegory out of consideration.[29] When Kahl does address the slavery imagery of Galatians 4:21–31, she argues that "Paul completely confuses the traditional groups of binary polarities of Jewish and non-Jewish, slave and free, male and female."[30] She sees the Hagar–Sarah allegory as belonging to a broader sociorhetorical strategy of Paul, whom she thinks is extricating human identities from their positioning as binary opposites in a hierarchical order, without abolishing differences between human beings. Paul, according to her reading, is advocating a "non-repressive, egalitarian and communitarian Christian identity and unity" in which the "hierarchy between dominant and dominated is transformed into community."[31] One can appreciate how her "difference without hierarchy" model would allow for an egalitarian community between men and women within a narrow definition of gender, but one must seriously doubt whether it can be applied to slaves and free persons. After all, the difference between slave and free is by definition a hierarchical one, since outside the hierarchy of slavery there are no slaves and freedom has to be reconceptualized as something other than not being a slave. Apart from this conceptual difficulty, there still remains the problem of accounting for the harshness of Paul's description of Hagar and her son. Unfortunately, Kahl does this by claiming that the historical reality encoded in the allegory is the "highly marginalized and persecuted Pauline vision of a universal and egalitarian messianic Jewishness which tries to defend itself against the superiority claims of a violently exclusive branch of pre-70 Judaism."[32] Schüssler Fiorenza has pointed out that Kahl's "argument needs at least certain segments of Judaism as a negative foil."[33]

Kahl does, however, have a second line of argument in which she connects Paul's abandoning of the dichotomy of slave and free in Galatians 3:28 with Paul's depiction of Christian behavior in Galatians 5:13–6:10. Here she believes that Paul subverts any notion of Christian community built on hierarchy and supplants it with one of a community founded on mutuality, in which the members serve one another. Quite correctly, she translates *douleuete allēlois* in Galatians 5:13 as the call to perform "mutual slave service," but is she right in assuming that this would subvert the hierarchy of slavery?[34] Two caveats spring immediately to mind. First, this is an injunction addressed not specifically to slave owners and slaves but to all members of the community. It is setting up very generalized standards of behavior and does not deal with how Christians should view a person's legal status. Second, in the Greco-Roman world it was not uncommon for free persons, even members of the elite, to describe themselves metaphorically as slaves.[35] This is not to deny that Galatians 5:13 did have implications for the relationship of slaves and slave owners but to question whether one should see this verse as such an unequivocal subversion of the hierarchy of slavery.

Comparison to 1 Corinthians can be helpful in determining what Paul intended to say here about the relation of an ethics of mutuality to social hierarchy. We have already seen that in Paul's application of the hierarchy of the physical body to roles and functions in the Christian community in 1 Corinthians 12 he certainly wants those with inferior status within the hierarchy not to be subjected to degradation but to be shown honor (12:23–25). Paul would have expected Christian slave owners to avoid the brutal excesses that slavery as a system of social degradation entailed. However, Paul in 1 Corinthians, as in Galatians, confuses the language of freedom and slavery without questioning the continued existence of slavery in the Christian community. 1 Corinthians 7:22 provides a definitive example of how Paul rhetorically complicates the language of slavery and freedom without undermining the social institution: "For whoever was called in the Lord as a slave is a freedperson belonging to the Lord, just as whoever was free when called is a slave of Christ." There is no doubt that Paul accepts in 1 Corinthians 7:21–24 the continued practice of slavery among Christians, but he also believes that the relationships of the patriarchal household (marriage and slavery) are redundant as a framework of meaning in which Christians view their lives. Paul's apocalyptic reasoning in 1 Cor 7:29–31 permeates his attitude to the patriarchal dual system of slavery and gender, inscribed in the patriarchal household. To view Paul as a social conservative or social egalitarian ignores that Paul's ideological lens for viewing social relationships is primarily apocalyptic. He is neither a defender nor a detractor of the ancient social order, which he believes is passing away.

CONCLUSION: LOOKING FOR
THE *EKKLĒSIA* OF WOMEN AND SLAVES

I do not want to let Paul have the last word, because when his text becomes the measure of early Christian identity, community, and practice, then we give up trying to reconstruct the other voices that historically were present in first-century Christianity. Although I have characterized Galatians 3:28 as concerned with overcoming hostility, this does not preclude an egalitarian implication either today or in the first century. Indeed, women, slaves, and members of other socially subordinated groups in the early Christian churches may have been less willing than Paul to leave the hierarchical social order intact during the interim before Christ's return. Many would have had little stake in preserving the reified and subjugated identities assigned to them by the social hierarchy. They would have been more likely to perceive that the hierarchical social order was often unable to deliver on its promise of harmony because they would have borne the brunt of the conflicts it engendered. Hence, some of them would have viewed baptism as the overcoming of hostility through integration into a nonhierarchical unity where the identities prescribed by the kyriarchal society no longer defined them. Baptism would provide a new social practice through which the Christian *ekklēsia* would be differentiated from the household and the city with their hierarchical divisions.

Not all early Christian women, slaves, and other subordinated persons would have adopted an emancipatory and egalitarian interpretation of the baptismal formula in Galatians 3:28. Many would have clung to the relative "privilege" afforded them by their status in the patriarchal household as freeborn wife, or well-placed slave, or freedman of a wealthy man of the elite. Many would have hoped for Paul's solution of an amelioration of the harsh and brutal conditions of the slaveholding patriarchy in their particular situation, especially if they were owned by a Christian householder, while waiting with expectation for its disappearance at Christ's return. Christ did not return, and the patriarchal household endured, casting a long shadow even over the institutions of contemporary society. Yet the patriarchal household's victory was never complete. One enactment of the baptismal formula of Galatians 3:28 is to be found in the story of Thecla. The *Acts of Paul and Thecla* relate how this elite young woman refuses marriage and quits her place in the patriarchal household even under the threat of death. She cuts her hair, effacing her gender status not only as a woman but also as a free woman. Jennifer Glancy has pointed out that the sexual availability of slave women is the backdrop for the incident in which Thecla is physically and publicly embraced by the free elite male Alexander.[36] She resists his embrace, which leads once more to her being sentenced to death. After yet another miraculous rescue in the arena she does not return to safety and to her high status within the patriarchal household. Instead, wearing male clothing she takes up the life of a wandering apostle. The legend of Thecla led to further stories of women who abandoned the patriarchal household and went on pilgrimage alone or without male protection to the shrines of Thecla. They too risked sexual assault because they now belonged to those marginalized women who could be treated as slaves. Behind these stories of Thecla and her followers are the historical lives of itinerant women ascetics and the reality of women's piety in late antiquity.[37]

Long after the New Testament *Haustafeln* had been written, women continued to resist the patriarchal household, defying its prescriptions on female behavior which distinguished between honorable free women and those who could be dishonored like slaves. The trajectory of Galatians 3:28 does not begin in the Pauline text or end within the boundaries of canonical scripture. Androcentric and kyriocentric New Testament texts and later readings of those texts could erase the historical memory of those who through the baptismal formula preserved in Galatians 3:28 subverted the identities assigned to them within a hierarchical social order and performed new Christian identities within an egalitarian and emancipatory early Christian community. The historical possibility of an egalitarian and emancipatory performance of Christian identities could not be eliminated. To hold up the possibility of an emancipatory and egalitarian appropriation of the baptismal formula in Galatians 3:28 in first-century Christianity is, as Elisabeth Schüssler Fiorenza has argued, not to romanticize Christian origins but to recognize that Christianity has always been a pluriform movement and the site of sociopolitical contestation.[38]

NOTES

1. See, e.g., Neil Elliott, *Liberating Paul: The Justice of God and the Politics of the Apostle* (Maryknoll, N.Y.: Orbis Books, 1994), x–xi. He says that it is Schüssler Fiorenza's "public appeal to biblical scholars to engage their professional activities in a broader struggle for justice that informs the approach that I take here. This book is an attempt to apply such politically engaged interpretation to the legacy of Paul."

2. Owing to limitations of space, I will not be discussing 1Corinthians 6–7 here, but I have addressed elsewhere the intersection of slavery, gender, and sexuality in these chapters. See Sheila Briggs, "Paul on Bondage and Freedom in Imperial Roman Society," in *Paul and Politics: Ekklesia, Israel, Imperium, Interpretation: Essays in Honor of Krister Stendahl* (Harrisburg, Pa.: Trinity Press International, 2000), 114–17.

3. Elisabeth Schüssler Fiorenza, *In Memory of Her: A Feminist Theological Reconstruction of Christian Origins* (New York: Crossroad, 1983), 217–18.

4. See the chapter "Discipleship and Patriarchy" in Elisabeth Schüssler Fiorenza, *Bread Not Stone: The Challenge of Feminist Biblical Interpretation* (Boston: Beacon, 1984), 65–92; also the chapter "Justa—Constructing Common Ground," in Elisabeth Schüssler Fiorenza, *But She Said: Feminist Practices of Biblical Interpretation* (Boston: Beacon, 1992), 102–32.

5. Schüssler Fiorenza, *But She Said*, 114–15. She argues: "an 'adding on' method conceptualizes the patriarchal oppression of women not as an interlocking, multiplicative and overarching system, but as parallel systems of domination which divide women against each other. To list parallel oppressions, or to speak of 'dual system

oppression' (patriarchy and capitalism), or even of the triple oppression of women in patriarchal societies, obscures the *multiplicative* interstructuring of the pyramidal hierarchical structures of ruling which affect women in different social locations differently." She then uses the definition of "multiplicative" found in the black feminist thought of Deborah K. King. It is not simply the case that some women suffer multiple oppressions but that these various oppressions multiply one another.

6. Schüssler Fiorenza, *Bread Not Stone*, 89–90. Here she refers to the work of the feminist political philosopher Susan Moller Okin.

7. "The patriarchal order of the house, when applied to the order of the church, restricts the leadership of wealthy women and maintains the social exploitation of slave-women and men, even within the Christian household community" (Schüssler Fiorenza, *In Memory of Her*, 291). "When I speak of the *ekklēsia* of women, I have in mind women of the past and of the present, women who have acted and still act in the power of the life-giving Sophia-Spirit" (p. 350).

8. Schüssler Fiorenza, *But She Said*, 108–13. She discusses here the work of Tamsin E. Lorraine and Teresa L. Ebert. She concludes, "If ideology conceals not only its own inconsistencies and contradictions but also its very own construction, then it becomes important to destabilize even further the illusion of a unified, stable subjectivity that patriarchal hegemony constructs. This must be done, I suggest, by specifying patriarchy not just in terms of gender but also in terms of race, social status and civilization" (p. 113).

9. Elisabeth Schüssler Fiorenza, *Rhetoric and Ethic: The Politics of Biblical Studies* (Minneapolis: Fortress, 1999), 149–73.

10. Ibid., 151–54.

11. Ibid., 155–56.

12. Aristotle laid the foundations of this mode of thinking about the human person and society. His *Politics* set out the connections and differences between city and household, gender relations and slavery and how the subordination of inferior to superior is natural and the natural basis of social relationships.

13. Schüssler Fiorenza, *Rhetoric and Ethic*, 157.

14. Part of the social reality of slavery in the Roman Empire was the memory of enslavement. Whether one was freeborn, a slave, or a freedperson, one learned accounts of enslavement as one witnessed the everyday degradation of slaves. For example, the Corinthian Christians lived in a city that was one of the major slave markets of the ancient Mediterranean and which had been founded as a Roman colony in 44 B.C.E. by Julius Caesar and mainly settled by Roman freedpersons. First-century inhabitants of Corinth would also know the fate of the earlier Greek city, which Pausanias relates in his *Description of Greece*. When the fall of Corinth to Roman armies took place in 146 B.C.E., the defeated general, Diaeus, committed suicide after he had "killed his wife with his own hand, just to save her from being taken prisoner" (7.16.6). Ancient readers (and many modern ones) would not need to be told the reason for Diaeus's killing of his wife. Captured and enslaved, she would be

subject to sexual violation and she would thus lose her honor (and also her husband's), a lot quite literally worse than death in the mind of this freeborn elite man. The fate feared by Diaeus for his wife overtook many of the inhabitants of Corinth, who had not fled the city when the Romans captured it. "The majority of those found in it were put to the sword by the Romans, but the women and children Mummius [the Roman commander] sold into slavery" (716.8).

15. *Women and Slaves in Greco-Roman Culture: Differential Equations,* ed. Sandra R. Joshel and Sheila Murnaghan (London/New York: Routledge, 1998), 3–4.

16. For a recent treatment, see Jennifer A. Glancy, *Slavery in Early Christianity* (Oxford/New York: Oxford University Press, 2002), 24–27.

17. Ibid., 27–29.

18. Susan Treggiari has disputed the claim that Romans thought of women's chastity in terms of honor, but Thomas McGinn has argued for the existence of honor/shame categories in Roman society. He has argued that the laws on marriage (especially adultery) and on prostitution developed in tandem and that prostitution became a legal foil for marriage and the distinction between honorable women and those who lacked honor. Since the majority of prostitutes were slaves, and slaves and prostitutes were grouped together in several legal regulations, especially of dress, the contrast between honorable women and those without honor was linked to the binary opposites of freedom and slavery. See Susan Treggiari, *Roman Marriage: Iusti Coniuges from the Time of Cicero to the Time of Ulpian* (New York: Oxford University Press, 1991), 311–13; Thomas A. McGinn, *Prostitution, Sexuality, and the Law in Ancient Rome* (New York: Oxford University Press, 1998).

19. For the Roman law of concubinage, see Jane F. Gardner, *Women in Roman Law and Society* (Bloomington: Indiana University Press, 1986), 56–60.

20. See Richard P. Saller, "Symbols of Gender and Status Hierarchies in the Roman Household" in *Women and Slaves,* ed. Joshel and Murnaghan, 89.

21. See Sarah B. Pomeroy, *Goddesses, Whores, Wives, and Slaves: Women in Classical Antiquity* (New York: Schocken Books, 1975), 196; Antti Arjava, *Women and Law in Late Antiquity* (New York: Oxford University Press, 1996), 220–27. Although having sex with one's slaves constituted *stuprum* (unlawful sexual conduct) or adultery, if the woman was married, there is only one extant legal case before the time of Constantine. Ancient writers rarely mention women having sex with slaves, and it was thought of as an obvious depravity (see n. 23 below). Freeborn women who cohabited with male slaves were to be reduced to slavery themselves according to a law passed by the Senate in 52 C.E. However, the motive here was to prevent dimunition of the slaveholder's property since children derived their status from their mothers. Therefore, the children of such a union would not belong to their father's owner but would be free. The women affected by this law were of humble origins, and it seems to have been only spasmodically enforced.

22. Although legal, the sexual use of slaves by free men did not escape moral crit-

icism from philosophers. Musonius Rufus (*Fragments* 12.221–22) condemned men who sought sex outside marriage and the common opinion that there was nothing wrong in having sex with one's own slaves. He pointed out that men would find it intolerable if married or unmarried women had sex with their slaves. Men, in his view, should hold themselves to the same standard, since their behavior should not be morally inferior to the weaker sex. However, his concern is not with the harm done to the female slave, as Susan Treggiari has pointed out (*Roman Marriage*, 313), but with the lack of self-control in the free man. Sexual excess belonged to the character of the slave, not to the free man, and undermined his moral authority over his wife and his household. Plutarch also argues against the double standard in marriage and that spouses should only have sexual intercourse with each other (*Moralia* 144b). Yet, shortly before this statement, he has advised a bride that she should not object to her husband having sex with a female slave because he can find in the slave an outlet for sexual acts that it would be shameful to practice with his wife (*Moralia* 140b).

23. See L. H. Feldman, *Jew and Gentile in the Ancient World: Attitudes and Interactions from Alexander to Justinian* (Princeton: Princeton University Press, 1993), 107–76.

24. The identity of Paul's opponents remains unresolved. Mark Nanos has recently made the proposal that they were the local Jewish communal leaders who wished to prevent provoking pagan mistrust and attack. Gentile Christians were an anomalous group, since they were neither proselytes to Judaism nor were they fulfilling their civic responsibilities as pagans. Gentile Christians blurred the boundary between Jew and pagan and could therefore exacerbate tensions between the two communities. See Mark D. Nanos, *The Irony of Galatians: Paul's Letter in First-Century Context* (Minneapolis: Fortress, 2002), 203–83.

25. See Wayne A. Meeks, "The Image of the Androgyne: Some Uses of a Symbol in Earliest Christianity," *History of Religions* 13 (1974): 165–208; Hans Dieter Betz, *Galatians: A Commentary on Paul's Letter to the Churches in Galatia* (Philadelphia: Fortress, 1979), 189–200; Dennis Ronald MacDonald, *There Is No Male and Female: The Fate of a Dominical Saying in Paul and Gnosticism*, Harvard Dissertations in Religion (Philadelphia: Fortress, 1987).

26. On women and slaves, see Holt Parker, "Loyal Slaves and Loyal Wives: The Crisis of the Outsider-Within and Roman *Exemplum* Literature," in *Women and Slaves*, ed. Joshel and Murnaghan, 152–73. Apuleius in *The Golden Ass* relates numerous tales of disloyal wives and disloyal slaves, including the story of the baker's wife who compounds her moral turpitude with impiety by worshiping only one God; that is, she is either Christian or Jewish (9.14).

27. The most famous example and one frequently quoted in the literature on 1 Corinthians 12 is the speech of Menenius Agrippa, who in the early Roman republic prevented a rebellion of the plebeians against the patricians with a parable about the body. The other members of the body revolted against the stomach, which

seemed to do nothing except eat what the rest of the body worked hard to obtain. They went on strike but soon found that they all suffered when the stomach received no food (Livy, *History of Rome* 2.32).

28. Brigitte Kahl, "No Longer Male: Masculinity Struggles Behind Galatians 3:28," *Journal for the Study of the New Testament* 79 (2000): 38.

29. Ibid., 43. "While I cannot go into the debate of the free-slave polarity at this point, the effect of the allegory in terms of male and female is quite clear."

30. Brigitte Kahl, "Gender Trouble in Galatia? Paul and the Rethinking of Difference," in *Is There a Future for Feminist Theology?* ed. Deborah F. Sawyer and Diane M. Collier (Sheffield: Sheffield Academic Press, 1999), 68.

31. Ibid., 67.

32. Ibid., 68.

33. Schüssler Fiorenza, *Rhetoric and Ethic,* 165.

34. Kahl, "Gender Trouble in Galatia," 66. "One of the most striking examples of this paradigm is the subversion and 'conversion' of the hierarchical polarity of slave and free. After Paul has established 'our' identity as children 'not of the slave woman but of the free woman' in 4.31, this freedom a few verses later is explained precisely as doing slave service to one another–through love (5.13)" (Kahl, "No Longer Male," 47).

35. Numerous examples can be found in literature, philosophy, and politics. Of course, Paul describes himself using the metaphor of slavery in 1 Cor. 9:19. For the connection of Paul's usage to the figure of the enslaved leader in ancient rhetoric, see Dale B. Martin, *Slavery as Salvation: The Metaphor of Slavery in Pauline Christianity* (New Haven: Yale University Press, 1990), 86–116. See also Kathleen McCarthy, "Servitium Amoris, Amor Servitii," in *Women and Slaves,* ed. Joshel and Murnaghan, 174–92. She looks at elite men describing themselves as slaves in Roman love elegy. She concludes that the "objectification of slaves and women that I have argued is central to the genre's project obviously maintains the practices and values that were accepted as normal in this culture" (p. 189).

36. Glancy, *Slavery in Early Christianity,* 14.

37. Stephen J. Davis, *The Cult of Saint Thecla: A Tradition of Women's Piety in Late Antiquity,* Oxford Early Christian Studies (Oxford/New York: Oxford University Press, 2001), 49, 71–73, 133–48. Davis sees Thecla's transvestism as a "physical expression of the baptismal dissolution of gender distinctions mentioned in Galatians 3:28" (pp. 31–32).

38. Schüssler Fiorenza, *Rhetoric and Ethic,* 145–48.

12

Magdalene christianity

Jane Schaberg

———————

ELISABETH SCHÜSSLER FIORENZA TEACHES US TO BREAK SCHOLARLY stereotypes and boundaries: between writer/reader and scholar/literary theoretician; between the activist and the thinker; between the scholar of religion and the religious/spiritual person; between the believer and agnostic/atheist. I offer this essay in the hope that it might follow her lead and be of use not only to scholars but to wo/men[1] changing religion and politics in the twenty-first century.

My contribution here expands and revises three pages in my recent book *The Resurrection of Mary Magdalene*,[2] in which I argued that even if we may not be able precisely to locate its center(s), or identify all its leaders, we can imagine what I call Magdalene christianity, a movement or set of movements that continued, from the first century to the fourth and beyond, to exist and create on the basis of wo/men's insight, revelation, and leadership. In using the name of Mary Magdalene, which appears in the canon only in the Gospels, I am giving a name to something that was unnamed and associating it with the testimony of this specific named woman, testimony understood as central to the resurrection faith and as rooted in Jewish apocalyptic and wisdom traditions. Examination of the opposition to Magdalene christianity posed by Petrine, Pauline, and perhaps James and other traditions and versions will eventually give a fuller picture of the origins of Christianity, in particular of its struggles regarding egalitarianism.

By egalitarianism I do not mean the achieved ideal of a social organization that is without sexism, structures, and ideologies of domination, blindspots, and failures. I also do not mean an ideal that is clearly perceived by leaders or followers, or identical to the feminist ideals taking shape in our own time. Nor do I mean a society or ideology that ignores all issues of gender or is compatible with virulent misogyny and sexism. I mean rather a social reality characterized by the attempts of men and women to live and work together for a common goal as equals, in a variety of changing circumstances and understandings. In the religious sense, what characterizes egalitarianism is the attempt actually and fully to "incarnate" or embody certain beliefs such as the belief that all have equal access to salvation, that all are created in the image of God.

This is not what some have called the myth of Christian origins, the assumption that there was an original moment of perfect egalitarianism, from which subsequent history is a "fall."[3] Nor is it a version of the myth of matriarchal origins, which posits a woman-centered, goddess-centered culture of peace and harmony destroyed by "patriarchy." Cynthia Eller shows that there is *dis*confirming evidence of such a culture, that is, evidence of conflict and of a division of labor that was later associated with disproportionate value given to men's labors. There is also simple absence of proof positive, that is, no evidence that the original "matriarchal" society was utterly different from all that came after; no reason to expect that it would be so different; and no compelling explanation of why things changed drastically. Moreover, Eller criticizes such thinking as embedded in an unliberating theory of sex and gender that exaggerates differences between women and men, attributing complementary, (only) positive, nurturing characteristics to women.[4] Eller nevertheless knows that "matriarchal" myth is held up by things stronger than archaeological or historical evidence: by passionate hope and religious faith.

> [I]n theory, little can be said against the propriety of imagining a time—prehistoric if necessary—when women were treated well rather than badly, with respect rather than condescension or outright hatred. Envisioning a feminist future is arguably a necessary task. And insofar as envisioning a feminist past helps accomplish this—as it clearly does for many people—it would seem to have obvious merit.

It provides hope that male dominance can be ended, and it empowers women to imagine themselves as capable of leadership, autonomy, and creativity. But the problems and dangers, as Eller sees them, undercut the benefits. Origin stories tend to reduce historically specific facts and values to timeless archetypes, to offer solutions tailored not to specific cultural environments but to a totalizing image of "patriarchy," to project onto the past a vision of the world as it ought to be, to be convincing only to those who already ardently hope it is true, to trap women in archetypes of the Great Good Mother, and to create nostalgia for the lost past which is usually escapist rather than functional. These are staples "of right-wing antifeminist rhetoric." "Myth is not history capable of teaching us how to avoid past mistakes."[5]

The reconstruction of moments and phases of struggle that are proposed here is not about the perfection of a mythical time. Nor is it about the perfection of a mythical Jesus' attitudes and actions. Nor is it about an egalitarianism that came from nowhere, flashed into history, and was ended. Its roots are in Judaism's egalitarian impulses, and it is submerged in later history, but not ended. Nor is this reconstruction an overly optimistic invention of the past, wishful thinking based on a distortion of the evidence. Although there is healthy disagreement over the interpretation of certain texts, that disagreement has led to reassessment and sharper interpretation, imagination grounded in sober historical assessment. The claim is not that early Christianity and the Judaism from which it sprang and within which it took shape were not patriarchal or kyriarchal. The claim is that there were egalitarian movements struggling within—movements in which male domination was not total and women were active participants, with roles in creating some traditions that later centuries inherited. This is very different from projecting an ideal back into the past, and very different from nostalgic escapism. Evidence of women's leadership in early Christianity does not draw on stereotypical, archetypal ideals of women; it is accompanied always by evidence of opposition to women's leadership and multiple strategies for suppressing it. Knowledge of this history can help us imagine a different future and take steps to secure it. In this short essay, I make some broad speculations that cry out to be supported or challenged by detailed exegesis—thus the many maybes, might-bes, might-have-beens, perhaps, which indicate that I do not want my imagination cut free of evidence (as well as indicating that I see my historical reconstruction as tentative, possible, at the most probable). My frustration lies here in the need to wrestle this article and cut it to fit the present format, where it is only a sketch.

In my opinion, without the dimension of Magdalene christianity, conflicts in the canonical epistles, within the Gospels themselves, and in the apocrypha, including some so-called gnostic materials, make less sense. Just as important, with an exploration of Magdalene christianity, aspects of concepts and beliefs, such as the "Human One" (the Son of Man), are made more multidimensional and somewhat more comprehensible. The apocryphal materials function as a lens through which to view women and gender roles in the earlier *basileia* movements. Claims made for early egalitarinaism and the prominence of women are more possible, even more plausible or probable, seen through that lens. Our understanding of the conflict and variety that Walter Bauer argued for in early Christianity and its documents[6] is deepened by this complexity.

The value this may have for present-day reform movements can be likened to, for example, the value the uncovered memory of women healers has for the medical profession: contemporary medicine would change without this memory; but the past is part of the profession, and change is empowered and corrected by it. The future does not rest on, nor is it determined by, historical precedent. But we have an obligation to know and honor the past, to retrieve the memory of wo/men's struggle and agency.

The struggle for egalitarianism is situated in several contexts: (1) within individual communities, and in their different stages, (2) among them, in their efforts to work out what is later called orthodox and heretical, inside and outside, and (3) with outsiders like Celsus, who ridiculed the resurrection faith as based on the witness of "a hysterical female, as you say, and perhaps some other one of those who were deluded by the same sorcery" (Origen, *Contra Celsum* 2.55). (4) The struggle is situated also in later history and our own time, in multiple dimensions. Trying to give shape to what has been lost in the past is inextricably linked to contemporary enterprises, but recognition of this link does not necessitate a fall into ahistoricism or antihistoricism, oversimplification, or impatience with ambiguity, in the promotion of any particular agenda. "The legacy of history as history retains its ability to affect everyday lives by determining the weight of the past."[7] The weight of the particular past examined here is both ballast and burden, inspiring and depressing.

The figure of Mary Magdalene brings this past into focus. With growing popular awareness of the distortion of her image into repentant whore, and of correction of that distortion, she has been reinvented as a symbol for church reform: for example, for the ordination of Roman Catholic women, and not just for ordination.[8] This is an instance in which feminist historical criticism—diluted or pure—is getting out of the seminary and university into the workshop and discussion group and reading club and activist movements of wo/men. This scholarship, both a vehicle and a site for education,[9] involves transforming, transgressing, translating the tradition, and challenging fundamentalism. The harlotization, demonization, and taming of Mary Magdalene, and her rehabilitation, have parallels with the fate of Joan of Arc and a multitude of women, in their histories and representations. "The burning of Joan was an attempt to deaden a great deal more than a young woman with pretensions of prophecy. It was also an attempt to eradicate the nascent possibility of agency in a woman, of a possible weakness in the dominant discourse, requiring constant vigilance and cleansing, lest it be uncovered."[10] These attempts at eradication (short-lived in Joan's case, centuries long in Mary Magdalene's) failed. Neither was domesticated by canonization or by scholarship. Feminist work moves through the legends, the art, the distortions, to traditions of the Jewish woman Mary Magdalene who witnessed the crucifixion and death of Jesus and the empty tomb, and whose claim is at the core of the resurrection faith. It reads the canonical texts differently in the light of the surprisingly many noncanonical texts in which she appears[11] and vice versa. Movement beyond the canon—in particular, familiarity with the *Gospel of Mary*—persuades me of an ancient and widespread tradition about Mary Magdalene which the canon also reflects.

Reading the canonical Gospels against the current of much contemporary male criticism in which the women at the tomb disappear from history and/or their role disappears from serious theological consideration, some feminist interpreters' educated assumption is that an androcentric telling and stereotypes in the past and present have garbled and diminished the contribution of women.[12] This directs us to read gaps and slippages in the texts, in order to map out ancient and contemporary strategies of suppression and resistance. Three of the major insights of feminist scholarship of the last twenty-five years are relevant to our discussion:

1. The *basileia* movement associated with Jesus can be historically reconstructed as one of several renewal or revitalization groups[13] within Judaism (such as the Therapeutae, John the Baptist's group, the Essenes of Qumran, Simon ben Giora's revolutionary movement). Membership could cross social, economic, cultural, and religious gulfs.

2. These movements included women and men. They can be called "egalitarian" in the sense of struggle, meaning that there was certainly a spectrum of perceptions and roles on the part of the participants. In the case of the movement associated with Jesus, some women functioned historically as what the Gospels call disciples, even though the texts do not give them this title. Or—it has been suggested[14]—they may have been more than disciples: companions, even co-leaders. The paratactic structure of Luke 8:1–3 can be

read to mean that, along with Jesus, the Twelve and "certain women" pro-claimed and brought the good news of the kingdom.[15] A significant number of women are mentioned without reference to husbands or sons, a fact that may indicate that these relationships did not define the women, or that the women were without these relationships.

3. The memory of important women was distorted by a wide variety of strategies and "accidents," such as loss of the name; confusion and merging of identities; silencing through unreported speech, which means the erasure of their contribution; boxing the women characters into stereotypes and ideal types; nudging the reader's imagination in the direction of a negative evalua-tion of the women; and androcentric perspectives that put men at the center of events and women on the periphery (if in the picture at all). Even in the crucifixion/tomb narratives, the sheer number of verses in all four Gospels concerning the betrayal of Jesus by Peter far outweighs the number of verses paying attention to the women and signals how much more fascinating Peter was than they were, in this androcentric perspective.

With some minor differences, in the canonical Synoptic Gospels, Mary Magdalene is mentioned most prominently among the ministering women who followed Jesus from Galilee, though there is no narrative of her call, nor any narrative in which she plays an active role or speaks or is spoken to in the ministry. In the company of other women, she is said to have stood by at the crucifixion and burial, and to have come to the tomb. In the Gospel of John, her first appearance—unexplained—is at the cross; she is not said to witness the burial, but to come later, alone, to the tomb. Garbling, distortion, inven-tion, and loss—the signs of tension and importance—are evident in the telling of subsequent incidents at the tomb and afterwards, which involve the emptiness of the tomb and angelic revelations (all the Gospels), an appear-ance to her of the risen Jesus (only Matthew and John), a commission to tell (in all but Luke), and a telling (Luke, John, and the Markan Appendix, implied in Matthew; unbelieved in Luke and the Markan Appendix) or a silence (Mark). Mary Magdalene's testimony is trumped by appearances to male disciples and their commissioning in all the Gospels except Mark, which ends at the empty tomb with the women fleeing and saying nothing to any-one out of fear. Mary Magdalene is not named as one to whom the risen Jesus appeared in Paul's list in 1 Corinthians 15, nor is she named in Acts or in any other Christian Testament writing except the Gospels.

Apocryphal texts mention Mary Magdalene in ways that are strikingly dif-ferent from the picture of her in the canonical Gospels, to say nothing of the ways in which legends about her developed in Western Christianity. Most intruiging is the *Gospel of Mary [Magdalene]*.[16] Out of nine elements, at least four of which appear in each one of the twelve noncanonical texts that mention her, I created a profile of the gnostic/apocryphal Mary: (1) Mary is prominent among the companions of Jesus; (2) she exists as a character, as a memory, in a textual world of androcentric language and patriarchal ideology; (3) she speaks boldly; (4) she plays a leadership role vis-à-vis the male disciples; (5) she is a visionary; (6) she is praised for her superior understanding; (7) she is identified as the intimate companion of Jesus; (8) she is opposed by or in open conflict with one or more of the male disciples; (9) she is defended. In only one text, the *Gospel of Mary*, are all nine points found.[17]

Of the many issues raised by the gnostic/apocalyphal materials, four overlap: (1) How do noncanonical treatments of Mary Magdalene relate to the treatments in the Christian Testament, and to the historical woman Mary? (2) What does her apocryphal prominence indicate, if anything, of the roles of women in the communities in and for which the materials were produced? (3) Is there a relationship between her prominence in both canonical and noncanonical traditions and the canonical evidence in the letters of Paul of women's leadership in the earliest decades of Christianity? (4) Can a study of several elements (the historical women companions of Jesus; claims of their presence at cross and tomb and of a resurrection appearance to them; the women leaders mentioned in Romans, 1 Corinthians, and elsewhere; and the earliest controversies over the roles of women as documented in 1 Corinthians and the Pastorals) coalesce to help us begin to delineate aspects of an early egalitarian form of christianity? It is these last two questions that interest me here. More specifically, are there dots connecting the Gospel women, Mary Magdalene most prominent among them, the women prophets of Corinth, and Mary Magdalene in the *Gospel of Mary?*[18] What follows is an experiment in connecting the dots I think do exist, and in describing the image that results when the dots are connected. It will be obvious how incomplete this work is.[19]

There is enough evidence of her prominence to make it reasonable to assume that Mary Magdalene was understood and presented by some in the first to fourth centuries as a model or, rather, an inspiration to which later women connected their claims of authority and leadership. Since some women in the Judaisms (and Greco-Roman religions) of the time were leaders, Mary Magdalene would not have functioned as a ground-breaking precedent, but as an empowering memory and unfinished work.

Putting together the bits and pieces of evidence, with acute awareness that there would have been critical differences with regard to time and socio-religious locations, we can attempt a sketch of Magdalene christianity as an early alternative to Petrine and Pauline Christianities. The sketch is specula-tive, tentative, explorative, searching, full of (untyped) question marks.

1. In Magdalene christianity, women spoke boldly, with authority. Joanna Dewey argues that in the egalitarian Jesus movement women must have spo-ken as much as men. But their active role was reduced in the composition and selection of texts, a process in the hands of a small minority of literate men.[20] Surely, however, the speaking women companions of Jesus experienced androcentrism and efforts to silence them as well. The distinction between speaking in public and private contexts breaks down when we consider that women spoke in the synagogues and in Christian assemblies. In the list of names in Romans 16, almost half are the names of women well known in the community, known even to Paul, who had not visited Rome. The letters of Paul to the Corinthians clearly show that the church there in the fifties expe-rienced conflict over the roles of women, especially with regard to their prophetic speech.[21] The speech such of women was listened to, remembered, passed down, and developed by some. It was teaching.[22]

Paul is nastily sarcastic in the two rhetorical questions (1 Cor. 14:36) that follow his attempt to silence the Corinthian women prophets: "Or did the word of God originate with you? Or are you the only ones it has reached ($\bar{e}$ aph' hymōn ho logos tou theou exēlthen $\bar{e}$ eis hymas monous katēntēsen)?"[23] The questions are the reverse image of the question of Miriam and Aaron: "Has Yhwh spoken only through Moses? Has he not spoken through us also?" (Num. 12:2). Paul is mocking the Corinthian women for their extraordinary confidence, their speaking as a source and exclusive destination of God's word. He insists on the contrary that his own preaching carried from Pales-tine and based on authentic tradition (1 Cor. 15:3–11; 11:23–26) has been the source of all they know and has reached many. He is the origin; they are merely receivers; it is a one-way communication.[24] Antoinette Clark Wire points out that the masculine plural of the word "only" (monous) shows that Paul "cannot mean the women of Corinth are claiming to be the font of wis-dom against the men of Corinth. The context suggests an inclusive mascu-line in which the women addressed represent all those in Corinth who claim through prophecy to be an independent source and destination of God's word."[25]

Did the Corinthian women prophets, by presenting themselves as the or a point of origin and the point of destination of God's word in Corinth, mean only that God speaks in their prophecy? Or was there also some connection between them and Galilean women as the origin of their resurrection faith? Others besides Paul brought information and teaching to Corinth, including the itinerant Jewish preacher Apollos (1 Cor. 1:12; 3:4–6, 22; 4:6; 16:12), who, according to Acts, was familiar with the baptism of John and was instructed by Priscilla (Prisca) and Aquila (Acts 18:24–26; cf. 1 Cor. 16:19). Apollos may have had no personal contact with John the Baptist, but his knowledge may have come from disciples of John or from "a fragmentary report of the events in Palestine" between 25 and 30 C.E. L. D. Hurst thinks that Apollos's information probably included "*the* account of the resurrection" (emphasis mine) but "seems not to have included any knowledge about what took place immediately after Jesus' ascension; i.e., the coming of the Holy Spirit."[26] Let me modify this statement by suggesting that Apollos's information included an account of the resurrection stemming from the Galilean women, which had an understanding of the Spirit different from that of Paul (and Luke), and was probably indebted in some way to Prisca and Aquila.

If the Corinthian women prophets made any reference to Mary Magdalene and the other women, to the story of the empty tomb and the appearance to the women, then the absence of reference to these by Paul in 1 Corinthians 15 may be pointed, intended to undercut them. Wire thinks Paul's closed list, ending with himself, omitted mention of Mary Magdalene and other women probably in order to counter the claim of Corinthian women prophets that they experienced the risen Christ and spoke for him, to discourage their speech. Paul wished "not to provide support for women who prophesy in Corinth from the *news* [emphasis mine] that women's word was the genesis of the resurrection faith." But perhaps it was not news at all. Paul may have chosen not to mention anything connected to what the four Gospels consider the first resurrection accounts "because of some meaning of these stories in Corinth."[27]

Claiming a connection between, on the one hand, the historical role of Mary Magdalene and other women as witness to the death and burial of Jesus and as initiators of faith in the resurrection of Jesus and, on the other hand, the women whose leadership has left traces in the Christian Testament is not claiming that the figure and tradition of Mary Magdalene was the only model, source, and inspiration of this leadership. But if the witness of Mary Magdalene is historically and theologically central to early Christianity,[28] her later influence may bear some important relationship to the strong traces of women's prominence, their claims, and their agency in the first-century communities, especially in their speech.

2. Magdalene christianity sprang from and developed Jewish apocalyptic and wisdom and prophetic traditions, which are intellectually distinct but were existentially and chronologically intertwined, interrelated. This heritage especially fostered a type of mysticism and insistence on justice before and after death. By this mysticism, I mean a knowledge of God and self from contemplative or ecstatic experience, "lived out seriously in everyday life" and connected with resistance to injustice.[29] Mysticism was honored, with charisms open to all and nonhierarchical. Enthusiasm existed within a specific kind of order: the just order of Wisdom.[30] Prophecy (associated with Mary Magdalene in John 20:18[31]) was accepted as a gift that could be received and exercised by women and men. The belief that Jesus is risen was experienced in visions and free speech, in dress, and in common life. Communities open to hearing from men and women of all classes were democratic or democratizing,[32] with power, the "gifts," and authority (and their economic and educational aspects) decentralized and not in the hands of a few males. A reconstruction of such communities answers the question Jeffrey Kripal asks, "[W]hat would a religious or mystical tradition look like that took democracy seriously, and I mean *really* seriously?"[33] This is the question, What would an ancient mystical tradition of wo/men look like?[34]

With men and women in authority, it was not likely that the priesthood would have been of any literal interest,[35] since the Jerusalem temple priesthood was limited to men and involved animal sacrifice.[36] Only one apocryphal text associated with the name of Mary Magdalene has anything to do with the Eucharist (in the *Apostolic Church Order* Mary's laughing or smiling is given as a reason for banning women from the celebration of the Eucharist).[37] Perhaps in Magdalene christianity the Eucharist was understood not as a sacrifice but as an expression of communality, not as a representation of death but as a celebration of passover freedom. Unmediated access to God and the Spirit given freely were stressed. Succession was prophetic,[38] not linear and/or genealogical, and not as understood in Acts and the Pastorals and later.[39] The Spirit was believed to be given through baptism. In such communities, leadership had a chance of emerging in a spectrum of roles that emphasized nonhierarchical working together and serving together.

Silvia Schroer proposes that sources of the baptismal account in all four canonical Gospels were conceived in terms of Wisdom theology: the dove as symbol of Wisdom rests on Jesus. John the Baptist and Jesus are both Wisdom's children in Luke 7:31–35 (Q). Wisdom of Solomon's portrayal of the suffering, death, and translation of the just one influenced the Christian Testament crucifixion/resurrection traditions.[40] Wisdom theology, which inclusively identified the risen Jesus with Sophia, informed the understanding of the Corinthian wo/men prophets (cf. 1 Cor. 1:24–30), perhaps as preached by Apollos and drawn from a Palestinian source. Probably connected with baptism, their theology was misconstrued by Paul. Note that Mary Magdalene is called "the spirit of wisdom" in the *Manichaean Psalm Book* 2.194.19.[41] These separate but connected loci of Wisdom imagery and thought,[42] are instances of Sophia theology, which has been regarded by Elisabeth Schüssler Fiorenza as "the decisive factor" that made a community of equals, a liberating praxis, possible.[43]

3. Images of the Human One or Son of Man, derived from Jewish apocalyptic literature and developed in mystical traditions, were central to the *basileia* movement of Jesus and his companions, and to Magdalene christianity. The figure of the Human One (later narrowed to refer to the individual Jesus alone) was understood as corporate, and incorporating. Phillip B. Munoa III argues that the vision of Stephen in Acts 7, the throne scene in Revelation 4–5, and the series of visions in the early-third-century work *The Passion of Perpetua and Felicitas* demonstrate how a *merkavah* vision became associated with martyrdom.[44] In my opinion, this association was already in the spirituality and thinking of this *basileia* movement as an expectation of the suffering and resurrection of the Human One. A corporate, not individualistic, understanding of the Human One underlay and survived within certain interpretation(s) of the death and resurrection of Jesus. It grounded the belief seen in Corinth and elsewhere that the resurrection of the dead is in some way the resurrection of the living.

While the phrase *ho huios tou anthrōpou* does not appear in the Pauline writings (or anywhere outside the Gospels in the Christian Testament except Acts 7:56 [Stephen's vision] and Rev 1:13; 14:14 [John's visions][45]), for the prophets of Corinth, the metaphor of the body continued the function of the Human One: creating unity, shared authority, and joyful courage. But Paul used the body metaphor in a different way, stressing that the body has different parts related to different charisms (stratified, individual), and warning of the possibity of amputation. Egalitarian diversity was suppressed in favor of what Paul saw as the common good, in a kind of leveling that paradoxically reinstated ranking and hierarchy. The Corinthian prophets thought that they already bore the image of the one of heaven (the Human One); Paul thought that this lay in the future (1 Cor. 15:49).[46]

The masculine language ("Son of Man"), of course, must have alienated women, forced them to double-think in order not to regard themselves as excluded. But many women were and are good at that resistance, at paying that price. Androcentrism is an aspect of the imagination and utopian vision that is deformed by sexism and kyriarchy; but the deformation is not total, not fatal. That a woman could imagine herself or be imagined as included in this corporate figure leaves traces in Perpetua's metamorphosis into a "man" (*Passion* 10.7)[47] and even in sayings such as *Gospel of Thomas* 114, in which Jesus makes Mary Magdalene "male." Within the streams of tradition flowing from Daniel 7, this was not simply optimistic belief in the human species, the solidarity of the human race; it was rather an apocalyptic expectation and experience that conquered the sense of aloneness and the fear of death and empowered action.

Esther A. de Boer holds that the *Gospel of Mary* "advocates egalitarian discipleship in the sense that all disciples have been made *true Human Being* and all received the instruction to preach the gospel . . . and . . . all are prepared to preach the gospel of the Kingdom of *the Son of Man* [emphases mine]."[48] Karen King translates such phrases inclusively because the language has that connotation in the context of this work.[49] It has that connotation, I think, wherever else "Son of Man" traditions strain to become expressions of full humanity.

4. Magdalene christianity was focused on an understanding of baptism related to this corporate figure. John's coming one (*ho erchomenos*) would baptize with fire, in which Lars Hartman sees the fire streaming from the throne in Daniel 7:10.[50] John's own apocalyptic-prophetic baptism was linked with a program of social justice that "challenged the very foundations of the social order" (Luke 3:10–14, 16–17). "He asked the baptized to forsake the normal socially accepted ways of acting and living and to take up new ways."[51] These new ways were a renewal and rethinking of Israelite ideals of justice. Such a program was expressed and developed in the pre-Pauline baptismal formula of Galatians 3:27–28: "As many of you who were baptized into Christ have clothed yourselves with Christ. There is no longer Jew or Greek, there is no longer slave or free, there is no longer male and (*kai*) female; for all of you are one (*heis*) in Christ Jesus."[52] The last phrase, using *heis* (masculine) instead of *hen* (neuter), and referring to Christ Jesus, makes the formula androcentric, and Paul further integrates it into a patriarchal

framework.[53] But I think *heis* was used originally in reference to the Human One, *ho erchomenos* having come, that is, with language that is still andro-centric but inclusive. You are all one in the Human One, one in a "person" (the concept and word "person" not yet available), not one in a "thing." Com-pare the reference to clothing oneself "with perfect humanity" (King transla-tion) in *Gospel of Mary* 10.11, and putting on "the living human being" in *Gospel of Philip* 75.21–24. Because the formula in Galatians mentions Jew/Greek (and not Jew/Gentile), it is believed to have been formed in a Jewish-Hellenistic community, perhaps coming from the pre-Pauline mis-sionary movement centered around Antioch. But it is possible that the for-mula has a Palestinian provenance. Josephus (*Life* 66–67) refers to the "Greek" citizens of Tiberias who were massacred during the war of 66–70.[54]

The phrase "neither male and female" (missing from 1 Cor. 12:13 and Col. 3:11, where patriarchal marriage is affirmed) need not be understood as extinguishing the spark of sexuality, sublimated or not. That is, although it is open to an ascetic interpretation and implementation, the phrase need not be read as insisting that human beings must relate in asexual, nonsexual ways, with gender differences abolished. Schüssler Fiorenza reads "neither male *and female*" as meaning "neither husband and wife": that is, as abolishing patri-archal marriage, which she sees as at the root of the sociopolitical system of status that reproduces kyriarchy and is produced by it. The *ekklēsia* envi-sioned and attempted to practice a marriage-free ethos. Galatians 3:27–28 was a "radical theological claim to equality" announcing the invalidity of kyriarchal gender ideology and of ethnic, religious, and status differences.

The "oneness" in Christ, in this reading, was not otherworldly, spiritual, and nonpolitical; rather it was a stand against disparities, barriers, cleavages, false distinctions, hierarchies, and differences that divided slave from free, Jew from Greek, men from women. It stood against notions of the mental, social, and racial biological inferiority and weakness of subalterns: it defied the political powerlessness of slaves, Jews, wo/men. Extolling "the social one-ness of the messianic community," it rejected all structures of domination, all social, cultural, religious, national, and biological gender divisions and status differences. Galatians 3:27–28, Schüssler Fiorenza claims, was "a realistic program of action and unconventional living," with political, economic, gen-der, sexual, sociocultural, philosophical, and theological dimensions.[55]

The mention of many women in the Gospels without reference to male husbands or sons (as in Luke 8:1–3 and the crucifixion/tomb narratives) does not necessarily indicate that few of Jesus' companions were or had been married[56]or that they were were celibate, though it may signal aspects of autonomy and independence that were part of the pre-Pauline tradition. Questions abound. To focus here on gender relations:

> If the notion "no longer male *and* female" meant that patriarchal marriage was no longer constitutive for the new creation in the Spirit, this was bound to create difficult practical problems in everyday life. In light of it people might have raised questions such as: Did baptism abolish all previous marriage relationships? Could one, especially a wo/man, remain marriage-free even though this was against the law?[57] If one remained married to a pagan, what about the children? Did it mean that one could live together without being married? Did it imply that one should live as a celibate and abstain from all sexual intercourse? Was marriage only legal, and not also a religious affair? Did wo/men just like men have control over their own body and life?"[58]

Further, how could a couple work to abolish structures of domination in their relationship and interactions? Could some sexual partnerships be egalitarian? If so, how? How could a single woman (unmarried, divorced, or widowed) survive in society? How did men and women experience differently these possibilities, requirements, and choices? The choice, for example, of celibacy or virginity was quite different for a woman than for a man, as was childlessness. Marriage and nonmarriage had to do not just with sex but with inheritance, education, safety, and travel. How could God be imagined and conceptualized without acceptance of structures of domination and subordination? How could unity-in-diversity be symbolized? How could a community be ordered without the structures of domination? How could power be contained? What reparations, reeducations would be necessary? What speaking, what listening? And again: What about children?

A community baptized into freedom from social expectations of all dominance and subordination would have to wrestle with these questions and many more. The fact that we can see them being wrestled with in many Christian Testament and apocryphal[59] texts, and see them lying just below the surface of texts,[60] convinces me that such a reading of Galatians 3:27–28 is one that "can do justice to the text in its historical context."[61] Moreover, the reading does not "fix the meaning" because undoing the structures of domination had and has multiple meanings, multiple interpretations, multiple consequences, multiple applications, multiple problems. It *cannot* be dogmatically ursurped, *cannot* be reduced to the experience, interests, assumptions, worldview, or practices of any individual or group.

5. A low christology (a Jesusology?) may have been characteristic of Magdalene christianity and may have been linked to the centrality of belief in the Human One—linked, that is, to a corporate christology. Understanding Jesus as member of, an instance of, the Human One precluded focus on him as an individual who was above all other human beings and separate from them. Historical reconstruction that has wo/men at its center yields a christology quite different not only from Paul's christology but also from overriding general impressions of the canonical Gospels and the christology of each of them. The Gospels present Jesus in a unique Father–Son relationship with God. No human character is represented as equal to Jesus. Like a cowboy, he has no wife, no lover, no partner, no intimate companion, no colleague, no fully mutual human relationship. He is unique in terms of exclusivity, privilege, and superiority.[62] Contemporary feminist criticism insists that the understanding of Jesus as feminist come to liberate women from Judaism is both a misrepresentation of the evangelists' interpretation of him, and a historically flawed reconstruction. In my opinion, also flawed in this respect are aspects of the "hero" or divine ideal. Low christology can be assessed by feminist scholarship not as something to be superseded but as something valuable that was lost.[63]

The pervasive but submerged Wisdom theology in the Christian Testament may articulate early understandings of Jesus, perhaps even something of his own prophetic understanding of himself. Jesus and John the Baptist are understood as among the "children" of Wisdom (Luke 7:35 [Q]), and it is implied that Jesus is a prophet and an apostle of Wisdom (Luke 11:49; cf. 13:34) who speaks as or for Wisdom (Matt. 11:19; 11:28–30; 23:34; 23:37–39 par Luke 13:34–35) as do others (see Prov. 9:1–6). There is little christological development and a low sophiology in the Q material, with "relative lack of emphasis on Jesus himself."[64] Traces of his "ordinary" connections with others appear in the Gospels. Two women are depicted as standing up to him in conversation (the Syro-Phoenician woman in Mark 7:24–30; the Samaritan woman in John 4:1–42). He is said to have "loved" some (John 11:5), called some "friends" (15:14–15), and promised them empowerment equal to and even superior to his own (14:12). The fact that women are not called "disciples" in the Gospels (although the title may be given them by readers) opens up, as we have seen, the possibility that they are colleagues, which means that Jesus can be thought of as something other than dominating Master who is superior and privileged.

Jesus the Human One "came not to be served but to serve" (Mark 10:45;

par Matt. 20:28; cf. Luke 22:24–27: "I am among you as one who serves"). "Serving" is work that male disciples are never said to do in the Gospels,[65] though they are called to do it. Women and angels (Mark 1:13; par Matt. 4:11) do it,[66] and of course so do servants/slaves.[67] *Diakonoun* connotes social subordination; it "refers almost exclusively to the menial labor of women and slaves, performed for the people of higher rank on whom they are economically dependent."[68] This layer of meaning persists when the verb acquires the technical meaning of "ministering" in the *ekklēsia*. While Jesus is depicted only as "serving" in grand and symbolic fashion (the feeding of multitudes, the washing of disciples' feet) or miraculously (curing, not caring for the sick), and as not preventing women from serving him or the disciples (Luke 8:1–3), he can still be reconstructed as representing Wisdom as a wo/man. Not a "real man," but rather a marginalized man, "struggling against oppression "at the bottom of the kyriarchal pyramid"[69] with his co-servers.

Sayings such as "Who made me judge?" (Luke 12:14) and "Why do you call me good? No one is good but God alone" (Mark 10:18)[70] are not just examples of a low christology that later reflection and insight outgrew. As Martin Buber remarked, "[A]nyone who thinks of Jesus neither as a god only apparently clothed in human form, nor as a paranoic, . . . will not regard his human certainty about himself as an unbroken continuity." He was subject to "attacks of uncertainty," "attacks of self-questioning" (Mark 8:27ff.), and real despair (Mark 15:34 par).[71]

The Gospel of John presents the highest christology (John 20:28), but also contains a low-key, flexible christology articulated by women. His mother makes no faith statement, but implies that she believes in his powers when she informs him of a need for wine at the wedding at Cana (2:3, 5). The Samaritan woman remarks tentatively, "I know that Messiah is coming (who is called Christ); when he comes, he will show us all things . . . Can this be the Christ?" (4:25, 29). In response to Jesus' statement that he is the resurrection and the life, Martha says, "I believe that you are the Christ, the Son of God, he who is coming (*ho eis ton kosmon erchomenos*) into the world"; but then she hesitates to have Lazarus's tomb opened, expecting a stench (11:27, 30). There is a contrast here in the Martha and Mary traditions to the christology associated with Peter in Mark 8:27–33 and parallels, in which messiahship is separated from the suffering Human One. Martha's sister Mary says merely what Martha says before her, "Lord, if you had been here, my brother would not have died" (11:22, 33). Later she silently anoints his feet, anticipating the foot washing at the Last Supper, and the action is said to prophesy his burial (12:3–8). Recognizing the risen Jesus when he speaks her name, Mary Magdalene calls him (only) "*Rabbouni*" ("little rabbi"; 20:16). She is given the leveling message to deliver to his "brothers": "I am ascending to my Father and your Father, to my God and your God" [20:17]). Her claim in v. 18 is simply "I have seen the Lord." None of the women characters in the Gospel of John are singled out for condemnation as "Jews," nor are their christological statements condemned by "Jews."

We can speculate that the Jesus of Magdalene christianity was not remembered as domineering, dominating; that is, not primarily as "Lord" in this sense. Jesus was not the only one who talked, decided, judged, and healed; and as an aspect of the Human One, he was not the only one who suffered and rose from the dead. Like the corporate concept of the Human One, the egalitarian understanding of baptism seen in the pre-Pauline formula of Galatians 3:27–28, and the inclusive sophiology of the Corinthian prophets, this low christology all but faded away. How it may or may not relate to apocryphal christologies, such as that of the *Gospel of Mary*, needs careful analysis.

6. Resurrection was at the spiritual core of Magdalene christianity. Suffering was not central, nor were repentance, guilt, or individualistic "born-again-ness." The Gospel format of Peter's story (denial, rehabilitation, authorization) and Paul's (persecution, revelation, transformation) is quite different from the format of the story of Mary Magdalene and the other women (steadfastness, fear and courage, revelation, authorization). The latter stresses connection, interconnectedness, lives challenging boundaries and barriers. Resurrection was understood to be about striving to live lives that move beyond the deaths of division, and beyond the fear of death. The moving, of course, involved suffering, but suffering was not the focus of attention. Eyes were on the prize. Even maybe, at times, hands were on the prize.

To the claim that resurrection can be experienced in the present, and to the lifestyle built on that claim, Paul responded by locating resurrection in the future and by calling believers to face suffering now, a call unnecessary and stifling for the powerless. It is striking that in the Gospels the resurrection faith was articulated at the empty tomb by those who had experienced up-close a gruesome execution. If we have a desire "to witness the witnessing of revelation—to try to see how such a totality was experienced,"[72] we are directed by Magdalene christianity to the extremes of poverty and death as the place of resurrection insight.

7. Magdalene christianity was opposed at every stage that we can reconstruct historically, and was ultimately all but defeated. Almost completely

erased from memory and use were the components we have analyzed: the prophecy and leadership of women, the corporate concept of the Human One and even this title, the importance of the Wisdom and mystical traditions, the understanding of baptism as challenging social barriers and inequities, the low christology(ies), the Corinthian prophets' experience of resurrection, and the heritage of Mary Magdalene. I see these as submerged traditions[73] of an Atlantis, coherent. They surface from time to time.

Why Magdalene christianity was opposed is far more mysterious to me than the resurrection faith itself. The search for reasons for the opposition is interesting, but yields no final answers; however logical, the opposition is basically irrational. The desire of the privileged to protect their status, perks, and distinctiveness; the desire to conform congregations to (nonegalitarian, unjust) social norms; the desire to protect christianity from association with what were seen as "orgiastic, secret, oriental cults that undermined public order and decency"[74]—all these were certainly aspects of opposition. Add also misunderstanding and ignorance (willed and unwilled); fears of many kinds; inconsistencies, jealousy, lack of courage, and brutality; superficial religious sensibilities; and the real, continued weakness and powerlessness of wo/men—economic, social, political—whose task was to transform these structures, to transfigure "the given world," not to escape from or deny it.[75] Energy and confidence must have ebbed and flowed in the protracted struggle for freedom, [76] the struggle, that is, to live in the freedom believed to be already won.[77]

But Magdalene christianity was never quite defeated, at least on the fringes. Reconstruction of the lost options forces a radical rereading and reassessment of the history of Christianity, in which some margins may appear over centuries as the (true or truer) center. Feminist scholarship provides clues and directions in the past about roads not taken, roads abandoned. These are, interestingly, roads rediscovered or retraveled by some smaller Christian groups in history and in modern times. Such reconstruction may be today "history capable of teaching us how to avoid past mistakes."[78]

8. Magdalene christianity was not Christianity but a developing form (one of many) of first-century C.E. Judaism. It may be true, of course, that none of the types of what became Christianity had broken from Judaism and formed a radically separate religion by the end of the first century C.E., and true that different responses to the power of the Roman Empire fostered the split from post-70 C.E. Judaism.[79] But Magdalene christianity seems to me to have

certain features that, so to speak, resist the split; it looks less on its way to becoming Christianity than some other early types. To oversimplify, Magdalene christianity is in many ways closer to the Enumah type of faith (trusting someone) than to the Pistis faith (acknowledging something as true) as described by Buber in *Two Types of Faith: A Study of the Interpenetration of Judaism and Christianity*. The former depends primarily on a "state of contact with the one in whom I trust"; the latter can lead to such contact. The former is communal, the latter individual; the former is a "persisting-in," the latter a "facing-about," a conversion, a leap from the absurd. Buber understood the former to involve "an actual relationship which essentially transcends the world of the person" and a finding of eternity "in the depth of the actual moment,"[80] but he did not associate this with the "mystical," which he judged (I think wrongly) to be about union which destroys dialogue, about a swallowing up of the I by the You, an alienation from the world.[81] The intimate connection between mysticism and apocalyptic expectation of the overcoming of death, I have argued, is context for the resurrection faith of the women at the empty tomb.[82] It can be seen also as context for the experience of the Corinthian prophets, the theologian(s) of the *Gospel of Mary*, and the long line of their spiritual descendants.

The post-Holocaust perspective of Margie Tolstoy produces the two-pronged insight that "Christianity is an orphaned religion unless it returns to the Judaism of Jesus and reconnects with contemporary Judaism and Jewish scholarship."[83] Tolstoy links her insight with the witness of Mary Magdalene at the empty tomb of Jesus, which she reads as stressing the unfinished character of salvation, placing Jesus alongside rather than above people, providing an "alternative reality" to the one that stresses obedience to an all-powerful Being who rescues.[84] What might be the ways of such a return and a reconnection? Krister Stendahl once advised Christians to ask Jews, in spite of all the anti-Judaism of Christian history, "whether they are willing to let us become again part of their family, a peculiar part to be true, but, even so, relatives who believe themselves to be a peculiar kind of Jews."[85] An unfolding of Magdalene christianity, in its history and its present possibilities, might be a road of return for Christians and Christian theology to the new departure Stendahl thought necessary.

Let me go back briefly to my earlier remark that this essay names something that was unnamed. The absence of the name of Mary Magdalene in places where one might expect it (1 Corinthians 15; Acts 1), is not only evidence of erasure, negative evidence that the name was important, controversial. It can also be seen as aspect of the resurrection faith:

Belief in the Resurrection has never been merely about what may have happened *then,* for it is more about what those who listen to and interpret the story of the Resurrection of Jesus *do* about it for themselves. . . . *There is no privileged moment when a favoured few saw face to face while the rest of us have to make do with seeing in a glass darkly. . . . Resurrection faith will not permit the abandonment of the hope of the transforming power of God's justice in history.*[86]

The absence of the name may indicate that Mary Magdalene was not seen as a model to be imitated,[87] or someone in whose name prophecy and creativity were justified and authorized. The absence can also serve as a reminder that so much is lost.

What happens to the Christian Testament and our readings of it when we take this reconstruction of Magdalene christianity into account? It looks and reads to me something like a draft, as Rachel Blau DuPlessis writes a draft. It becomes a collage of fragments, aborted ideas, blackouts, white spaces, instructions, verbal experimentations, doodles, dots. Some words and phrases are in bold type, some tiny, some in caps, and there may be two or three columns interacting or not. It is "mudrush" (draft 6): "It is they that speak/silt/ we weep/silt/ the flood-bound/ written over and under with their /muddy marks//of writing under the writing."[88]

> The "primary" text shows its fragments, repetitions, gaps and intertextual snippets and multiple voices that unsettle the notion of a "true version of events." . . . [This pushes readers] beyond orderly reading practices, our expectation of easy connections and transparent access to information [to what DuPlessis calls the] random recovery / of unresolved tidbits . . . [that] can never be assimilated within social norms and institutions.[89]

DuPlessis is interested in what is and will always be unfinished, "the possible slippage between something that takes place and / something that is spoken of. . . . The 'unsaid' is a shifting boundary / resisting even itself."[90] When as wo/men we read defensively, so as not to be harmed; when we read creatively, so as to speak, we read "mudrashically." We learn to read and value fragments.[91] This is one of the many things Elisabeth Schüssler Fiorenza shows is possible, exciting, and politically worthwhile.

Notes

1. Schüssler Fiorenza's term for all women and oppressed and marginalized men (*Jesus: Miriam's Child, Sophia's Prophet: Critical Issues in Feminist Christology* [New York: Continuum, 1994], 191 n. 1).

2. Jane Schaberg, *The Resurrection of Mary Magdalene: Legends, Apocrypha, and the Christian Testament* (New York: Continuum, 2002), 347–49.

3. See Kathleen E. Corley, "Feminist Myths of Christian Origins," in *Reimagining Christian Origins,* ed. Elizabeth A. Castelli and Hal Taussig (Valley Forge, Pa.: Trinity Press International, 1996); eadem, *Women and the Historical Jesus* (Santa Rosa, Calif.: Polebridge, 2002).

4. Cynthia Eller, *The Myth of Matriarchal Prehistory: Why an Invented Past Won't Give Women a Future* (Boston: Beacon, 2000).

5. Ibid., 182, 63, 185.

6. Walter Bauer, *Orthodoxy and Heresy in Earliest Christianity* (1934; Eng. trans. Philadelphia: Fortress, 1971).

7. *Shaping Losses: Cultural Memory and the Holocaust,* ed. Julia Epstein and Lori Hope Lefkovitz (Chicago: University of Illinois Press, 2001), editors' introduction, 1.

8. See "Blueprint for Vatican III," *National Catholic Reporter* (May 3, 2002): 11–18.

9. See, e.g., the pamphlet entitled "Jesus and Women" by Christine Schenk, project coordinator of the Women in Church Leadership project (no date). The pamphlet makes available to churchgoers some of the results of contemporary scholarship. Unfortunately, it is flawed by anti-Judaic perspectives and misinformation. See A.-J. Levine, "A Jewess More and/or Less," in *Judaism since Gender,* ed. Miriam Peskowitz and Laura Levitt (New York: Routledge, 1997), 154: "To see [the women of the Gospels] as rejecting Judaism (in this case characterized as oppressively patriarchal, misogynistic, repressive, spiritually dead, and so on) in favor of Jesus' (here not-'Jewish') movement, is an offense both to scholarly rigor and to Judaism."

10. Francoise Meltzer, *For Fear of the Fire: Joan of Arc and the Limits of Subjectivity* (Chicago: University of Chicago Press, 2001), 97.

11. From Nag Hammadi, *Gospel of Thomas, Dialogue of the Savior, First Apocalypse of James, Gospel of Philip,* and *Sophia of Jesus Christ.* Discovered previously, *Pistis Sophia, Gospel of Peter, Gospel of Mary, Psalms of Heracleides, Epistula Apostolorum, Apostolic Church Order,* and *Acts of Philip.* I wonder if the figure of Mirai in Mandaean texts might also be a conflation of Mary the mother of Jesus and Mary Magdalene (see Jorunn Jacobsen Buckley, *The Mandaeans: Ancient Texts and Modern People* [Oxford: Oxford University Press, 2002]).

12. See Tal Ilan, *Integrating Women into Second Temple History* (Tübingen: Mohr-Siebeck, 1999), 5.

13. This is Amy-Jill Levine's term ("Women in the Q Communit[ies] and Traditions," in *Women & Christian Origins,* ed. Ross Shepard Kraemer and Mary Rose D'Angelo (New York: Oxford University Press, 1999), 165.

14. See, e.g., Mary Rose D'Angelo, "Reconstructing 'Real' Women in Gospel Literature: The Case of Mary Magdalene," in *Women & Christian Origins,* ed. Kraemer and D'Angelo, 105–28. Contrast Richard Bauckham's sketch of the historical Joanna

(*Gospel Women: Studies of the Named Women in the Gospels* [Grand Rapids: Eerdmans, 2002], 194–98): she was healed by Jesus, actively participated in *his* mission, preaching *as he did*, healing and exorcising *as he did*. "She and the other women did not scandalize the people by preaching in public places, but she would talk to the women where they gathered at the well or the market stalls, visit them in their homes, relating some of *Jesus'* parables and sayings" (emphases added). Only when he mentions healing does Bauckham draw on women's own abilities: "She would be available for the people to bring the sick to her, as they were used to going to village women with healing skills" (p. 197).

15. So Quentin Quesnell, "The Women at Luke's Supper," in *Political Issues in Luke-Acts,* ed. R. J. Cassidy and P. Scharper (Marynoll, N.Y.: Orbis Books, 1983), 68. Bauckham (*Gospel Women,* 111) rightly finds this reading awkward and improbable in the context of Luke's writing, but does not explore the possibility that such grammatical ambiguities may be signs that Quesnell's reading is correct on a pre-Lukan level.

16. Translation and commentary by Karen King in *The Complete Gospels,* ed. Robert J. Miller (Sonoma, Calif.: Polebridge, 1994). See also Esther A. de Boer, "The Gospel of Mary: Beyond a Gnostic and a Biblical Mary Magdalene" (diss., Theologische Universiteit van de Gereformeerde Kerken in Nederland te Kampen, 2002).

17. See *Resurrection of Mary Magdalene,* 127–203. The elements of this profile have different values and meaning from text to text, when seen in the context of each work as a whole, and then when seen in the context of the codex in which a work appears.

18. Karen King's description of the theology of the *Gospel of Mary* reads like a description of the theology of the Corinthian women prophets: "It constructed Christian identity apart from social gender roles, sex and childbearing. It argued that direct access to God was possible for all through the Spirit. Leadership was exercised by those who are more spiritually advanced by giving freely to all without claim to a fixed hierarchical ordering of power. Jesus was understood as a teacher and mediator of wisdom, not as a judge or ruler, and theoogical reflection centered on the risen Christ, not on suffering as atonement for sin" ("Canonization and Marginalization: Mary of Magdala," in *Women's Sacred Scriptures,* ed. Kwok Pui-lan and Elisabeth Schüssler Fiorenza [London: SCM, 1998], 34). See also Karen Torjesen, "Wisdom, Christology, and Women Prophets," in *Jesus Then & Now,* ed. M. Meyer and C. Hughes (Harrisburg, Pa.: Trinity Press International, 2001), 186–200.

19. For example, we need to explore further how "resurrection" is understood by the Corinthian prophets and by the writer of the *Gospel of Mary,* and how this relates to (Does this relate to?) elements in the canonical accounts of the empty tomb and appearances to the women.

20. Joanna Dewey, "From Storytelling to Written Texts: The Loss of Early Christian Women's Voices," *Biblical Theology Bulletin* 26 (1996): 71–78.

21. See Elizabeth A. Castelli, "Paul on Women and Gender," in *Women & Chris-*

tian Origins, ed. Kraemer and D'Angelo, 224–26, on the questions raised by the references to women.

22. "To prophesy in the early church was to engage in some type of inspired teaching—to communicate God's will directly in the midst of the assembly" (Margaret Y. MacDonald, "Reading Real Women Through the Undisputed Letters of Paul," in *Women & Christian Origins,* ed. Kraemer and D'Angelo, 215).

23. On discussions of the authenticity of 1 Cor. 14:33b–36, see MacDonald, "Reading Real Women," 216–17.

24. See Antoinette Wire, "1 Corinthians," in *Searching the Scriptures,* volume 2, *A Feminist Commentary,* ed. Elisabeth Schüssler Fiorenza (New York: Crossroad, 1994), 2:187, 160.

25. Antoinette Clark Wire, *The Corinthian Women Prophets* (Minneapolis: Fortress, 1990), 33.

26. L. D. Hurst, "Apollos," in *Anchor Bible Dictionary,* ed. David Noel Freedman (New York: Doubleday, 1992), 1:301. "Thus the note in Acts 18:25 that Apollos was *zeōn tō pneumati* ('fervent in spirit,' RSV) cannot refer to the Holy Spirit, since this would be inconsistent with his subsequent experience with Aquila and Priscilla (v 26) and with Paul's subsequent experience preaching in Apollos' wake (Acts 19:1-7)" in Ephesus, where Luke says the disciples claim they have not heard there is a Holy Spirit. Contrast Peter Lampe's argument that pre-Lukan tradition knew Apollos as a "Christian pneumatic" ("Prisca," in *Anchor Bible Dictionary,* ed. Freedman, 5:468). See also Joan E. Taylor, *The Immerser* (Grand Rapids: Eerdmans, 1997), 72–76, 297: she thinks that Acts 19:1–7 may refer to people who were unaware of the notion that the Holy Spirit would be imparted at baptism, and that Apollos was a disciple of Jesus, not of John.

27. Wire, *Corinthian Women Prophets,* 162–63; eadem, "1 Corinthians," 189. She regards Apollos as an ally of the Corinthian women prophets.

28. I have argued that this reconstruction is plausible (*Resurrection of Mary Magdalene,* chs. 5, 6, 7).

29. See Dorothee Sölle's contribution to *How I Have Changed* (Harrisburg, Pa.: Trinity Press International, 1997), 27. Cf. "'Early Jewish and Christian Mysticism': A Collage of Working Definitions," ed. April D. DeConick, in *Society of Biblical Literature 2001 Seminar Papers* (Atlanta: Society of Biblical Literature, 2001), 278–304. Cameron Afzal writes, "Mysticism is erotic theology" (p. 281). What Phillip Munoa distinguishes as "vertical apocalypticism" and "linear apocalypticism" (pp. 293–94) are not separate in the Magdalene christianity I am reconstructing.

30. See Silvia Schroer, *Wisdom Has Built Her House: Studies on the Figure of Sophia in the Bible* (Collegeville, Minn.: Liturgical Press, 2000); Schüssler Fiorenza, *Jesus: Miriam's Child,* ch. 5.

31. "Mary Magdalene went and announced to the disciples, 'I have seen the Lord'; and she told them that he had said these things to her" (NRSV). Almost formulaic, the passage leaves out her report of Jesus' words.

32. See *Democratization and Women's Grassroots Movements,* ed. J. M. Bystydzien-ski and J. Sekhon (Bloomington: Indiana University Press, 1999), 9; the editors conceive of democracy broadly both as a political system and as a culture that allows for the fullest realization of human creative potential and enhances choices, a process "by which the voices of ordinary people can find increasing organized expression in the institutions of their societies. . . . In a sense, democracy can never be achieved in any final form—it has to be continually re-created and renegotiated."

33. Jeffrey Kripal, *The Serpent's Gift* (unpublished manuscript), 202.

34. The possibility should be explored that four apocalypses associated with the Virgin Mary (some containing *Merkavah* and *Hekhalot* traditions) might have originally been associated with Mary Magdalene, and thus related in some way to John 20 and the *Gospel of Mary.* Richard Bauckham has begun an analysis of these apocalypses (*The Fate of the Dead* [Leiden: Brill, 1998], ch. 13), but does not entertain this possibility. See Ann Graham Brock, "Authority, Politics, and Gender in Early Christianity: Mary, Peter, and the Portrayal of Leadership" (diss., Harvard University, 2000) on the substitution of other names, especially those of Mary the Virgin and Peter, for Mary Magdalene. The Marian apocalyptic material also contains references to the Trinity, which I think may be part of baptismal tradition flowing into and from Matt. 28:16–20.

35. See, however, the article by Joan Taylor in this volume, on the use of priesthood concepts and imagery for female Therapeutae.

36. See Nancy Jay, *Throughout Your Generations Forever: Sacrifice, Religion, and Paternity* (Chicago: University of Chicago Press, 1992), on the gendered aspect of sacrifice.

37. See *Resurrection of Mary Magdalene,* 166.

38. As John the Baptist, Jesus, Mary Magdalene, and others may have been seen as prophets in the Elijah/Elisha tradition. On Elijah as the Human One in Mark 9:9-13 par Matt. 17:9-13, see Taylor, *Immerser,* 281–87.

39. In a review of *The Resurrection of Mary Magdalene,* Pius C. Murray, C.S.S., says "Pope Mary Magdalene I. That in a nutshell is the conclusion of the interesting, thought provoking, new book by Jane Schaberg" (*Catholic Library World* [December 2002]). That in a nutshell was precisely *not* my conclusion; calling Mary Magdalene *a* not *the* successor of Jesus, I was not presenting a reading of John 20 that fosters structures of domination. Denise Kimber Buell discusses procreative and kinship (father to son) language used to depict the transmission of knowledge and authority (*Making Christians: Clement of Alexandria and the Rhetoric of Legitimacy* [Princeton: Princeton University Press, 1999]). Like the language of imitation, it "privileges sameness over difference and naturalizes a hierarchy of power relations among Christians" (p. 14). For Clement it provided a framework for presenting Christianity as an essential unity (sameness, conformity), originating in one source, and for excluding the "illegitimate" others (p. 18), silencing rival voices (pp. 180–81).

40. E.g., Luke 11:49; Matt. 27:43 with Wis. 2:18, 20; Mark 14:62 with Wis.

5:1–2; Wis. 5:5; Luke 23:47 with Wis. 3:l; Mark 16:19 with Wis. 4:10, 14. See Donald Senior, *The Passion of Jesus in the Gospel of Matthew* (Wilmington, Del.: Glazier, 1985), 134–35; Raymond E. Brown, *The Death of the Messiah: From Gethsemane to the Grave: A Commentary on the Passion Narratives in the Four Gospels* (New York: Doubleday, 1994), 2:995, 1451–52.

41. For different understandings of this phrase, see *Resurrection of Mary Magdalene*, 136.

42. Schüssler Fiorenza traces the submerged theology of Wisdom in the Christian Scriptures (*Jesus: Miriam's Child*, 139–55).

43. See Elisabeth Schüssler Fiorenza, *In Memory of Her: A Feminist Theological Reconstruction of Christian Origins* (New York: Crossroad, 1985), 130–40; Schroer, *Wisdom Has Built*, 153.

44. Phillip B. Munoa III, "Jesus, the *Merkavah*, and Martyrdom in Early Christian Tradition," *Journal of Biblical Literature* 121 (2002): 303–25.

45. Hebrews 2:6–8 quotes Ps. 8:4–6.

46. See Wire, "1 Corinthians," 190–92.

47. Munoa, "Jesus, the *Merkavah*, and Martyrdom," 321 n. 61: he says that her metamorphosis "may be understandable in terms of Dan 7" and in terms of the suffering Christians modeling themselves after and thinking of themselves as becoming like Jesus, a "man." In her ascent to heaven, overcoming of the dragon, and being welcomed and gifted by the seated gray-haired man, Perpetua is "patterned after" Daniel's "one like a son of man." "For most Christian readers the 'one like a son of man' is Jesus, the one who after his victory, achieved through suffering and death, went on to empowerment" (p. 319). Munoa reviews other explanations of her gender transformation, which I think may also be factors in the appropriation of this imagery: S. Maitland: Perpetua's manhood represents a suppression of feminine characteristics; D. Scholer: her transformation is an example of a woman's empowerment in the church; L. Sullivan: Perpetua appropriates imagery of the dominant in order to converse on the dominant's terms.

48. De Boer, *Gospel of Mary*, 192, 194.

49. See Karen King, "The Gospel of Mary," in *Searching the Scriptures*, volume 2, *A Feminist Commentary*, ed. Schüssler Fiorenza, 606–7; eadem, "The Gospel of Mary," in *Complete Gospels*, ed. Miller, 362.

50. Lars Hartman, "Baptism," *Anchor Bible Dictionary*, ed. Freedman, 1:584.

51. Paul W. Hollenbach, "John the Baptist," *Anchor Bible Dictionary*, ed. Freedman, 3:893–97. I have suggested elsewhere that Mary Magdalene may have been associated with John the Baptist (*Resurrection of Mary Magdalene*, 341–42).

52. For a summary of the variety of interpretations of Gal. 3:26–28, see Carolyn Osiek, "Galatians," in *The Women's Bible Commentary*, ed. Sharon Ringe and Carol Newsom (Philadelphia: Westminster John Knox Press, 1992), 335; Elisabeth Schüssler Fiorenza, *Rhetoric and Ethic: The Politics of Biblical Studies* (Minneapolis: Fortress, 1999), 149–73.

53. Schüssler Fiorenza, *Rhetoric and Ethic*, 163.

54. See Richard A. Horsley, *Galilee: History, Politics, People* (Valley Forge, Pa.: Trinity Press International, 1995), 271–75, 78–79.

55. Schüssler Fiorenza, *Rhetoric and Ethic*, 149, 153, 155.

56. See Bauckham's discussion, *Gospel Women*, 116–21.

57. I do not know what law is meant here—Gen. 2:24?

58. Schüssler Fiorenza, *Rhetoric and Ethic*, 120. See n. 19 above, Castelli's questions about women's leadership.

59. Exploration of how baptism was understood and practiced in "heretical" groups, and how this related to Gal. 3:27–28, to visionary/prophetic experience, and to Human One imagery and language is obviously beyond the scope of this article, and complicated by the fact that we have little information about their social organization and religious praxis. See Karen L. King, "Sophia and Christ in the *Apocryphon of John*," and response by John D. Turner, in *Images of the Feminine in Gnosticism*, ed. Karen L. King (Philadelphia: Fortress, 1988), 158–86, and other chapters in this volume; Anne McGuire, "Women, Gender and Gnosis in Gnostic Texts and Traditions," in *Women & Christian Origins*, ed. Kraemer and D'Angelo, 266–67; de Boer, *Gospel of Mary*, 28, 68, 81–82.

60. And being wrestled with by interpreters. J. Louis Martyn's reading enshrines an ancient resistance to the interpretation offered here: "Religious, social, and sexual pairs of opposites are not replaced by equality, but rather by a newly created unity" (*Galatians: A New Translation with Introduction and Commentary*, Anchor Bible 33A [New York: Doubleday, 1997], 377).

61. Schüssler Fiorenza, *Rhetoric and Ethic*, 27: "An ethics of critical reading changes the task of interpretation from finding out 'what the text meant' to the question of what kind of readings can do justice to the text in its historical context."

62. See Schüssler Fiorenza, *Jesus: Miriam's Child*, 131, for the distinction between seeing Jesus' uniqueness in terms of particularity and distinctness and in terms of exclusivity, privilege, and superiority.

63. C. F. D. Moule points to "three paradoxes in New Testament convictions about Jesus—his humiliation and exaltation, his continuity with and discontinuity from the rest of humanity, and the individuality and yet inclusiveness of his person" ("The Manhood of Jesus in the New Testament," in *Crisis in Christology: Essays in Quest of Resolution*, ed. W. R. Farmer [London: Truth, 1995], 48). I look forward to feminist participation in the discussion and perhaps reformulation of these paradoxes.

64. Levine, "Women in the Q Communit(ies)," 153.

65. In conrast, women are not said to serve in Acts, but only men (Acts 6:2; 19:22; cf. also the noun *diakonia* in 1:17; 6:1, 4; 11:29; 12:25; 20:24; 21:19). This is an indication that "official" ministry is in the process of being reserved to males.

66. Simon's mother-in-law (Mark 1:31 parr.); women traveling with Jesus (Luke 8:1–3); Martha (Luke 10:40; cf. John 12:2); women at the cross (Mark 15:41; par. Matt. 27:55).

67. Luke 17:8; cf. the noun *diakonos* in Matt. 22:13; John 2:5.

68. Luise Schottroff, *Lydia's Impatient Sisters* (Louisville: Westminster John Knox Press, 1995), 205.

69. Schüssler Fiorenza, *Jesus: Miriam's Child*, 14. See Susannah Heschel, "Jesus as Theological Transvestite," in *Judaism since Gender*, ed. Peskowitz and Levitt, 192. Her primary interest in this article is in how the transvestism of Jesus questions the constructs and destabilizes the boundaries between Judaism and Christianity.

70. Martin Buber comments on this saying: it is as if Jesus warded off divinization (*Two Types of Faith: A Study of the Interpenetration of Judaism and Christinity* [New York: Harper, 1961], 116).

71. Ibid., 31.

72. Meltzer, *For Fear of the Fire*, 33, on secular postmodernism's nostalgia for religious texts of the Middle Ages and before.

73. See Schüssler Fiorenza, *Jesus: Miriam's Child*, 132, on laboring "beneath the headlamp" to mine submerged traditions.

74. Schüssler Fiorenza, *In Memory of Her*, 232.

75. Amos Wilder, "Eschatological Imagery and Early Circumstances," *New Testament Studies* 5 (1958–59): 234.

76. Orlando Patterson remarks on the decisive role women played "in the Western social invention of *personal* freedom and in its history" (*Freedom* [New York: Basic, 1991], 1:xv).

77. John J. Collins comments: "It is in the nature of apocalyptic eschatology that it can never be fully realized in this life. Even when the hopes could be realized in principle, they most often failed to materialize. . . . Apocalyptic hope is invariably hope deferred. Nonetheless, it has persisted as a recurring feature of Western religion for over two thousand years. While it can never deliver on its promises, it continues to speak eloquently to the hearts of those who would otherwise have no hope at all" ("From Prophecy to Apocalypticism," in *The Encyclopedia of Apocalypticism* [New York: Continuum, 1999], 1:159). See n. 32 above, on democracy.

78. Eller, *Myth*, 185.

79. See Dieter Georgi, "Was the Early Church Jewish?" *Bible Review* (December 2001): 33–37, 51–52; idem, "The Early Church: Internal Jewish Migration or New Religion?" *Harvard Theological Review* 81 (1995): 35–68.

80. Buber, *Two Types of Faith*, 8, 10, 21, 34.

81. See Pamela Vermes, *Buber* (New York: Grove, 1988), viii: "He nevertheless belongs to Jewish mystical tradition" (p. 11).

82. See *Resurrection of Mary Magdalene*.

83. Margie Tolstoy, "Woman as Witness in a Post-Holocaust Perspective," in *A Shadow of Glory: Reading the New Testament after the Holocaust*, ed. Tod Linafelt (New York: Routledge, 2002), 125.

84. Tolstoy refers to the article of Melissa Raphael ("When God beheld God: Notes toward a Jewish Feminist Theology of the Holocaust," *Feminist Theology* 21

[1999]: 59), who finds a different form of religious imagination in accounts of Jewish women's support groups in the camps "where through mutual care and kindness Shekhinah is made present . . . in the very abyss of profanity."

85. Krister Stendahl, "Judaism and Christianity: A Plea for a New Relationship," in *Disputation and Dialogue,* ed. F. E. Talmage (New York: Ktav, 1975), 337. Contrast Jacob Neusner, "How Judaism & Christianity Can Talk to Each Other," *Bible Review* (December 1990): 32–41, 45.

86. Christopher Rowland, "Interpreting the Resurrection," in *The Resurrection of Jesus Christ,* ed. Paul Avis (London: Darton, Longman and Todd, 1993), 69, 79.

87. See Elizabeth A. Castelli, *Imitating Paul: A Discourse of Power* (Louisville: Westminster John Knox Press, 1991), 16.

88. Rachel Blau DuPlessis, *Drafts 1-38, Toll* (Middletown, Conn.: Wesleyan University Press, 2001), 36.

89. Linda A. Kinnaban, "Experiments in Feminism," *Women's Review of Books* 19 (May 2002): 14.

90. Du Plessis, *Drafts 1-38,* 75.

91. See Walter Brueggemann, "A Fissure Always Uncontained," in *Strange Fire: Reading the Bible After the Holocaust,* ed. Tod Linafelt (New York: New York University Press, 2000), 71–73; Jane Flax, *Thinking Fragments: Psychoanalysis, Feminism and Postmodernism in the Contemporary West* (Berkeley: University of California Press, 1990).

13

Rising Voices

The Resurrection Witness
of New Testament Non-Writers

Antoinette Clark Wire

TWENTIETH-CENTURY RESEARCH MADE GREAT ADVANCES IN SHOWING us the wide range of perspectives of New Testament writers. It greatly sharpened our reading to see how each writer speaks with a distinctive voice to an intended audience. Less attention has been paid to the narrow range of the whole population represented by ancient writers. A recent study by William V. Harris on ancient literacy estimates that in the Mediterannean world very seldom could more than 10 percent of the population read; in Rome's eastern provinces less than 5 percent.[1] Literacy was the privilege of the few urban males whose families did not need their labor—and who were able to pay for private tutors. This meant that virtually all women, rural people, and many urban men were non-writers, yet they carried on responsible lives. If Jews, they would hear, sing, and tell stories about Moses and the prophets. Many such stories that survive from Hellenistic and Roman times and are not found in the Bible show how creative the storytellers were.[2] Stories about Jesus circulated for decades in this oral environment before Gospels were written, and what survives in the texts is only the tip of the iceberg, both in terms of quantity and in terms of social perspective. So we find, for example, that the Gospels all exonerate Pilate and blame the local Jews for Jesus' death. This is the way that people who could write would write in a Roman province soon after the suppression of a massive revolt.

221

Most scholars are content to leave it there—a nod of the head to the submerged voices that generated our tradition as we write about those who wrote. When we do this, we settle for hearing every story from the perspective of a writer, although it is without doubt that these educated men expose only in a very select way the great mass of storytelling they heard. But some scholars have not been so easily satisfied. We particularly honor the persistent work of Elisabeth Schüssler Fiorenza, who has investigated every genre in the New Testament, proposed and revised relevant methodologies, and offered hypotheses about non-writers from village women seeking healing to Hellenistic widows ministering at tables, from singers of hymns to tellers of visions.

Much work remains to be done to establish on a firm foundation the witness of such non-writers. The most basic tasks that need to be undertaken are to clarify adequate methods and to apply them in intensive analysis of specific texts, but there is also value in reviewing what has already come to light. This can both inspire us to pursue the task and provoke us to improve the work. Here I want to draw together some proposals about non-writers who witness concerning resurrection in New Testament texts. I will first look at the stories of Jesus' raising of the dead. Then I will consider the early women's witness to Jesus' resurrection, and finally the resurrection witness of Christian women prophets in Corinth twenty years later. In each case I will try to indicate how we hear their voices through the writings of others and what kinds of claims they were making. A healthy by-product may be to see that we do not know in advance what resurrection means.

I begin with the stories of Jesus raising the dead—Jairus's daughter, the widow of Nain's son, and Mary and Martha's brother Lazarus. These stories do not focus on the three who die and rise but on the bereaved—the father, the mother, and the sisters. It is the mother's weeping in the funeral procession that gets Jesus' attention for her son, the sister's sending for Jesus and complaining when he comes too late that brings him to Lazarus's tomb, and Jairus's "Come before my daughter dies" that makes Jesus follow him. Though elaborated by the writers, the tellers' stories remain recognizable, a fact best seen in the stories about Jairus that survive in three Gospels (Matt. 9:18–19, 23–26; Mark 5:22–24, 35–43; Luke 8:41–42, 49–56).

When the synagogue ruler Jairus begs the street preacher Jesus to come save his daughter, we hear not only a single story but a broader story type. There are a number of stories from this period about great religious leaders who ask poor village teachers to heal their children.[3] In one such story

Hanina ben Dosa heals a famous rabbi's son and the rabbi's wife asks, "Is Hanina greater than you then?" and the rabbi answers, "No, but he is like a servant before the King, and I am like a lord before the King." Apparently a servant's intimacy is more use than a lord's status when it comes to getting God's ear.

Once Jairus recruits Jesus to come heal his daughter, word arrives—from the mother perhaps—that the daughter has died and there is no need to bother Jesus. Yet Jesus tells the father, "Don't be afraid, just believe," leaves behind most of his followers, and tries to make a quiet entrance at Jairus's home. But the hullabaloo of village mourning is in full swing. When he tells them the child is not dead but sleeping, their wails turn to laughter. Even Matthew, who pares down this story to four sentences does not omit the laughing mourners. It is a poignant and comic scene that also confirms that they know the child is dead. Jesus puts them all out of the room except the mother and father; he takes the child's hand, and Mark has him say, "*Talitha kum,*" Aramaic for "Girl, get up," which is then translated, "Little girl, I say to you, rise." In a village telling, of course, no translation would be needed.

Mark adds here that she is twelve years old—the age of marriageability in the Greco-Roman world and one of the crisis points in a woman's life about which we have many ancient miracle stories.[4] Will she make it through this transition from being a girl to being a woman? The story answers: "immediately the girl got up and walked around." Jesus says to tell nobody and to give her something to eat. Food makes him sound practical—a good prescription this doctor writes—but is it practical to tell no one in a house where she is known to be dead? This silencing has a wider meaning in Mark, but in the context of many healing stories it reminds us that the people who press Jesus for healing are told not to tell because they are the ones expected to tell—in this case the father, who did not give up at the news of death, and the mother, who may have sent him for Jesus in the first place. So the parents are presented as the non-writers whose story the teller claims to tell. Ironically, the father as synagogue head was probably literate—though not his wife—but he did not write this kind of story. This is a non-writer's story in the sense that we are all non-writers in 90 percent of our lives. One can assume that they told the story in celebration, praising God. Far from being Jesus' story, this was a story told on Jesus, and a story told so well that he could not silence it.

It is significant that all the stories of Jesus raising the dead are told as healings, healings *in extremis* of course, but there is no separate story type for raisings of the dead. The teller's point in both healings and raisings is the same.

The person who presses for God's life-giving strength is like the servant before the king, or the child before the parent, powerless and hence irresistible to God. In response, those who receive what they ask for cannot resist telling the story. We can say that they become witnesses to the one God on whom all depend, who, as Paul says, "makes the dead live and calls what is not into being" (Rom. 4:17). We do not see how this happens, but we do trust that this mother and father are not deceiving themselves or us. For them, resurrection is life in the face of death, and at such news we can only join their rejoicing.

Resurrection witness of non-writers appears again in the stories about the women who come to Jesus' tomb (Matt 28:1–10; Mark 16:1–8; Luke 24:1–11; John 20:1–18).[5] A sign that these stories are oral tradition is that, though Matthew and Luke may be dependent on Mark, Mark and John cannot be traced back to a common literary source. Paul's omitting the women's stories in his list of resurrection witnesses does not prove that these stories were late or a literary creation, but suggests that he discounts women as legal witnesses or did not want to confirm women's authority in Corinth (1 Cor. 15:3–8). The presence of non-writers at the graveside would be expected in Palestinian Jewish practice, considering women's traditional roles in mourning and anointing the dead. And the fact that this story was about women being sent to tell the story further points to women as probable first tellers.

A single common oral account cannot be fully reconstructed. Mark says that the women saw a young man inside the grave; Luke says two men; John two angels; and Matthew one angel sitting outside on the stone. Yet in spite of the different tellings, there is a certain shape that the story retains. In its first scene women (or a woman) come(s) to the tomb before dawn after the Sabbath. There is no hint of this death as a ransom for sin or as a model of self-sacrifice. The women's leader has been executed without cause and they have come to mourn and/or anoint their friend. Perhaps the tone of telling would reflect their anger, or just their fear and frustration about the heavy stone, because they are met by a bright presence who recognizes why they have come and encourages them: "Don't be afraid." "Don't be alarmed." "Why do you weep?" "Why seek the living among the dead?"

Second, in each story they discover that Jesus is not there. Either they are told, "He is not here . . . , see the place where they put him," or a woman complains, "They have taken my Lord and I don't know where they put him." Jesus' corpse was put here and it is now put somewhere else, and until they find it there will be no comfort in mourning or anointing. The point is not that the absence of a body proves resurrection, but that it prevents closure and they cannot "do the right thing by him."

But third, they are told that Jesus is risen and where he is going—yet not so as to give them the inside track on finding him. Rather they are told to tell his disciples, in Mark and Matthew, "Go tell his disciples that he is going ahead of you into Galilee. There you will see him as he told you." Back to work, it sounds like. Galilee is the place in the wider story where the disciples and these women had spent years with Jesus, teaching and healing, and Matthew reminds us Galilee is proverbial for its Gentiles, to whom the news is to be carried (Mark 15:40–41; 13:10; Matt 4:12–22; 10:18; 28:19). But this women's story says nothing about how Jesus will be present with them except that he is going ahead, or one can translate, he is leading them to Galilee where they will see him. Matthew goes on to tell that the women meet Jesus himself as they leave the tomb and he repeats the angel's message, "Don't be afraid. Go tell my brothers to go to Galilee and there they will see me." So the women's story in some tellings includes seeing Jesus, but the message is still to tell the whole group where Jesus is going so they can follow.

When Luke and John retell the women's story, the place that Jesus is going shifts. In Luke, Jesus reminds the women that he predicted his death and rising in Galilee, but only when he appears again to the eleven and the women does he tell them where to go (Luke 24:49). They must stay in Jerusalem, he says, until they are clothed with power from God. So the women's story is adjusted to Luke's geography, but it tells where to go to receive Jesus, or God's empowering Spirit. In John's account, Mary Magdalene gives up on the angels and goes after a gardener to tell her where they put Jesus—and the gardener turns out to be Jesus. He says to tell his brothers where he is going—not Galilee or Jerusalem but, "I am going up to my Father and your Father, to my God and your God." Jesus then appears to his followers and breathes the Holy Spirit on them, and we see how they are to meet him: the Spirit becomes Jesus' presence with them while Jesus becomes their presence with God (John 20:19–22; 14:15–17, 25–26; 15:26; 16:7–15, 23–28; 17:1–26).

But what happens to the women's message? On this the Gospel writers are not encouraging. Mark says they say nothing to anyone because they are afraid, and that ends his Gospel. Luke says that they tell the disciples, but no one believes them. Matthew doesn't even say if they tell. And when the disciples do meet Jesus in Galilee, the women's sending seems to be superseded by the great commission to the eleven. Only in John do we get a bit of narrative: Mary goes and tells the disciples, "I have seen the Lord," and she tells them what he said—but John does not tell us what she tells them.

So are the women silent? Or disbelieved? Or superseded? Or do they tell but we do not get to hear their voices? Clearly, the Gospel writers cut off the women's story. Yet by this time we have already heard their resurrection witness: they are welcomed at the tomb, they find Jesus' body gone, and they are sent to tell his followers how to meet the risen Jesus. After this witness, when you think of it, who needs more resurrection stories? The appearance stories are redundant when it is known how to meet Jesus. Jesus was "going ahead of them" in one way of speaking or another. For Luke, they would follow by remembering and telling what Jesus said and did through God's empowering Spirit; for John, they would follow by speaking new things from Jesus through God's Spirit breathed into them; and, for Matthew, by baptizing and teaching all nations Jesus' promise, "I will be with you always." Mark simply ends with the women's story and their mute fear. But the story has said that Jesus went ahead of them into their home territory, where they could see him.

In all these ways the writers say that Jesus' resurrection is about a telling that leads to presence. It is not restricted to that time and place—one day or forty, Galilee or Jerusalem—but happens where Jesus leads or God's Spirit comes. So, although the Gospel writers cut off the women's story, they do keep it going in their own idiom. One can say that it is a story of Jesus going ahead, of how to see his back ahead of them again, which is what keeps followers going.

A third kind of non-writer's resurrection story is found among the women prophets in Corinth's house churches.[6] This is the most difficult to access because there are no oral stories that can almost be heard through their several written versions. Instead we have a letter, Paul's First Corinthians, and from Paul's effort to persuade the Corinthians, we can reconstruct certain aspects of their life and thought. Apparently some leading Jewish families from the synagogue whom Paul had baptized find themselves hosting in their homes crowds of Gentiles from every religious practice, including many women and slaves whose husbands and masters did not come. Paul's advice shows that these new converts often give up sexual partners in order to devote themselves to spreading the gospel. The women especially are doing this, because subordination to their husbands makes active ministry difficult and their prophecy suspect. In worship women as well as men prophesy revelations from God to the people and pray petitions and praises from the people to God, prayers sometimes so intense that they leave behind human words for what is called "the tongues of angels." The women apparently cook the common meal together in one place, and when it is ready they bless God and eat it without taking serving roles or waiting for everyone. Scholars tend to conclude from Paul's efforts to discipline the Corinthians on many fronts— eat before you come, each have your own spouse, women prophets cover your heads—that the Corinthians needed discipline. Today we might ask if they were developing a worship of Christ appropriate for Corinth.

Concerning resurrection, Paul argues in 1 Corinthians 15 that "some of you say there is no resurrection of the dead," and he mocks the materialistic skeptic. Because the letter shows that these Corinthian believers are not doubters, Paul's skeptic is probably a straw man set up to make his contrasting view appeal to the spiritual in Corinth. They may have rejected the resurrection of the dead because they experience the resurrection of the living. Paul himself taught them that they had died and were buried with Christ in the waters of baptism, from which they were raised up to newness of life (Rom. 6:3–4). Not that they are persuaded that this life will end at death— Paul implies that they baptized someone as a proxy for a person who died before baptism. But their focus is on the present and continuing experience of resurrection life. Paul responds to this by locating resurrection in the future after Christ's return, when the faithful will be rewarded for all their sacrifices.

This makes sense if we remember that sacrifices are the story of Paul's life since he himself was baptized into Christ—this Roman citizen with rabbinical education now living from pillar to post.[7] Like the synagogue families who gave up dignity and status to worship with Gentiles, Paul took losses; and this experience was constitutive for his theology of the cross. Our earliest intimations of Christ's preexistence come from Paul's claim that Christ might have grasped equality with God but chose instead humanity and slavery and death (Phil. 2:1–11). This downward path of voluntary loss on behalf of others that binds Paul to Christ becomes what he most wants to share with others.

But few in Corinth have the starting point for this. When called to believe, they are "not many wise, not many powerful, not many from honored families," and they could not choose to give up what they did not have. They are women and slaves and foreigners who serve in hierarchial households and workshops, where they have no political rights or educational choices. One could say that Jesus' cross is built into their lives. They quickly identify with Christ's death and find themselves raised up in Christ to share insight and power and honor in his community. Paul means to mock them when he says: "Already you are full! already you are rich! Without us you are ruling in God's kingdom!" (1 Cor. 4:8), but this reflects their experience of rising up in Christ. It is no surprise that they do not consign resurrection to the realm of the dead to assure future rewards. They are witness to it in their present lives, above all in speaking ministries of prophecy and prayer, the life-giving two-way communication that they articulate between God and these new people of God.

These short summaries about non-writing witnesses to resurrection raise two questions: What is resurrection? And how credible is it?

Though there are major cultural differences between village people who tell how Jesus raises the dead, itinerant women in the Galilee who follow Jesus to the cross and keep following, and rising urban women prophets, they do share at least three things. The resurrection they witness is a local reality, not distant in time or place. It happens among them and to them. So the mother and father witness Jesus' raising their own daughter. Those at Jesus' tomb carry their witness wherever they go, "there you will see him, as he told you." And Corinth's women prophets are raised up in Christ and inspire his living body, which meets in their homes. Second, resurrection is in each case a vocal reality, what we would call a communication event: telling the story reenacts the girl's rising; telling where Jesus is going makes it possible for someone else to see him; telling God's wisdom revealed to women and slaves draws others into the resurrection life.

Resurrection for them is local, vocal, and, third, it is the reality of Christ's life-giving presence in the face of death. Jesus takes a deadened hand and says "Girl, get up." From the grave he leads his followers back to their mission in Galilee and beyond. And those with dead-end lives he animates to become channels of God's wisdom to the people who echo thanks to God in "tongues of angels."

But how credible, how authoritative, is this local and vocal witness of non-writers to God's life-making presence in Jesus? Those who think that biblical writers speak with unique authority need to be reminded of other biblical non-writers such as Elijah and Job and Jesus. It is not writing that makes authority. But the question of credibility still stands because of the great distance between ourselves and the non-writing resurrection witnesses. We do not speak the same language as any of the three groups I have introduced— and I do not mean Aramaic or Greek, which we could learn, but the cultural and political langauges of our respective social worlds. We would like to teach them our descriptive language, our critical tools and careful judgments. Where our voices are reticent and probing, theirs are sharp and sure. But if we think we would do better with outside observers than these people so much implicated in Jesus' life, we might ask, Who would give us the best report of Bishop Romero's end, the nuns who were worshiping in the chapel with him when he was gunned down or the officials writing reports for the morning papers? Our informants also have the advantage of intimacy rather than distance, of full investment rather than control. By taking seriously those who are speaking, we could learn how to tune in and hear these and other rising voices.

NOTES

1. William V. Harris, *Ancient Literacy* (Cambridge, Mass.: Harvard University Press, 1989), 264, 272–73.

2. For a selection and discussion of such storytelling, see my *Holy Lives, Holy Deaths: A Close Hearing of Early Jewish Storytellers* (Atlanta: Society of Biblical Literature; Leiden: Brill, 2002).

3. Babylonian Talmud *Berakhot* 34b; Wire, *Holy Lives,* 131.

4. Antoinette Wire, "Ancient Miracle Stories and Women's Social World," *Foundations and Facets Forum* 2/4 (1986): 77–84.

5. On the oral provenance of the stories of Jesus' appearance to the women, see Holly E. Hearon, "Witness and Counter-Witness: The Function of the Mary Magdalene Tradition in Early Christian Communities" (Ph.D. diss., Graduate Theological Union, 1998), forthcoming in 2003 from Liturgical Press.

6. On this section, see further evidence in my *The Corinthian Women Prophets: A Reconstruction through Paul's Rhetoric* (Minneapolis: Fortress, 1990).

7. Ibid., 62–71.

14

Jephthah's Daughter

A Lament

Alicia Ostriker

I COME TO THE WORK OF ELISABETH SCHÜSSLER FIORENZA NOT AS a scholar of religion but as a feminist poet and critic who became obsessed with the Bible in the mid-1980s, and for whom the existence of feminist scholarship in religion was a revelation and a justification, telling me, and others like myself, that we have a right to wrestle with the Bible. That we have a right to write. My work on Jephthah's daughter is a tribute to Schüssler Fiorenza in three ways. First, there is her example of scrupulous reading of biblical texts—reading which always requires that we pay attention to issues of power and powerlessness as they play themselves out in language. I have tried at all times in my own reading to be as clear-eyed, or one might say as hawk-eyed, as she. In the story of Jephthah's daughter, this issue seems to be right there on the surface, but there are also subtle connections or parallels I have tried to bring out, for example, between the language of religiously based militarism and the languages of domestic abuse and misogyny. Second, Schüssler Fiorenza gives a name, "kyriarchy," to the principle in every form of religious (and intellectual) orthodoxy that I find myself most repelled by and struggling against, in my life and in my writing. Like her, I refuse to worship what demands to be worshiped. William Blake, my earliest teacher in such matters, called this principle "Urizen." But Blake, despite the power of his dissent, never dreamed that the female, in religious matters, should be anything but subordinate to the male.

So, third and most important, I am inspired by the concept of the sacred collective creativity of women which Schüssler Fiorenza calls women-church. Here we turn from pain and rage to a vision of strength and hope that is biblically based, for me as for Schüssler Fiorenza. "We must go forth in mourning / We will return in joy" are the words I give my women's chorus. As a Jew, I do not use the term "church." But in the close of Judges 11, immediately after the sacrifice of Jephthah's daughter is so succinctly announced—"And it came to pass at the end of two months, that she returned unto her father, who did with her according to the vow which he had vowed"—we have the earliest example in recorded history of the fact of women gathered together in an annual ceremony: "And it was a custom in Israel, that the daughters of Israel went yearly to lament the daughter of Jephthah the Gileadite four days in a year." At the time of this text, the custom was evidently already obsolete. I would like to see it revived. *Jephthah's Daughter: A Lament* is a text or libretto for a women's ceremony which offers an opportunity to grieve the sacrifice of Jephthah's daughter and of all women who have been literally and figuratively sacrificed to the laws and wars of the fathers, and in our act of mourning to begin a turn toward change, toward joy.

The Book of Judges recounts the history of the Israelite people after settling in the promised land, as the tribes struggle against neighboring peoples such as the Canaanites and the Perizzites, the Ammonites and the Moabites.

The story of Jephthah's daughter (Judges 11) tells us that Jephthah the Gileadite made a vow to the Lord before going into battle with the Ammonites. He vowed that if he succeeded in battle he would offer up to the Lord as a burnt offering whatever first came forth from the doors of his house to meet him. When his daughter (who is unnamed in the text) comes out with timbrels and dances to greet him, he rends his clothes, saying that she has brought him very low and troubled him, but that a vow to God cannot be retracted. She does not protest, but obtains permission to spend two months in the mountains with her companions, to bewail her virginity. When she returns, Jephthah fulfills his vow. An epilogue tells us that it was a custom for the daughters of Israel to lament her death for four days each year.

Jephthah's Daughter: A Lament offers an opportunity to grieve the sacrifice of Jephthah's daughter and to ponder the meaning of her sacrifice for us today. Groups of women are invited to experiment with the text. A group may choose to read or perform the entire *Lament,* or it may select sections. A setting of a version of this work as a cantata, composed by Moshe Budmor, is available from the author.

JEPHTHAH'S DAUGHTER: A LAMENT

And it came to pass at the end of two
months, that she returned unto her father,
who did with her according to the vow which
he had vowed; and she had not known man.

And it was a custom in Israel, that the
daughters of Israel went yearly to lament the
daughter of Jephthah the Gileadite four days
in a year.

—Judges 11:38–39

(Performers come onstage to this chant, which may be repeated between sections of the performance.)

Going forth in mourning
Returning in joy

Going forth in mourning
Returning in joy

Going forth in mourning
Returning in joy

* Mountaintop *

(The chorus is motionless. Two voices read, the italicized voice interrupting.)

Sacrifice: The act of offering something to a deity in propitiation or homage, especially the ritual slaughter of an animal or person. A victim offered in this way. The forfeiture of something highly valued for the sake of one considered to have a greater value or claim.

The heart asks pleasure first. Let him kiss me with the kisses of his mouth. And then excuse from pain. And then—

Considered to have a greater, as they say, value or claim. A grander. A greedier. Such as a father. Such as a vow. A sequence of special higher-than-legal-more-sublime. Words. Such as a father might utter to One. The relinquishment of something at less than its presumed value. Something so relinquished. *Such as a daughter.* A loss so sustained. *The father has. Lost the daughter.*

The father has sacrificed the daughter.
He has—
we have—   beloved one   blessed are
lost her.

Holocaust: Great or total destruction, especially by fire. Widespread destruction. Disaster (bad stars). A sacrificial offering that is entirely consumed by flames. Cf. Holokaustos, burnt whole.

Sacer, sacred + *facere,* to make. It is made sacred by sacrificing it.

* Sunrise: We Emerge from the Forest into a Clearing *

(Full chorus, almost dancelike, but uppercase is shouted.)

Into a clearing
from the forest of our lives
every year it is
a wild high climb

Light stands on the mountain
almost too bright
like a truth from which
we hide our eyes

The presence of God
is in the rocky ridge
the wildflowers the stunted pines
the ghostly wind

Today we do not remember
the angel, the ram, the thicket
we remember the war
and the death of our sister

The sons of Ammon were coming
we feared their army
we begged Jephthah
be our leader

The spirit of God was upon him
he made a great slaughter
when he returned home he was
greeted by his daughter

For he had one daughter, no other
to praise him after the war
so the child danced out with timbrels
and with dancing from the door

But Jephthah rent his clothes he said
you have brought me very low
if a man open his mouth to God
he must fulfill his vow

Then the child asked leave to go
two months in the mountains
to bewail her virginity
among her companions.

Two months in the mountains.

AND JEPHTHAH HOME FROM SLAUGHTER
WAS GREETED BY HIS DAUGHTER!

* Little Fugue *

(A section for several voices: A begins loudly then continues softly under the voice of B, who speaks her section twice, then yields to C, who speaks very quickly, etc. Variations can be tried; in any case the overall effect should be one of cacophony, but each voice should be heard clearly at least once. The final section is to be said in unison by all speakers. The duration of this piece should be no longer than one minute.)

A. She weeps in the night
   her tears are on her cheek
   my eye, my eye runs down with water
   because the comforter is far from me

B. The Lord is become an enemy
   he has swallowed up Israel   (2x)

C. He actually blames her claims she
   made him compelled
   do to her this awful thing
   can you believe
   never otherwise
   lament

D. Fault stands in door fault fault
   fist is his whoever cries be hit   (2x)

E. Obedience shallow law
   repeat repeat a tale of terror repeat
   comply complain
   complain comply
   deny deny

OMNI: Want to say no
   want to jump in
   want to say stop
   stop stop

want to stop
being afraid, want
the power
to say no

* INTERROGATION AND REPLY *

(The implicit question asked by this section is what keeps someone in an apparently oppressive or abusive situation when the option of walking out seems possible. The question has many resonances, including the issue of the feminist within a patriarchal religion, and the issue of God in a post-holocaust age. The structure of the piece is modeled on the alphabetical acrostics of the Book of Lamentation)

In the beginning, the wound is invisible.
—Edmund Jabes

A question to pose to the celebrants. The participants. You women, of outraged eyes and grinding teeth, resemble birds whipping themselves against the walls of a room into which they have accidentally flown. In its frustrated attempts to escape, a bird becomes frenzied. It leaves bloodspots on the walls. But here no walls exist. Against what do you fling yourselves so extravagantly?

—Against this very question, hurling ourselves at it in vain. This irresistible, unanswerable question encloses us like the swaddling blanket around the squirming infant. Like a Polish chimney. Like a used star. Like a crown and a balloon. Like a glass bell jar.

—Because walls of stone or plaster would include windows from which to climb, doors to unlock, keyholes to squint through, we are not permitted images. Instead, we inhabit a penitentiary of fire (or alphabets) which is a cage of cages.

—Chained to earth from before the beginning of the world, the destiny of the human heart is to ache. We alone offer it the exalted thin wind of the mountaintop.

—Do you think you are immortal? Do you think you are innocent? We will die but we cannot abandon our sister. Do you claim we are extravagant? Do you believe we are strident? Have you heard that if you save one life it is as if you saved the universe? Down the collapsed mineshaft of time we call until our voices grow hoarse, we are coming though we delay. We beg our sister to breathe, to forgive our slow machinery.

—Expert at stillness, we are whirling in place like Sufis. We are dancing on the inflamed heart. As it heaves we almost fall.

—From the forest of our lives
into the clearing
lightning rapes the mountaintop
violent   like the truths
of which we only dream
forgetting
the ancient screaming of God
answers our scream

—God who is One warns us that to escape is to perish. Beyond these nonexistent walls they have removed the air! Did you not know that? Nothing is outside but vipers and tigers.

—Her desire was for her beloved. Her boyfriends, her girlfriends, her life.

—If a baby is beaten by a parent, and then put down on the floor, the baby will crawl, not away from the parent, but toward. So we— So we—

—Just then I stood in the doorway of a ruined stone castle. A tuft of thick grass lay beneath my feet. The Mediterranean sun hammered against my forehead until it felt like a brass amphora. I offered my brass forehead as a bride. Here, I said, is the soul. Before me tumbled the hillside of grass and boulders to the sea edge. The blue sheerness offered itself as a husband.

—Killing God, killing God. . . . if I walk away God will commit suicide. He threatens it. I cannot risk it.

—Lovely little lies. The truth is that we are afraid of our passions. And afraid of history.

—More lies. The truth is that we are terribly, passionately hopeful. The truth is that we are tethered like fiery-eyed horses. The truth is a mystery. The truth is, it is a mystery. The truth is that the razor is in my pocket.

—No, the truth is that we are on vacation. Lament, for us, is recreational. A pilgrimage is an excuse for adventure, look at Chaucer, look around, women in every culture pursue some religious rites or other, groveling massively, doing novenas, wearing veils, lighting candles, you must perceive that this is not simply a matter of oppression. Of course they are oppressed. Of course we are. The ritual of lament faithfully encodes our oppression and we enact our part faithfully. On another mountain you might see women from a neighboring oppressive culture excising the clitorises and labia of their daughters. We might exchange signals from our twin peaks. Or not. And for Jephthah's daughter, we get four whole days off from work.

—One may not desert the sickbed of a friend. Or of a nation.

—Perhaps the story has been edited, perhaps the daughter was a priestess, perhaps the vow was not an accident: what then?

—The Question always is how to go on living after the holocaust. Each and every holocaust. How to value life *enough*. Is Palm Beach *enough?* Are the Catskills *enough?* Is the mooing cow on the kibbutz enough? How about Carnegie Hall and the invention of land-of-the-free America by Hollywood? And being dredged from the Mississippi riverbottom with your black and white companions?

—Riverbottom mud, the unassuaged, the infinite screaming of the moon.

—Since Isaac was saved, they can pretend that men are not wounded. Since Jephthah's daughter was a woman, they can pretend that her murder was insignificant. Since Adonai transcends the body, they can sacrifice the planet. These imbecilities make us, too, writhe as if bound upon an altar.

—To let go, we once knew, was to plunge into the abyss. Suddenly we learn that there is no abyss, or rather that the abyss is everywhere. Now we cling with desperate arms and legs, because we love the smell of God. The milk-yielding nipples of God. God's tongue.

—Underneath everything we are women. Hear us sigh. Do not call us *sweetness.*

—Very often we meet on the mountaintop for the same reason that we perform in the theater of religion. Here we are allowed to wear masks. And if you question people in their masks, they will tell the truth. And we love the truth.

—What strategies we have used to survive. How inventive our means, how diligent our metamorphoses. We use even the moon. Even the mountaintop.

—X = the unknown that may yet be discovered, the truth that may yet be born, for the sake of which I am prepared to pierce a hole in the membrane of God. Let him not dare to show his face. I would reach into his gizzards and drag out the Goddess concealed there, all these centuries, even if he himself denies that such a Goddess exists. He is ignorant of her existence because of his terrible busy memory.

—You remember that it is the obligation of every Jew to remember.

—Zero my fate, infinite my dream.

* Rain Falls on the Mountaintop *

Can these bones live?
—Ezekiel 37:6

No one bears witness for the witness.
—Paul Celan

(To be performed slowly, with grief.)

She has no name, has neither face nor eyes
they were drowned in blood
they were burnt
by fire

She is a garden shut, a fountain sealed
She sought her beloved and found him not
no kisses of the mouth no child at breast
no belly of heaped wheat
she is the song of nothing
and never

She loved the man she called father
a great a mighty warrior
a rock an outstretched arm his enemies fled
she ran after his love she praised she danced
hallelujah father but he
was angry

He said she hurt him, she caused him grief
he took her she consented he raised the knife
she lay on stone and showed her throat she said
blessed be he who protects and saves
who comforts the captive and raises up
the dead

Her father will die at a good old age
but where was the angel to stop his hand
where was the sacred messenger
who is this God of stone and knife and fire
why does he hide, what can he see
when a woman prays

will he ever hear

From the forest of our lives
into the clearing
rain falls on the mountaintop
soaking the wordless stone
year after year
like the truth of tears

* In Time *

(Three voices together speak the epigraph, then one by one the separate parts.)

Of our own accord, with our intelligence
and understanding, we can distinguish
between good and evil, doing as we choose.
Nothing holds us back from making this
choice.
—Maimonides

So then there was a moment in time

the knife might fall

or it might

not fall

So then there is a moment

in time

the knife may fall

or it may not fall

there is
a moment
in time

* FIRE *

(Chorus divided into portions. May be a sequence of alternating or mixed alto and soprano voices.)

To cause to burn! To add fuel to! To maintain or intensify a fire in! To bake in a kiln! To arouse the emotions of! To detonate or discharge (a firearm, explosives, or a projectile)! Fire a rifle! Fire an electron! Informal: to discharge from a position; dismiss!

Catch fire. On fire. Under fire. Firepower.

The Lord thy God is a consuming fire

and that which passes through the fire
returns to its nature
the beauty of fire, the beauty   of fire, the beauty

and the secret of fire is that to burn something is to send it back,
released from its body, to the energies of the other world.
To see a fire raging is to see the process of
transformation

whereby matter returns to spirit, with one's own ecstatic eyes—
wood, cloth, flesh, what were they before the cosmos was formed?
They return in glory and fury. The smallest campfire, or the
smallest flame in a domestic oven or wood stove,
proves that Death is everywhere, vividly
enacting his rights and exerting his
powers and prowess
and that to die is to be unwritten, ravished and ravishing

and they say that whenever something is burned
it is an outburst of the violence of God

who is light, rock, flame
who is creation's roar behind all sound

* SHE REFUSES TO BE COMFORTED *

(A single voice)

Yes I am dead
Yes I was a daughter of Israel
Yes I am nameless

Yes my father was a very great warrior
Yes the spirit of the Lord came upon him
Yes the Ammonites were delivered into his hand

Yes I ran after his love I praised I danced
Yes he had opened his mouth to the Lord
Yes he felt pain he blamed me

Yes I went with my companions on the mountains
Yes for two months I lamented my virginity
Yes I was a girl I wanted love

Yes I wanted a man to push into me
Yes like a long flash of light and babies to push out
Yes my companions kissed me and embraced me

Yes the men lay me on stone like a sheep
Yes I was naked like a sheep
Yes I cried God God Mama

Yes the angel of the Lord rescued my ancestor Isaac
Yes the Lord sent a messenger to stop the father's hand
Yes he would save a boy but not save me

Yes we are born into a theater of war
Yes the violence of my father
is a mirror he holds to the face of God

Yes I was unblemished
Yes I was a proved virgin
Yes I am very long dead

Yes I am weeping
Yes what else do you want of me

* LAMENT *

We look into Torah with regard to women,
and we see that women are perceived as lesser,
and are thereby dehumanized. . . . There is no
immutable moral principle to countermand
what humankind will do if left to the willful-
ness and negligence and indifference and cal-
lousness of its unrestraint.
                                        —Cynthia Ozick

Holocaust, from Gr. *holokaustos,* a sacrifice
wholly consumed by fire; a burnt offering.

(Full chorus, call-and-response, crescendo)

how is she slain
who was full of life

        holocaust
        holocaust

our eyes run down
with bitter water

        holocaust
        holocaust

never to be scholar
worker leader

        holocaust
        holocaust

physician judge
rachmanes din

        holocaust
        holocaust

image of God
denied rejected

        holocaust
        holocaust

how many daughters
sisters mothers

        holocaust
        holocaust

how to lament
the unremembered

        holocaust
        holocaust

is there any sorrow
like this sorrow

* HEARTBREAK *

(Full chorus, immediately following the previous section.)

sorry for him
    feel   feel
        sorry for him
son
  of a whore

sorry for him
    he opens
        he opens
sorry for him
    feel
the poor bastard
the poor bastard

it hurts him
        it hurts him, feel
           sorry for him
the poor despised bastard

the despised rejected   lonely bastard   feel it

inside every heartbreak
    an older heartbreak
inside every injustice
    a deeper injustice

he opens   his mouth

        sorry   sorry   feel it

* DEATH AND THE MAIDEN *

(This call-and-response section should be considered optional. If performed, it may be best to speak it almost in a whisper, implying a tone of desolation comparable to that of "Lament." The verb may remain present tense, "We sacrifice . . ." or may be changed to past tense, "We sacrificed. . . .")

We sacrifice this girl in the theater of war
    For the Lord your God is a jealous God
We sacrifice this girl in order to spell our names
    See now that I, even I, am he
We sacrifice this girl to strengthen our hearts to combat the enemy that
  surrounds us.
    Thou shalt break them with a rod of iron,
    Thou shalt dash them in pieces like a potter's vessel.
We sacrifice this girl today because we sacrificed her yesterday, last year,
  a thousand years ago, it is a tradition of holiness.
    For the Lord our God is holy
We sacrifice this girl because her hair is long and powerful
    Sin began with a woman, and because of her we all die
We sacrifice this girl because she danced at the wrong moment
    Her filthiness was in her skirts
We sacrifice this girl that blood surge from her cut throat.
We sacrifice this girl that her soft new body become ash and cinders,
        and we smash what remains of her pelvis.
    And let her put away her harlotries from her face,
    and her adulteries from between her breasts
We sacrifice this girl to protect ourselves from impurity.
    For the lips of a strange woman drop honey
    And her mouth is smoother than oil
We sacrifice this girl because she asked for it.
    For all his ways are justice.

* Mountaintop *

(Full chorus for the words in roman type. The italicized words may be understood as the voice of the wind, of the spirit, ruach—the voice of God who finally replies. It should be played from a tape and seem to come from everywhere and nowhere.)

> I desired mercy and not sacrifice, and the
> knowledge of God more than burnt offerings.
> —Hosea 6:6

Going forth in mourning
returning in joy

From the forest of our lives
into the clearing
weeds grow on the mountaintop
between the stones

Birds fly from shrub to shrub
the spirit of God
is in their twittering
like a truth that is sweet

Wind increases
shiver and listen
is it the wind
is it a voice

You who lament
you are the one
you be my angel
you be my messenger
you stop the warrior's hand

it will take ages
it will begin today

you will die many times
you will slip in blood
you will be humbled
you will fail
it will take all your strength
it will appear to take forever
it will begin today

we must go forth in mourning
we will return

in joy

* AN UNCLOSED CLOSURE *

("Mountaintop" may conclude the performance of Jephthah's Daughter: A Lament. *Performers will freeze for applause. They will then walk toward the audience but instead of bowing, an option is the following naming ceremony.)*

The performer who has read the part of Jephthah's daughter steps forward one step, and speaks:

Remember me
and tell me
what is my name

The other performers step forward one by one to stand at her side. Each states her own name.

When they have all done so, it may be possible to gesture toward the audience, inviting members of the audience to state their own names.

Contributors

ALICE BACH is Archbishop Paul J. Hallinan Chair of Catholic Studies at Case Western Reserve University in Cleveland, Ohio. She is the author of *Women, Seduction, Betrayal in the Biblical Narrative* (1997) and the editor of *Women in the Hebrew Bible: A Reader* (1998). Her new book, *Bible and Popular Culture: Cracking Open the Geode*, will be published in 2004.

ATHALYA BRENNER is Professor of Hebrew Bible/Old Testament at the University of Amsterdam, The Netherlands. She is the editor of *The Feminist Companion to the Bible Series* from Sheffield Academic Press, which has published twenty volumes in the series between 1993 and 2001. She lives in Amsterdam and in Haifa, Israel.

SHEILA BRIGGS is Associate Professor in the School of Religion at the University of Southern California. Her fields are theology and the history of theology, investigated from a feminist perspective. She has written extensively on slavery in early Christianity.

ELIZABETH A. CASTELLI teaches in the Religion and Women's Studies departments at Barnard College/Columbia University, including courses on the New Testament, early Christianity, religions in the Roman Empire, gender in Christian history, feminist theory, and theory and method in the study of religion. Her publications include *Imitating Paul: A Discourse of Power* (1991), *The Postmodern Bible* (with the Bible and Culture Collective, 1995), *Reimagining Christian Origins* (edited with Hal Taussig, 1996), *Women, Gender, Religion: A Reader* (edited with assistance from Rosamond C. Rodman, 2001), *Martyrdom and Memory: Early Christian Culture-Making* (forthcoming in 2004), and numerous articles on feminist biblical interpretation and early Christian women's history.

UTE E. EISEN is a Wissenchaftliche Assistentin at the Institute of New Testament Studies and Ancient Judaism at the University of Kiel, Germany. She has a doctorate in theology from the University of Hamburg. Her teaching and research areas are biblical studies, history of early Christianity, narratological analysis of Luke-Acts, methodology, and gender issues. She is author of *Women Officeholders in Early Christianity: Epigraphic and Literary Studies* (English translation, 2000).

ESTHER FUCHS is Professor of Judaic Studies at the University of Arizona in Tucson. She is the author of two books in Hebrew on S. Y. Agnon, and numerous essays on both modern and biblical Hebrew literature. Among her books are *Israeli Mythogynies: Women in Contemporary Hebrew Fiction* (1987), *Women and the Holocaust: Narrative and Representation* (1999), *Sexual Politics in the Biblical Narrative: Reading the Hebrew Bible as a Woman* (2000), and *Israeli Women: A Reader* (forthcoming).

TAL ILAN was born in Israel. She studied at the Hebrew University in Jerusalem and wrote her Ph.D. thesis on Jewish women in Greco-Roman Palestine. Her publications include *Mine and Yours Are Hers: Retrieving Women's History from Rabbinic Literature* (1997) and *Integrating Women into Second Temple History* (1999).

PUSHPA JOSEPH is a research scholar in the Department of Christian Studies, University of Madras, where she has submitted her doctoral thesis entitled "Indian Feminist Hermeneutics: A Contextual Application of the Reconstructionist Method Proposed by Elisabeth Schüssler Fiorenza." Her M.Phil. thesis is entitled "Indian Biblical Hermeneutics: The Contribution of Georges Soares-Prabhu."

ALICIA OSTRIKER is a poet, critic, and midrashist, author of *Feminist Revision and the Bible* (1992) and *The Nakedness of the Fathers: Biblical Visions and Revisions* (1994). Her poetry has been widely anthologized and appears in numerous collections of Jewish poetry. Her most recent book of poems is *The Volcano Sequence*, a meditation on God and on the figure of the mother. Ostriker is a professor of English at Rutgers University.

TINA PIPPIN is an activist educator and Professor of Religious Studies at Agnes Scott College. She is the author of *Apocalyptic Bodies: The End of the World in Text and Image* (1999) and coeditor (with Ronald Schleifer and David Jobling) of *The Postmodern Bible Reader* (2001), among other publications. She works in community partnerships with teen parents at Decatur High School, Decatur Cooperative Ministries (homeless women and children), and with Refugee Family Services. She also helps facilitate the Living Wage Campaign at her college.

ADELE REINHARTZ is Dean of Graduate Studies and Research at Wilfrid Laurier University, Waterloo, Ontario, Canada. Her main area of research is Judaism and Christianity in the Greco-Roman world, with specialization in the Gospel of John. She also has interests in feminist biblical criticism, literary criticism, and, more recently, in the interplay between the Bible and film. Her most recent book is *Scripture on the Silver Screen*, which is a study of the use and misuse of the Bible in recent Hollywood films, and she is currently working on a book entitled *Jesus of Hollywood*.

JANE SCHABERG is Professor of Religious Studies and codirector of Women's Studies at the University of Detroit Mercy. She is the author of *The Father, the Son, and the Holy Spirit (Matt 28:19)* (1982), *The Illegitimacy of Jesus: A Feminist Theological Interpretation of the New Testament Infancy Narratives* (1992, 1994), *The Resurrection of Mary Magdalene: Legends, Apocrypha and the Christian Testament* (2002), and numerous journal articles on biblical studies and feminist interpretation.

JOAN E. TAYLOR is Adjunct Senior Lecturer in the Department of Philosophy and Religious Studies, University of Waikato, Hamilton, New Zealand, and also Honorary Research Fellow in the Department of History, University College, London, U.K. She is the author of *The Immerser: John the Baptist within Second Temple Judaism* (1997) and *Jewish Women Philosophers of First-Century Alexandria: Philo's 'Therapeutae' Reconsidered* (2003).

ANTOINETTE CLARK WIRE is the Robert S. Dollar Professor of New Testament Studies at San Francisco Theological Seminary and at the Graduate Theological Union in Berkeley, California. Her research interests include early Jewish oral traditions, women in early Christianity, Hellenistic miracle stories, Pauline theology, and contemporary Chinese biblical interpretation.

She is the author of *The Corinthian Women Prophets: A Reconstruction through Paul's Rhetoric* (1990) and *Holy Lives, Holy Deaths: A Close Hearing of Early Jewish Storytellers* (2002). Her recent sabbatical was spent in China, where she taught at Nanjing Theological Seminary and studied indigenous Christian oral songs.